"As a participant in many of Boston's programs over the past 20 years, I am moved to read these compelling stories of her life journey and understand how she became the gifted teacher and inspiring role model she has been for me and so many others. "Out of Bounds" is the perfect title for Sandra's memoir, as she has dedicated her life to teaching and modeling taking risks, speaking one's truth, and creating a vibrant women's community and culture. "The reason we're here is perfectly clear... We're ridin' the edge, again and again" could well be her theme song." —Robin Weingarten, LICSW, Full Moon Rising sister, Pilgrim Warrior graduate

"Sandra's gift to her grandchildren tells a remarkable story of the personal and social evolution of a spirit-led peace activist and women's empowerment trainer. As she journeys from jungles to war zones, and ashrams to women's circles, she lives out her determination to experience God as compassionate action for freedom and justice." —Cheryl Fox, friend & peace activist

"Boston takes the reader on a high speed, compelling world tour, skillfully telling the story of her life choices while also sharing how she works with women in many cultures to validate their vibrant uniqueness and choice to live their truth. The impact of her story stayed with me long after I stopped reading, giving me the courage to fully embrace my own life choices and go out of bounds. Kudos!!" —Jan Dziadzio, Business consultant

"This is a tale of a life fully lived. Boston's authenticity and willingness to share her journey—from difficult family relationships to daring physical challenge, dedication and service –reveals a heart that knows what this world really needs." —Gurunam Khalsa, God's Sweet Pea, Full Moon Rising sister

"Sandra's journey through life is an extraordinary tale of curiosity, openness and determination to witness firsthand the diversity of cultures on this planet. What is remarkable is her generosity and wisdom in pursuit of connection, and her unfailing commitment to a vision of love, equality and justice in the world."
—Georgina Forbes, Artist, psychotherapist and activist

"Out of Bounds is a book of stories that you won't want to put down. Masterful! Marvelous! One is transported through time from the '50s to the present as a sidekick to the author—a most original, courageous and self-reflective woman who knows who she is and who we are. She knows the problems of the world that need witnessing and response from all of us. Boston shows us the courage to stand up for what we know is true in our society, both the sacred and the profane. A must read for the generation that inherits this world from us!"—Becca King, community activist and retired family therapist

"Every paragraph has a thought expressed or an experience shared that makes me want to call someone I know and say "Hey, listen to this. . . ." I am going to read it a second time, this time aloud with my son Gillis. It would be fabulous for the kids in our homeschool network to have a chance to hear from and ask questions of someone who has pondered so many important issues and met life with such courage and deep faith. Sandra is a true heroine and model, a wise elder, and spiritual leader. I'd love for our kids to be exposed to her phenomenal gifts and wisdom." —Eveline MacDougal, homeschool coordinator, Amandla Community Chorus director.

Out of Bounds

Sandra Boston

OUT OF BOUNDS

Adventures
in
Transformation

ISBN 978-0-9885927-5-9

Printed in the United States

Booksmyth Press
Shelburne Falls, MA

Invocation from *The Box* by the Terma Company, 1992.

Front cover photograph by Jane Spickett
Cover design by Jim Sadler, Jim Sadler Designs
Book design by Maureen Moore, Booksmyth Press

Dedicated to

my mother, Sylvia,

whose tenacious holding onto the boundaries of respectability as she understood them pushed me to wed my own truth, weather the heat of our differences, and live my authentic self.

my once-husband Bruce,

who weathered the changes my quest brought to our marriage, and stretched into holding the integrity of family with me and our three sons, his new partner Jean, and her children and parents for fifty-one years.

all those

who have participated in the co-creation of my ministry as they met me at the edge of limitless possibility, followed their heart, and did something courageous and original.

> *"Freedom is an inside job."*
> Sam Keene

> *"I respond, although I will be changed."*
> Eugen Rosenstock-Huessy

> *"For God, to me, it seems, is a verb, not a noun."*
> Buckminster Fuller

Contents

Invocation

*A prayer for you, the reader, and for all those who will follow
the path we open with our courage, creativity, and wonder:*

*May all who enter here be protected by those who have gone
before and can show the way.*

May great courage accompany those willing to cross the River of Sorrow.

*May all who read these words be freed from the bondage
of fear and denial.*

May our eyes remain open even in the face of tragedy.

May we not become disheartened.

*May we find in the dissolution of our apathy and denial,
the cup of the broken heart.*

*May we discover the gift of the fire burning in the inner
chamber of our being—burning great and bright enough
to transform any poison.*

*May we offer the power of our sorrow to the service
of something greater than ourselves.*

May our guilt not rise up to form yet another defensive wall.

May the suffering purify and not paralyze us.

May we endure; may sorrow bond us and not separate us.

May we realize the greatness of our sorrow and not run from its touch or its flame.

May clarity be our ally and wisdom our support.

May our wrath be cleansing, cutting through the confusion of denial and greed.

May we not be afraid to see or speak our truth.

May the bleakness of the wasteland be dispelled.

May the soul's journey be revealed and the true hunger fed.

*May we be forgiven for what we have forgotten
and blessed with the remembrance of who we really are.*

Prologue

I want to be a remarkable ancestor to my descendants. They deserve to have the stories of the powerful times that I have lived in the second half of the 20th century, when struggles for personal and political freedom were breaking out all over the planet—and inside me as well. I want the next generation to learn from the sacrifices we made for our victories, the intensity of our determination, and the poignancy of our loves and losses. I want to offer what we have honed as wisdom to guide them in their own struggles, for surely they will have theirs. I want them to know our humor, our foibles, our shames and our transformations. I want women to know what it is like to act as an equal in a society that does not yet believe in equality for women— and to pay the price. I want them to understand the struggle for children's authentic selves that my generation waged in a culture that still taught boys not to cry and girls not to be angry. I want them to see how passion guides action and opens doors, keeping us focused on what is most true and most important to our journeys along our chosen paths.

I recently sat in a ritual circle called a "Blessing-way," held to honor a woman about to give birth, Each of the twelve of us were to introduce ourselves as the daughters of as many mothers as we knew from our family tree. All but one of the twelve of us could only go back two generations. The lives of our great-grandmothers were shrouded in mystery. I realized then that in just 100 years all memory of my lifetime may also be lost. The dreams I made a reality, especially those of new possibilities for women's lives, might seem ordinary. The courage I mustered to go out of bounds and challenge the status quo in order to live life more in line with my values than present social norms offered, would be but an echo of norms later either taken for granted or forgotten. The stories of how change happens would be lost.

Is there something in us beyond the reaches of nature and nurture that explains who we become? James Hillman, in The Soul's Code (1996), says yes, and calls it an acorn. He describes the acorn as a uniqueness in each of us that is already present when we arrive on this planet, and pushes out from the inside to be lived. He says the acorn sets up a yearning such as E.T. felt for "home" that ultimately shapes our character more than who our parents are or how we grew up. In my seventh decade, I am reaching back into my origins to find those moments of yearning, of pushing from within that guided my way into crafting the life I wanted to live. Surely we all have those gems of experiences that reveal the core of our passion—our acorn. This memoir is my odyssey to gather together my transformative experiences, glean the wisdom they impart, cherish each one, and share them with you.

Born during World War II, my childhood came during the "golden era" of the 1950s, with a post-war booming economy and my country seen as the hero of the world. My teen years were just ahead of the curve of the radical 1960s, when our culture turned somersaults on what was right and wrong. Free love, spreading like dandelion seeds in a steady wind with the arrival of "the pill," added more fire to the movements sweeping our country for black civil rights, women's rights, and gay rights. I joined the women who were throwing away their bras and no longer shaving their legs, both choices seen as ways to claim our freedom in a society that would keep our power crippled by shame about our bodies. Men let their hair grow to their shoulders, grew beards, and wore beads, rejecting the same scripts of the corporate culture that had kept them marching in lock-step in suits and ties to get ahead. Eighteen-year-olds were burning their draft cards in public and refusing military service in what was seen as an illegal, imperialist war in Vietnam. My mother's generation had seen our country be a military hero; I was seeing my country be a military villain. Our generation gap was enormous, and led to painful impasses in our family life as we struggled with our often conflicting needs for belonging and autonomy. Affirmative action was breaking the silence on racism. Neighborhoods were integrating. People were finally talking about class differences and how they affected education, employment and housing opportunities. Women, who were being paid seventy cents on the dollar for the same work men were doing, demanded equal pay (which they still haven't gotten fifty years later). All those held back by the control of dominant groups were screaming to be understood, and to have their circumstances and opportunities changed in the name of justice.

New cultural norms were rising out of the fire of pent up rage being released as more and more groups cried out their demand for change. Wheelchair ramps and accessible bathrooms started appearing in public places. Smoking was no longer allowed in any public places. (In my lifetime, our culture went from smoking allowed everywhere, to being corralled in limited areas of restaurants and airplanes—imagine!—to only outside entire buildings, to no longer being allowed on entire college campuses, airports, and all manner of public spaces.) Women were becoming news commentators on television for the first time. Divorce was no longer seen as a calamity. Unmarried couples were cohabiting. By the early 1980s, we even thought this country was ready for the Equal Rights Amendment to our national Constitution that would protect women from discrimination in the workforce.

We were mistaken on that count. Ratification failed, in spite of a fifty-four day hunger strike in the Illinois State House by over fifty women with the whole world watching. We also failed to make significant change in the arena of domestic violence, a field I would work in for eight years. The same statistics of one in three women raped in their lifetime, and one in four children molested, still stands today after forty years of battered women's shelters, restraining orders, court accompaniment, and prevention education in all age groups. I will never forget the thunderous, ear-pummeling sound of hundreds of women marching through the underground subway of Philadelphia, beating on pots and pans and demanding an end to violence against women during our annual "Take Back the Night" march in 1975. The best we have to show for all our work in that field is rape kits available in every emergency room to help prevent pregnancy. Politicians still argue on today's evening news over whether that protection should be allowed if getting pregnant by whatever means is the will of God.

Social change—or justice—is at the heart of my calling, and organizing for it is the most frustrating yet compelling action I have ever undertaken. I am still trying, now focused on climate disruption and waking people up to the urgent need to change how we use fossil fuel in time to preserve a livable climate for our children and their descendants. The forces of resistance are mighty. Only those with political, monetary, and military power and control can risk injustice. We who seek justice—a fair deal for everyone—have to understand other kinds of power. My memoir explores these "experiments with Truth" as Gandhi called them.

I did not plan my life—I opened to it. Jesus said, "Knock, and the door shall be opened." I knocked. I said "Yes" to those who crossed my path unexpectedly, bearing gifts of vision and possibility. I just showed up with all my imperfections, willing to be a Pilgrim, open to learning, feeling pain, growing, and paying the price demanded by the powers that be from those who go beyond the consensus of what is good and acceptable. A quote by Buckminster Fuller that I have had on my office wall for fifty years reads: "For God, to me, it seems, is a verb, not a noun." These words connect me at seventy to the young woman I was when I first headed out to make those words my reality. I can say I have given all I have. I offer the story of my life journey to you as a testimony to the presence of a guiding Spirit in our lives, which may indeed be that mysterious acorn planted in us from the beginning.

A life is given, and it must be given back. The first section of this memoir tells the stories of what I have been given. The second section tells about what I have given back—my sense of mission. The third section is again about receiving, about the special opportunities I have had to savor life, to explore art and nature, and travel to foreign lands for the sheer joy of drinking in the unique gifts of those places and their people. All these experiences took me way out of bounds, out beyond the familiar suburban, nuclear family life that was expected of women and mothers in my day, out to work camps, jungles, mountain peaks, war zones, jails, communes, a sexual identity shift, and celebrations of sisterhood with women in many foreign lands.

I call out to my grandchildren—Katie, Jake, Ben, Bodhi, Finian, Anabel, Sammy, Aaron, Carmen and Anika—to remember and cherish the lives of your ancestors. Don't find yourself, as I do, wondering about the beliefs, the dreams, the guts and the tears that shaped the world and culture into which you were born. Here are some of the stories of where you came from. Take up the legacy made for you, and wear it like a mantle of protection. Hold it like a candle to light your way. Yes, your path will be different, the questions beyond my imagining. But I trust you will need the courage that has been hewn into the genes for you. I hope my stories will help you know where to invest your faith and trust. One day, I hope you, too, will want to sing your song to your descendants. You, too, will want to give your gifts as Holy Grail to the passionate wanderer who hears your whisper in the stars.

I
Discovering My Path

Taproot

I sat upon a hilltop high,
And watched this earthly world go by.
I thought of all the things I'd missed,
Of fruitless striving, leading to this,
That nothing was mine which I had sought.
But then I remembered what God has taught,
That just as we are, we're all He asks,
To go out in His world and to do His tasks.

Then striving shall unselfish be,
Hopelessness gone, and love the key
To all that makes the world His way
"Go out into my world," He said, "and stay
Till I call you home when your work is done,
Life's struggle ended, your peace be won."

No longer I sat on hilltop high,
Watching this needy world go by.
Up I jumped, to be on His way,
My hand in His, the path to lay!
Others I've found, who have His purpose, too.
Together we'll make a sturdy crew.
Never to finish, but only to start.
Not seeing the end, but knowing our heart.

Sandy Waymer, 1954
Ten years later Sandra Boston

Taproot

I was a very motivated Christian at the age of fourteen. I cherish this poem as one of the sparkling gems I am gathering into this web of memoir. That acorn is clearly showing up here, pushing out, and announcing its presence. I treasure the innocent trust in guidance I find in the words, and the openness, courage, and determination so ready to partner with Spirit. Surely this one was ready to hear a calling that would carry her to many foreign lands, to deportation and civil disobedience, to the edges of innovation, and always  home to herself, to what was true and real for her, regardless of what society, or authorities, or her mother might think. She did indeed know her heart.

From my earliest memory, going to church on Sunday was one of my favorite times of the week. We were Congregationalists, Methodists or Presbyterians, depending on which minister my parents liked best whenever we moved. I loved dressing up, and everyone piling into the car together after breakfast. I loved the music, the stained glass, the presence of fresh flowers—all things I didn't see any other time of the week. I especially loved all the holidays like Christmas eve with pageants and Easter with bonnets, new outfits and baskets for egg hunts. My third grade Sunday school teacher, Mr. Sunberg, made a taproot impression on me when he told me that being held in the love of God was like being a drop of water suspended half way between the top and the bottom of the ocean. I trusted him, and that was all I needed to know in order to join the host of believers. In the junior high youth group, I discovered I was good at composing spoken prayers and singing out. By the time I reached high school, others were turning to me for leadership. I happily led our Senior High Fellowship and preached the Youth Sunday sermon, while also singing in the adult choir. The church was a second home for me.

My mother, Sylvia Bontecou Waymer, was the holder of the bounds beyond which I would travel. She was a housewife who never worked outside the home until my brother headed to college and I was just two years behind. She went to work for The Reader's Digest as a hole punch operator. Most of her married years were spent tending our home and decorating it with her paintings and hooked rugs. She used our upright piano for her easel and copied pictures from the National Geographic. She painted a Grandma Moses-like mural on our dining room wall (she let me paint the cow), and she hooked rugs for the stairs to the basement, with each riser depicting a family motif like our dog or our summer campsite. Dinner was roast chicken, peas and mashed potatoes—nothing fancy or original. No favorite recipes were passed down. Everyone who knew her would describe Sylvia as the nicest person they knew.

Sylvia, born in 1918, was from a wealthy family with live-in maids, oriental carpets and a huge crystal chandelier in the front hall. Her father worked for I.B.M. (International Business Machines) when it was a cash register company, before it became a typewriter rental company, precursor to the globalized computers of today. His ancestors were among the first mariners from Holland to round the Cape of Good Hope in 1607 with a fleet of seven ships. They were also in the court of Louis XV of France when he expelled the Protestant Huguenots and they migrated to New York with their merchant ships. Sylvia had two brothers who both fought in World War II. Her childhood and adolescence were marked by the Depression of 1929, the New Deal government helping to rebuild the country, and the build up to World War II when she experienced our country heroically "saving the world for democracy." These very formative experiences would set the stage for one of our biggest challenges, as I came of age during the Vietnam War and saw my country as an imperialist force fabricating reasons for escalation, spraying Agent Orange on everything, and killing millions of innocent civilians. My mother could hear none of my point of view. She even suspected I was a communist sympathizer. This impasse was my first powerful lesson in how we all see what we are looking for—how our perception is shaped by the lens we choose to look through.

My mother once told me, "Somebody has to wear the pants in the family and I'm glad it's not me." She also told me "Save all your kisses for the man you marry." These messages—seared into my being—were the beginning of my questioning her authority. They seemed to reign me in somehow, and were meant to show me how I was to belong and be acceptable. I didn't like hearing them. She had a made-up word—tallywacker—for a vagina. It was only used when going to the doctor, as in "Now the doctor needs to look at your tallywacker." I thought that was what it was called until I got to high school and started talking to the other girls. I also didn't know what the blood in my pants was until I had to leave the dinner table one night, at age twelve, because of a strange warm sensation between my legs. I called to my mother from the bathroom, and she came in and calmly explained that "it" was normal—normal? I didn't trust her. Sex education was absent from schools; it was considered the responsibility of parents to tell kids the facts.

I felt strangely lonely. As a blossoming young woman, I now had something to hide and hoped no one would know when I was bleeding. A box of Kotex was sold in an already-wrapped brown paper bag at the drug store. Even the merchants were colluding in the dirty secret. I was franticly embarrassed the first time I had to buy a box by myself. Twenty years later I would meet a woman—Betsey Wright—who, when she was bleeding, would spread a thumb-full of blood in the middle of her forehead so the whole world would know. I would gasp— half in embarrassment and half in wonder—when I saw this woman from the generation after mine being proud of her blood and her female body. Along with my shock came a wave of grief for all the shame I had inherited from my mother about mine.

My grandmother, Elsie, born in 1886, had a career outside the home as an accomplished pianist and didn't marry until she was twenty-seven—unheard of in her day. I count her as one of my remarkable ancestors. Because she had maids, she was able to practice the piano all day, so my mother never saw her do housework or deal intimately with the needs of children. She was also a teetotaler in the Prohibition era of the 1920s, so it was my mother as a young woman who would accompany her father to I.B.M. social events where drinking occurred. Sylvia knew early how to be a lady—an upper class lady. The family story—told to me by my mother's sister-in-law—is that Grandpa chose my father for his daughter because of his character (he was scoutmaster to the youngest son in the family, my Uncle George). When they married, Grandpa offered my father a job at I.B.M., which I imagine my mother expected him to accept. He turned it down. He was not attracted to business; his acorn was pushing out for service and character-building with boys. This may have been a shock my mother never quite adjusted to, with all the ensuing underground currents of a mixed-class marriage.

My father, Samuel Shoening Waymer, born in 1915, worked for the Boy Scouts of America as a field scout executive. His job was to move to a town that did not have a troop. He would start one and be the Scoutmaster. The following year, he would train the fathers in how to run the troop, and the third year we would move to a town without a troop and begin again. I lived six places by the time I was twelve. I emulated my father with all his leadership qualities in Scouting and the Church (he was Clerk of the Session in our Presbyterian Church) as well as our neighborhood (he founded a Neighborhood Association and convinced everyone to plant cherry trees in their front yard so it would look like Disney World in the spring.) I spent weekend afternoons digging in his vegetable garden as he weeded, or helping him prune our apple and pear trees. We were like two peas in a pod.

Whenever we moved, he would plant white dogwood trees in our front yard, which he would forage for in some woodland and transplant. They were our family trademark. He built a cage for my pet rabbit between two trees, with wire mesh for a floor so the poop could drop down. He also designed and helped build two of the houses we lived in. I thought he could do anything. His people came from Indiana farmers who had migrated here during the potato famine in Germany in 1848. His great-grandfather was an itinerant minister riding horseback across the state performing baptisms and funerals for rural communities. His grandfather owned the first cotton gin in St. Louis, where my father was born and from where he migrated at twenty-six to attend New York University night school. He paid his way through for seven years, working as a secretary for the Chief Scout Executive of the Boy Scouts of America. As far as I know, my father never returned to St. Louis or stayed in touch with his two sisters, who I met only twice. Once was a time they each visited us in the east, and once at my father's funeral. His younger sister, Margaret, told me on that occasion that my father had seriously considered entering the ministry—an unfulfilled family script left open for me.

There are many lost stories in this branch of the family. My father's mother died of a brain tumor before I was born. His father came to our house once when I was an infant. He came unannounced, which, as my mother tells the story, was so upsetting to her that she packed my brother and me in the car and took him to her parents' house—thirty minutes away—where he could be "properly" taken care of. Why was he unannounced, travelling from the Midwest to New England? Why did he come on a work day when my father was not even home? Where are the stories? A telltale trace of this farming family saga was in the painting that always hung over our fireplace no matter how many times we moved. It was called "The Angeles," and depicted a man and woman in work clothes out in a potato field, pitchforks in hand, pausing from their labor to bow their heads in prayer as the bells from a distant church chimed the hour. It spoke of the simplicity of hard work, connection to the land, and that faith with which I felt such a deep kinship as I grew up. I always loved that painting with the muted browns and grays of their clothing, the lumpy texture of the soil, and the quiet colors of sunset in the sky. I wonder now how that image—so central in our home—seemed to my mother, who grew up in an opulent home with such a different past.

There were other underlying dynamics in our family that made daily life hard. My father and my brother Sam Jr. did not get along. I don't know why, and no one ever explained it, but then I didn't ask either. My brother targeted me with his resulting anger and displaced physical attack. I would scream bloody murder when he would hit me for no apparent reason. My mother would say, "Wait until your father comes home." When Daddy came home, he would punish my brother—sometimes hitting him—for hitting me. Then he would leave again for work the next day and the dynamic would happen all over again. I had no adult protection and no understanding of why my brother hated me.

My brother's attacks were relentless. Sometimes it was a random punch in the arm, always with one knuckle extended to increase the pain. Sometimes it was hurling invectives like "You're so fat. You're so stupid!" When I walked behind him on the path to a neighbor's backyard ball field, he would turn around and shout "Go home!" with a frightening venom. I would cringe, but I wouldn't go home. Eventually I adopted a defense of "I don't care if you don't like me." But I really did. There was a lot of hurt stored behind that defense that I would get in touch with in my thirties and do a lot of crying about. I instinctively knew it wasn't safe to cry around Sam.

At forty-five, I would do an independent study in graduate school on my family of origin and sort out what I could of how conflict that is covert in one generation becomes overt in the next. It made me wonder more about my parents' mixed class backgrounds. My brother had taken the I.B.M. route, owning an airplane and two houses by the time he was thirty. I had followed in my father's footsteps leading training programs and living simply in community. Could it be that my brother and I never had a chance for a good relationship? Could we have been playing out between us a conflict that was really between my mother and father, but was being suppressed?

During this time I would also have a chance to ask my mother about her relationship with her mother. "Why do you want to know that?" was her first response. Then she answered, "She was always doing her music thing." I felt a sting, a tear in the fabric of our family. I had adored my grandmother, and had sat enraptured next to her on the bench in front of her Steinway grand piano as her fingers flew over the keys, bumping me when she would reach for the high octaves of a Chopin Etude. Clearly my mother did not share my admiration. Perhaps this was where the nurturing bond was broken that would have such consequences for our relationship?

I also asked Mom about a traumatic time when I was three months old and had pyloric stenosis—a spasm in the muscle at the bottom of the stomach—which led to projective vomiting and dehydration. She told me that our family doctor wanted to do surgery to correct my condition and she refused because I was so tiny. In such dreadful circumstances, my father worked out of town and my brother was a toddler. I asked if she had any support from her women friends during that time. "No," she told me, "I couldn't complain about my problems when the other women's husbands were going overseas and mine wasn't." I asked what her memories of my brother Sam were at that time. "I don't have any." That comment told me the answer I had sought for so long as to why my brother never liked me. I can't help but imagine that things between us went sour then. I think I terrified my mother; she was isolated, and probably feeling very incompetent since she had never seen her own mother deal with the hard stuff of life like this. My brother probably got lost in the chaos just at the stage when a child wants to leave his mother but also be able to come back to her. My mother's hands were full with cleaning up vomit and keeping me alive. My condition did resolve at six months when our doctor suggested feeding me lumpy farina. It stretched the muscle at the bottom of my stomach and the drama was over, but I suspect the fallout between the three of us from that experience lasted a lifetime.

The more I grew into someone who was going to test the limits of her world, the more alarmed my mother became. My ambition to be a leader and make a difference was unfamiliar to her sense of womanhood as follower and helpmate. She seemed to abhor women who "tooted their own horn" or wore pants ("It makes their fanny show!"). I would forever wonder why my father, so dedicated to the character development of young boys, couldn't find a better way to deal with my brother than beating him up for beating me up. Or why my mother couldn't/wouldn't see how unsafe I was and do more to protect me from being a battered woman at ten. Decades later, when he was twenty-two, my brother's son, Jim, would ask me to tell him about his grandfather because his father would never talk about him. Was this a repetition of my father never talking about his father?

My father died at forty-eight of leukemia after a six year fight. My ally in the family was gone at nineteen. In the throes of these dynamics, it is not surprising that I would choose to head out on my own to look for greener pastures and people who were more like me. That searching for true home would weave through all the ensuing tales of adventure and mission. As my acorn—the passion of my soul—pushed out from the inside, and guided me into a sense of mission—to make God a verb—my mother would try to reign me in, in her words to "provide balance" to my way of seeing things. We would struggle like two sparring martial artists, both wanting the relationship—but always on our own terms. Sometimes the struggle itself is what love looks like, so I bow to her as my loyal opponent who in some mysterious way brought out the best in me by making me reach—really reach—for what I wanted, and pay the inevitable price for being true to myself and that acorn.

Lessons from the Wind:
Mariner Scout
1954

We graduate from infant to toddler when we master balance in our bodies, but what about learning how to balance the forces from within and without that regale a life? What about learning how to deal with attempts at a goal that fail, or seeming progress in our ambition that takes a hit and gives us feedback about what we forgot or missed? It can be painful to be frustrated, disappointed, or confused while learning to be resilient with life's challenges. We all have special teachers—neighbors, parents or siblings—who give us important lessons about when to wait, when to push forward, and when to yield in dealing with people, dilemmas, and opportunities. One of my earliest teachers turns out to be the wind.

Every Friday after school my Mariner Scout troop meets. In the morning I don my bright blue uniform with the square, sailor-like collar and black neckerchief tied in a square knot (just like my Dad's). I slip my sash of merit badges over my head and it hangs across the front of my body. Talk about wearing your heart on your sleeve, this sash is my pride and joy. I have accumulated just about every badge in the handbook, so many that the badges cover the front of the sash and go halfway up my back. I head off to school proud to be part of this adventure.

I wonder as I write this if this arena of merit badges is where I formed the habit of being a jack of all trades and master of none. For me, there are too many potential adventures to worry about perfecting a final outcome. That pattern seems to have followed me throughout life, and has given me a willingness to risk, a leaning into my passion, and a wild love of learning and skill-building. A job completed is good enough. I'm still doing it at seventy-three as I recently learned how to make windserts for all forty-six windows in my house (custom wooden frames with polyethylene film stretched around them to block cold air from the glass.) Sure enough, most of the frames don't fit perfectly, but they do keep out the cold.

The 1950s are years when it is still cool to be a teenage Girl Scout. The pride in belonging, in achieving, in being part of an adventurous, bonding, learning community of women forms a platform for my life. It gives me specific rungs of a ladder to climb that builds self-esteem. Every rung takes me higher in the development of my leadership, my competence, and my love of learning. It is my first experience of women's community and of belonging to a global movement, both of which will become central to my life journey. (I still have my world friendship pin in the front of my desk drawer today, sixty years later.)

Our troop of twelve owns two sailboats, a Thistle and a Sailfish. We spend every Saturday morning on Lake Carnegie in Princeton, New Jersey, where I live. I ride my bike the short mile from my house down a dirt road to the path through a meadow that leads to our little boat house on the shore of the lake. The wind is almost always blowing down the narrow, three-mile stretch of water as we pull out the boat, mast, boom and rudder and begin hitching them all together for our morning sail. Our leader, Jean Lickleider, is a lanky, laid back mother of three herself, and she's smart as a whip. I absorb her ease and confidence as she shows us how to pick a point upwind on the far shore to head the bow of the boat towards. As the wind fills the sail, it tips the boat toward the sail. You want to ride with the edge of the boat as close to the water as possible, she explains to we eager but anxious newbie mariners, to get the greatest speed. But to get that speed you have to be willing to let the boat tip toward the sail. Too much tipping, and you will take in water or even capsize. Too little tipping, and the boat levels out. Then, you have a smooth sail, but you fall short of your intended destination point. She is teaching us to pay attention to our body intelligence, using our senses to guide our actions. Thus begin the lessons about risk and reward that will stand us in good stead when we need them in the wider arena of life.

Heading out from shore with the sheet (attached to the sail) in one hand, and the rudder (catching the resistance of the water) in the other, the pressure from the wind and the water meet right in your solar plexus. You are the master of your fate! An unexpected gust could tip you faster than you are ready for and send you into the drink—and believe me that happened. But by riding with the edge just touching the water's surface, and leaning out over the water on the opposite side of the boat to balance the pressure of the wind on the sail with your weight, you become one with movement born of balance. The boat roars forth, matching its speed to the force of the wind. Your muscles strain to hold the balance. Your feet brace against the center board box to secure your body as you lean out over the rushing water. The waves splash off the bow as it skips across the choppy water, hitting your face and arms and soaking your clothes and hair. The bow pounds into each wave like a tanner beating a hide, and the sail snaps in the wind, exciting all your senses. Your exhilaration is dizzying, your concentration fierce. There is rarely a more intimate bodily contact with the forces of Nature. Feeling that passion for connection with that force is what the love of sailing is all about.

Sailing is also an intimate connection with ropes and knots. Little do I realize as I "learn the ropes," that I am learning to handle the very things that made world travel possible to the ancient mariners. To those sailors, a knot that didn't hold cost lives. A rope that didn't bear the force of the gale wind sank the ship. Ancient traditions are being passed to us on these Saturday outings that none of us are wise enough to appreciate, yet we take in the knowledge and learn to trust our knots and our ropes just like ancient mariners. Soon enough we would learn that knots are good for more than sailing; they are a benchmark of skill in many endeavors, like pitching tents, mooring kayaks, raising flags, hanging hammocks, tying luggage on top of cars and dogs to leashes, and on and on. I learn how to tie a bowline behind my back. This skill is needed in case of capsizing, and needing to reconnect the sail to the mast underwater after emptying the water out of it. I never have to do that, but I'm glad I know how to tie that knot anyway. I will probably use that knot more than any other as I travel life's course. It's a wonderful thing to have the knowledge of knots at your fingertips whenever you need one. I probably wouldn't have learned knots without being a Mariner Scout.

Little do I realize at the time that readying the boat and heading out into the wind is great practice for all the challenging times coming in my life. I am learning a body wisdom beyond the mind. I am gaining a strength and focus from this intimate connection with nature. I learn to set a goal, but be flexible and know when to push farther and when to step back and assess or consolidate possibilities by listening, tuning in to the forces at work, and being patient with unpredictable dynamics. With people, those signals are more often looks on faces telling me whether they are with me like the wind in a full sail, or pushing back because I have gone too fast, like taking on water. Sometimes they just slough away like a wind that has changed its direction. I learn that a straight, even course with no tipping may be easy, but it's never as much fun—or as good a training for handling life's challenges—as an unexpected gust of wind.

The familiar adage "Don't rock the boat"—so descriptive of my mother's approach to life—now seems to me like a surrender of this vital life force. Having the willingness to rock the boat in spite of the risk—to learn from the unexpected—is what juices me. I don't get a merit badge for these lessons with the wind, but they are the most important lessons I learn in all my nine years of being a Girl Scout. They are probably what makes me love riding the edge of possibilities that takes me out of bounds more often than not as I venture farther on my life path.

Testing My Creativity:
An Entrepreneur is Born
1956

I have become an entrepreneur by the age of twelve, earning thirty-five cents an hour for babysitting. I am out several nights a week in high demand in my neighborhood. I take this endeavor to greater heights by the time I am sixteen by creating my own summer day camp in my backyard. I make $1000 the first season, but the money isn't as important as the dawning of my conscious creativity and my deepening trust in my connection to that source of wonder, play, and pleasure that would enable me to be self-employed for most of my adult life.

Our house has a basement recreation room that opens onto our backyard, and this is where the camp happens. With six- and seven-year-olds coming on Monday, Wednesday and Friday afternoons, and four- and five-year-olds Tuesday and Thursday—about twelve kids in total—what would the authorities today think of this unregulated, unapproved shenanigan? The parents trust me, and that is sufficient. I have to continually come up with a program. My father has a Boy Scout catalogue with all kinds of crafts for merit badge projects. He and I pour through the pages, finding simple handiwork like braiding lariats. We order the materials and when they arrive he teaches me how to make the lariat and weave it into a bracelet. Then I teach the kids. What a set up! I guess you would call him my production manager. I never realized until now how integral he was to my success. I thought I had done the camp all by myself!

The games are easy—Simon Says, musical chairs, Kick the Can, three-legged races and burlap bag races. I take all my stuffed animals--at least twenty of them--and mount them on green, sturdy tomato stakes (hmm, I wonder where I got those stakes from?) and turn them into puppets. With a big refrigerator-sized cardboard box (I wonder how I got that home…) for a stage, I climb behind it, open a curtain strung across an opening cut into the side of the box (did I do that cutting?) and put on a show. I have no idea when I start an episode what will happen next among the animals. "Hey rabbit," calls the dog, "Did you see bear riding a unicycle down our street yesterday?" "What's a unicycle?" the raccoon would ask. I don't have a plot. The animals just start interacting with each other and the audience, and a story arises in the moment.

I fearlessly trust this process in the same way that I trust my hand on the rudder. Of course, the stakes aren't very high with kids who still believe in magic helping me out on the other side of the box. They just start talking to the puppets and the story unfolds between us. "I know what it is!" one child would shout out. "How can you hold on without any handle bars?" another would ask the bear. The turtle would answer, "He does it by pretending he is a cloud." I have no idea where this story line is going, but it sure is fun.

Thirty years later, I would be doing the same thing with a group of women around a campfire as I don a mask and cape to impersonate Mother Earth searching for her daughters and finding them in that circle. The women, about to go out into the forest on a vision quest, would ask questions of Mother Earth just like the kids asked the puppets. The synergy of their suspended beliefs and my channeling of the archetype of the Great Mother usually produced surprising wisdom and insight. I never knew what She would say next, and it was often funny, always loving and courageous. She would end by walking into the night and calling back over her shoulder, "Fly, my daughters, fly." The sixteen year old in me knew very early how to fly.

I see in hindsight that I could not have done this dynamic and challenging endeavor without my father at my side. He never got ahead of me, telling me what to do. He was behind me, backing me up with resources and experience. He was the essence of Teacher, asking me what I needed to succeed and helping me find it. Many years later, I would read a study on women who became successful CEOs, and the main point of the article was that they all had fathers who believed in their ability and mentored them. I was so fortunate.

I also have reflected on the freedom I experienced at this age—that I could dream a dream and simply reach for what I needed to manifest it. There were no obstacles. None. The space, the resources, the help, the self-esteem born of experience, were all a function of the privilege I so unconsciously enjoyed from being a young, white, woman in a stable family, a safe neighborhood, with a good education and confidence born of that freedom. "To whom much has been given, much will be required" comes to mind. That's me. I'm ready. I'm willing.

As I search for the beginnings of what would become my calling, I see my budding entrepreneurial spirit—perhaps drawing on those ancient mariner genes—at the core. I have learned that imperfection is okay, and what matters is to follow my intuition, access my courage, and enjoy the adventure of discovery.

4

Opening to My Calling: National Student Christian Federation
1955

The fork in the road that changes the course of your life often shows up when you least expect it. This happens to me the summer between my freshman and sophomore year of high school. I'm settled down alone in my seat by the window for a seventeen hour train ride through the night that would carry me from Princeton, New Jersey to Grinnell, Iowa. I'm on my way to a National Student Christian Federation Conference with 1800 other teens from all over the country. I have very little sense of what I am heading into, never having traveled alone this far before. I feel safe, comfortable, and naively confident as I let myself be transported into the unknown.

My Presbyterian minister, Dr. David Crawford, is a very important person in my life. A true Scotsman, he has a bounce in his step and a thrill in being alive that is contagious. He encourages me to make this journey. I have been a very active and enthusiastic member of our teen fellowship group. My thirst for adventure along with his encouragement are a potent combo. You might say I am a poster child for Jesus. I love studying the Bible and singing in the choir. Mine is very down-home Christianity; I have never known anything else.

After countless hours of clickity-clacking through the night and into the next day, I find myself, suitcase in hand, standing in a strange railroad station. I feel like Dorothy landing in Oz. There are people to greet me, a college dorm room to find, and roommates to meet. Then I'm off to the big dining hall, and then I finally arrive at the cavernous gym where we hold the opening convocation. I am stunned by the spectacle of so many teens gathered in worship and praise that fills this space. I feel as expectant as a kid coming downstairs on Christmas morning. As we begin the week together, I go from one activity to another like someone at an "all you can eat" smorgasbord loading her plate to overflowing. Suddenly, everyone is a friend. Just looking into the faces of my peers, who are on fire with a passion for the message of Jesus and the call to service, I feel a new sense of identity—a belonging in a bigger world—beginning to coalesce. That busy acorn inside me seems to be jumping up and down, shouting "Come on, let's go!"

Before me in one of my first workshops stands a middle-aged white man wearing an ordinary suit and tie, but with a most extraordinary look in his blue eyes. He is sitting half on the edge of a desk in the front of a classroom full of rows of desks. He is a medical missionary in Nepal. He tells us stories about his life there with the gentle, sweet people and their Buddhist beliefs. His words seem to form a halo surrounding me; I am drawn into the sound of his voice and the kindness of his countenance. A dream is awakening in my core, a knowing without words. It is a feeling of belonging, of welcome, of a fate already in motion that I am seeing for the first time. The dream feels familiar, easy, big, and compelling. Suddenly, I know I want my life to be just like his. I am experiencing my calling.

I don't know his name; I simply take in his being. I become like him. No, it seems like I just become him. I am internalizing a sense of purpose for my life that I will never again be without. I know I want to be a missionary. This crossing of paths with a special stranger has the alchemy of timing, ripeness, and mystery that shows there is a plan—a path opening before me. I am experiencing a new clarity, born more from responding than from choosing. Where does this momentum come from that arises from beyond our conscious choosing and propels us forward onto the path opening before us? The acorn is beginning to lead, and I am a willing follower.

The teens from California have unknowingly brought the Asian flu with them to Grinnell. They start getting sick the second day, and by the third day, the authorities decide to send everyone home. I pack up and hastily embark on a train headed for Chicago. This time, I'm not alone; I have my fellow travelers for company. The germ does its dance on the train, and I, along with four other girls, am taken off the train in Chicago. Transferred by ambulance to the Municipal Contagious Disease Hospital, we spend the next five days in quarantine. After a few days of fever, we actually have a great time bonding around our most unexpected adventure, turning our quarantined ward into a gabbing slumber party that even the nurses enjoy joining in on.

For me, this twist of fate is the first of many where I would find myself turning up in places I don't expect with people I don't know as I follow the path I have chosen. It is also an initiation for my mother back in New Jersey, who is having her first experience of the alarming ups and downs my life would cause her, in which she could not help me, or fix a problem, or do anything but watch fearfully from afar as I spread my wings and fly. A few years later, when she realizes I am going to follow through with my intention to be a missionary, she would ask me, "Where did you get all this religion, anyway?" Now, many years later, I, too, ponder that question. I can only say that I did not "get" religion—it got me. It is what I said "Yes" to because I was touched by the Spirit moving through another person, through a life, and through history.

My return to Princeton is an anti-climax after the great adventure I have experienced. I feel like Marco Polo returning to Italy after seeing China. I couldn't possibly describe what had happened in a way anyone would understand. I could only show them. I would follow that vision for my life into my junior year of college abroad in Beirut, Lebanon with the Presbyterian Church, and then to Ghana to visit and work with missionaries for a summer after graduating from Goucher College. After completing a Masters in Religious Education at Princeton Theological Seminary at twenty-three, I would become a Frontier Intern missionary with the Presbyterian Church, and travel to Malawi, Central Africa with the same mission--to serve, to love, to learn, and to embody the Universal Church. I give thanks for that servant from Nepal who, in my young year, passed fire to me, and lit my way with a passion that would guide my steps for decades.

Innocent Abroad: Beirut, Lebanon
1960

How many lives are changed in the kitchen while washing dishes? Mine is. Shirley Lewis, a petite thirty-something with eyes that sparkle, is a guest at Thanksgiving dinner, a gathering attended every year by our family and three other Scout families. While she and I are in the kitchen washing dishes after the feast, Shirley tells me about the Junior Year Abroad (JYA) Program that her boss, Margaret Flory, has created for the Presbyterian Church. I am a sophomore in college at the time, and have never entertained the thought of doing a JYA, let alone one sponsored by a church. She goes on to explain that this program is intended to introduce interested young people to the mission of the church.

Now that strikes a deep chord in my being! I am intrigued as I wipe each dish Shirley passes me and stack it on the counter. Another thrilling synchronicity is unfolding: right person, right place, right time. Voila! A spark ignites, and that acorn inside me hits the ground running. Shirley makes it sound simple to apply. The only JYA programs I have ever heard of go to places like Paris or London. Margaret Flory's program goes to Lebanon, Ghana, India, Senegal and Malaysia. I can taste adventure. I decide before the last dish is dried that I will apply. It is curious in hindsight that with about fifteen other people attending this event, no one else came into the kitchen during our meeting of hearts and minds to interrupt what was happening or turn the chatting to something more trivial. Why did Shirley, the only guest at this traditional gathering, end up out in the kitchen washing dishes while everyone else was still chatting around the table? It is as if the waters of familiarity had parted, and something sacred was meant to happen in that opening in the kitchen.

I slyly warn my mother that I probably won't be accepted in order to allay her fear of such faraway places. One thing I will credit my mother with is that, in spite of how far I stretched her sense of the possible, she never stopped me from going where I felt led to go. So at twenty, having been accepted into the program, I cross the ocean and land on my first foreign soil in Beirut, Lebanon. I am actually on my way to a World Council of Churches work camp in Amman, Jordan for the month before school starts.

I am met and housed overnight by an American missionary couple, the Dotsons, who would be hosts to our contingent of eleven JYA students beginning in September. Getting from Beirut to Amman means crossing the desert by taxi. With courage born of innocence, I take a trolley down to the central plaza of Beirut, where I find a taxi going to Damascus. We passengers have to wait until the taxi fills before heading out on a six hour journey. Rolling hills of light brown dirt are all there is to see, it being the dry season. The air is filled with dust. Now I understand why Arab men and women wear scarves on their heads that they can easily pull across their nose and mouth when needed. No one speaks to me. We arrive after dark. The streets are full of people, cars, donkeys and bicycles. I grab my knapsack, walk quickly to the nearest hotel and book a room. It is a tiny eight by twelve foot room with a single bed, light stand and lamp. Dropping my luggage, I venture out to see what is nearby, as I don't dare get lost in this big, bustling place. I need to stay very near where I would catch another taxi the next morning to complete my journey to Amman.

I am surprised by the crowds of people out after 9 p.m. The

local souk (market) is teeming with people. For the first time I see women covering their entire bodies with black cloth. They seem to float along the sidewalk with a mysterious sameness. No features distinguish them, unless it is something they are carrying. Men sit together in open sidewalk coffee shops, and occasionally a shop owner calls out an invitation to sit and have coffee, but I am too much on my guard to accept such an invitation. I don't dare venture very far, so after a few blocks of gawking at brass pots engraved with Arabic writing and bolts of silk fabric hanging down from high perches on lashed together booths, I head for safety and sleep on an unyielding straw-filled mattress.

The next day, I journey across the Syrian Desert six more hours by taxi to Amman, again with no one speaking my language. I can't help but notice the hands of the woman next to me, extending out from her black shroud. They are dark brown, lined, and callused, telling a wordless story of survival and a woman's plight. I look at my own hands: young, smooth, very white. I never thought before of what our hands tell of our lives. I am sitting side by side with a woman just like me whose whole life has been lived in a different world of possibilities and obligations. She probably has little schooling, has many children, and maybe even multiple wives with whom she shares her husband. I have a college education, no children, freedom to travel, my own money, and a future of my choosing. So much shows in our hands.

The scenery is the same as yesterday—monotonous, yet intriguing in its strangeness to one who grew up in the verdant Northeast with rolling hills, mountains, and river valleys gushing with melt-off. At the border crossing, we passengers have to exit the taxi and undergo a body search, including the emptying of my purse on a table with two Arab women officers present, wearing their total body-covering garb. Among my possessions is a tampon. They have never seen one before and ask in Arabic what it is. I have to explain by demonstrating with my hands. We all have a shy giggle together as they take it all apart and then try unsuccessfully to put it back together. Three women meet that day at the level of female physiology, with knowing nods to suffice for our introductions.

Reaching Amman safely, tired and dirty, I join twelve others from Jordan, Egypt, Turkey, Britain, France, and the U.S. We will live in a school building, and work every day in the cloudless ninety degree August sun to help build a retirement home for the aged of a Christian community. We rise at five a.m., eat flatbread pita that we stuff with cheese and jelly—a new and quite delicious food combo for me. Fruit and yogurt are the other staples. Then we load into the back of a lorry ("truck" in British English, because Jordan had been a British protectorate between the two World Wars) and traverse the city of Amman with its mosque minarets rising far above any other structures in every neighborhood. Donkey carts and occasional camels with loads of merchandise travel the same roads as cars, taxis, and trucks of all kinds. Amman is a bustling city with steep hills throughout, and a white limestone façade on buildings old and new alike. The call of the Muezzins (prayer leaders) from the tops of multiple minarets follows us through the neighborhoods to our destination. We arrive at our work site by 6 a.m. in order to beat the sun's noontime intensity. Neighbors happily greet us, and vie with each other for who will offer hospitality for that morning's break around 9 a.m., which always includes Arabic coffee and sweets served on one of their cinder block verandas under umbrellas. They delight in feeding us and helping us find our first Arabic words like "please" and "thank you" and "where is the bathroom?"

We wield pick axes, shovels, and wheelbarrows, sharing tasks equally and drinking water almost constantly. I am mystified by the need for this retirement home in what seems like a traditional society, where I assume families take care of their elders.

The neighbors explain to us that younger families are migrating abroad for better opportunities, and sometimes disease will take the caretakers before the elders, so there is a need. We return home by lunchtime, eat and nap as is the local custom (a very sweet custom, as you know you aren't missing anything because everyone else is napping too.) We spend the late afternoon going on field trips to demonstration farms and historical sites. I attend my first and only camel race at a regular race track, and end up with the souvenir of my photo appearing in a local paper, surrounded by a report in Arabic of what this young American visitor thought of her first camel race. I can't remember what I said, and I certainly can't read it, but it is displayed proudly in my scrapbook.

My new Arab and European friends and I go out into the school yard one night when we hear that the Russian satellite "Sputnik" would be passing overhead. None of us had ever seen it before. We stand there together in the hot, dry desert air staring up at this strange flashing light travelling rapidly across the sky. In that moment, our world becomes one entity instead of many countries. How many times does a change of this psychological magnitude happen in a lifetime? I am mindful of sharing this pivotal moment with people from six different countries. We drop into a collective silence as what is happening penetrates our consciousness. Something that has become so ordinary and ubiquitous to us in the 21st century looks like an aberration this summer, something extraordinary. It changes our night sky forever. What was until then a place of mystery—a home of gods—has become a laboratory for scientists, and a racetrack for politicians. John, the other American in camp, says, "I guess the Russians will never let us forget this one." We have never known anything but the Cold War between our countries, and this is a big win for them if you are counting. Our Arab friends are puzzled by his comment. To them, it is just the first satellite.

As I hunt for the sparkling gems of this journey, one more

flashes before me. On one of the last days of our time together in Amman, our group has an audience with King Hussein of Jordan in his palace. We unload from the back of our lorry in front of a simple, one-story palace that is only distinguished by a wide staircase leading to a twelve foot high door, with the emblem of the Hussein family gilded in gold above it. We enter a chamber through a wide, marble-floored lobby and sit on wooden benches that face each other, resembling the British Parliament. The King enters and sits in an elevated oversized wooden chair situated at the end of the rows between the two facing sides. Wearing a western style suit and tie, at first glance he seems remarkably short—no taller than me. He has a mustache typical of this culture, and a big, comfortable smile. He listens attentively to our Arab minister leader's account of where we all come from, and what we have been doing for the community.

At the end of the interview, he very ritually tells us, "Thank you for serving the people of my country. If there is anything I can do for you, I gladly will." Being the innocent abroad that I am, I take him at his word and respectfully reply, "Well there is something you can do for us." In that moment I join the throngs

of those who have said things they shouldn't have. I'm sure the Jordanian minister stopped breathing in that moment. I am way out of bounds, but I don't know it. I go on to explain, "We all want to see the ancient ruins of Petra, but they are a six hour ride by car across a desert, and many of us are leaving in two days and don't have time to make the two day journey down and back. Could you help us get there?" He gracefully offers his private airplane and the next day we fly down, ride horses around the ruins for several hours, fly back, and then depart. I have a photo

caught by the palace photographer of the twenty-year old Sandra making her request to the King with her hands clasped in
front of her chest. I look like Anna in the movie The King and I.
I cherish that glimpse of the one who expected the world to be
her oyster and for the Universe to bless her on her journey. And
so it did, even if the group leader was embarrassed. He never
spoke to me about it.

When we land on the desert floor (no runway here), we are
met by guides holding horses for each of us. I mount the horse
as if I know what I am doing—which I don't. No one asks if I
do—a blatant cultural shock. I hope for the best and stick close
to the others so my horse will know what to do. Seeing the majestic walls of Petra with pillars and cornices adorning buildings
literally carved into the fifty-foot high cliffs of pink limestone is
startling and awesome, unlike anything I have ever seen before.
There are at least ten of them, with cliff dwellings as homesteads
located even farther above the buildings. They aren't real buildings—but they are. This place has been an oasis in a desert, a city
poised to be a destination for caravans from all directions in an
era when travel was by animal and sources of water marked the
routes taken. I am standing at a crossroad of the ancient world,
and the perfectly rounded pillars and streaks of pink marble
across the ceilings of the inner chambers tell the story. Like so
many other important places, when the water dried up, the people left. What remains is the shell without the pulse of life. Only
we few tourists scuttle about between the mansions where once
throngs from many lands crossed paths and, no doubt, palms.
My world is forever bigger and older, and the context of my life
changed by the depth of history in this place.

At the end of August, I move on to Beirut and the American
University, where I would meet the other ten participants in the
JYA program. When I enter the Student Christian Center, which
is to be our home base and where our American missionary advisors live, I see Bruce Boston through a doorway, sitting on the

edge of a desk. He is wearing jeans, a navy and white striped tee shirt, and white buck shoes—a mark of the 1960s. His presence is sparkling. His platinum blonde crew cut shows off his sky-blue eyes, and his smile—relaxed and confident—welcomes me. I don't remember words spoken, only a feeling of gladness that this new person would be an instant friend in a foreign land. So much more would come with that smile.

A week later, as I am waiting in a long line in the hall of a three story classroom building to register for classes, I suddenly feel ill and drop to the floor. I don't even remember how I get to the hospital where I would spend the next three weeks recovering from Hepatitis B. I had drunk contaminated water somewhere in Jordan. I don't feel sick, but am told I can't put my feet on the floor. I have to give my liver time to recover. I'm fine, but I find out much later that my mother was a wreck. Mail takes three weeks by ship, and she has no information that the hospital I am in is the most modern in the Middle East. I'm not in any trouble, but once again she has to cope with powerlessness. She is being given an assignment she didn't ask for and is not prepared to weather. I wonder, sometimes, if she ever forgave me for frightening her so much.

I do have one shocking experience while in the hospital. This is a teaching hospital, and the medical students have such trouble drawing my blood that I would have a mini-anxiety attack whenever I hear the jiggling bottles on the tray on wheels coming down the hall. One day, the head doctor, actually an American, comes into my room with a rubber tie and syringe in hand. He is determined to have me get over my fear by having me draw his blood. Yikes! I am horrified by the prospect, yet mildly intrigued. "Here I go again, way out of bounds," I think. He rolls up his sleeve and hands me the tie. I draw it tightly around his upper arm, just as I have seen it done so many times before. Then he hands me the syringe and says, "Go ahead." He is calm, like there is nothing to this. I guess that's what he wants me to experience, but I am still busy being appalled that he would ask such a thing. I begin to stick the needle in where I can see his vein bumping up against his skin. I don't push far enough. The vein is slippery; it slides away from the needle. Clearly something else is required. He coaches me to push harder. I am amazed at how much pressure it takes to penetrate the vein, but I do succeed. The blood comes gushing into the syringe. I pull it out, without knowing to hold the point of the needle up, so blood spills all over the bed and him and me. "Oh well," he says, "You did what I came here to accomplish. There now, that wasn't so bad was it?" he asks. I don't think he is really asking me; he is telling me. I'm not convinced that my experience of the blood-letting will be any different, but I certainly have had my mind blown by this unusual style of doctoring.

My grandfather dies during the three weeks I am hospitalized, but I don't find out about it until I receive a letter that has been traveling for all that time. The funeral is over by now, and everyone has gone back to their lives. No one even contemplated a phone call. It was probably possible, but we didn't know how. It is a strange experience to grieve all by myself, among people who have never known Pierre Bontecou, our family patriarch. Grieving alone is like being in a mirage; it is a reality no one else is sharing. My mind chases after facts but can't be sure. He had died on the operating table. He had lung cancer. So what were they trying to do? Could they have saved him with an operation? There is no one to get the full story from. My mother's letter doesn't share anything about her loss or her grief. I realize how much grieving is a communal event. We need each other to mirror the reality that the mind wants to jump away from, so it can pretend that something else is true.

I revisit in my mind how my father had died two years previously, and how similar this experience is of how my family does death. He also had cancer, but he had lived with a kind of leukemia for six years, so we had all colluded in the belief that he might be all right. He was working; and life seemed normal when he drove me back to college after Christmas break my freshman year. A week later, I was called down to the Dean's office from class and told that my father had died that morning. My mother was on the phone. I was so stunned I didn't feel much of anything. It was unreal. I had just seen him being fine. He had been in the hospital for three days with pneumonia, and died because his body couldn't fight the infection.

I had felt for years after his death that I had been left out of the loop, prevented from being at his side because of my mother's unwillingness to admit what was happening. Now this death feels the same. The message is "Here's the basic information; deal with it yourself." She shares nothing of her experience of the loss. It would take me until JFK's assassination three years later to let the depth of my grief about my father that was my true experience come to the surface. I decompensated so dramatically for the three days of JFK's funeral that I had to go see a therapist. It took that counselor about five minutes to put the three stories together and invite me to finally grieve–with his attention and validation–for the loss of my father and grandfather. Years later I would be able to ask my mother why she didn't call me when my father went into the hospital, and why she went through that traumatic experience alone when I was two hours away by train. Her answer was, "I didn't want to bother you. We both thought he would be all right." It took me more years to truly accept her story and not attribute it to denial.

Bruce becomes my daily visitor in the hospital, even as he is making his way in this new place. One day, he shows up with Winnie the Pooh and reads to me. I am charmed. By the time I am released from the hospital, a very special spark has been struck between us. It becomes a daily challenge for us to find ways and places to connect amidst all our responsibilities as students, program participants, and dorm mates. We also realize we are in a culture that has no places for unmarried couples to spend time together. It just doesn't happen. One day we are walking along the promenade by the Mediterranean Sea, and an Arab man comes angrily up behind us and pulls Bruce's hand away from his grip on a decorative belt on the outside of my winter coat. It is a brisk reminder that our American behavior is out of bounds in this Arab culture. Our most romantic moments are shared in the apartment of our missionary sponsors, who discreetly give us the privacy they as Americans understand we want.

I am living in a women's dormitory surrounded by tropical plants, palm trees, and a view of the Mediterranean Sea from my bedroom. I live with a Syrian roommate, Iktimal Makdisi. She is delightfully warm and welcoming to me, the stranger in her land. Our dorm room is just wide enough for two single beds,  two desks, and built-in closets. Iktimal prepares Arabic coffee for me every morning as soon as we rise, using a dainty cup the size of an egg, with a quarter inch of grounds in the bottom. It is potent stuff, and not having been a coffee drinker until then, it is a jarring culture shock to learn that one never refuses when a cup of coffee is offered. I am a Sociology major, and I will attend classes on the clash of cultures that are caught between modern and traditional values. Iktimal embodies these clashes on a daily basis. She piles her long, bleached blonde hair on top of her head, wears mini-skirts and high heels, applies tons of eye make-up, and speaks fluent English. Yet she has been betrothed since she was twelve to a man twenty years her senior, who is waiting for her to graduate, return to her village, and marry him.

My fellow students are from all of the Middle Eastern countries and South Asia. Imtiaz Hudin Hussein is a tall, lanky classmate from Hyderabad, India, with a cocky swagger and eyes that dance with delight. He always wears a tie and sports coat. I meet him when I join the field hockey team, not knowing it is an all-male activity in this part of the world. Imtiaz is very open-hearted and jovial. He becomes my best friend. He is enchanted by the sounds of Western city names. He loves to recite "Ann Arbor, Meee-cheee-gan" or "Sas-ka-tooooon, Sas-kaaaa-tche-wan," or "Tullll-sa, Ok-la-hommm-ma" as if they are a love song. He challenges me to find out facts about India. Almost daily he seeks me out on campus amidst the throngs of students to tell me an important fact he wants me to know.

Over a semester break, I travel home with Iktimal to her village, Safita, with its crumbling Crusader castle a-top a hill overlooking olive orchards and one-story mud-stucco homes that spiral from the base of the hill up to the top. I meet her father, an engineer who rides horseback to all his construction sites and keeps his financial books in his head. I journey to Turkey, Egypt, and all over Lebanon, travelling through mountains covered with the Biblically famous cedars of Lebanon to the ancient Roman city of Baalbek, and to coastal towns where the ancient Phoenician mariners' blue dye vats are still visible among the ruins. I am awash in history, wailing Arabic music, and the spicy smells of the exotic foods of an ancient land. I am experiencing a taproot of civilization. Something mysterious and quiet is stirring in my soul—perhaps my own remembering?

Amid the storied ancient ruins and the warm hospitality of the people here, there would be some very uncomfortable lessons waiting for me. One is learning the truth about the origin of the Israeli-Palestinian conflict from people who had lived through the flash point of its origin just twelve years before, but which still rages today, sixty-six years after Israel was formed as a nation. Britain, which had been the colonizing power of this region between World War I and II, withdrew overnight from their post as the governing body, and left Israel free to declare its nationhood in the land it had shared with Palestinians for more than two millennia.

This take-over of the land that had been Palestine has been rewritten by the Zionist movement in my country; few Americans know what I am told. When Israel declared itself a State on the very land that Palestinians had occupied for millennia, the Arab citizens were left unarmed to fend for themselves as Israelis stole their land, destroyed their homes, bulldozed their villages (534 of them to be exact), and threatened their lives. When the Arabs pushed back, defending their right to their homes and land, they were called terrorists, and they still are today. My country took Israel's side, aligning with its right to protect itself from attacks while the American press erased the Arab side of the story—that these Arab attacks against Israelis were meant to right a wrong. Iktimal's boyfriend, Samir, a Palestinian, calls Israel "Jewish- occupied Palestine." I am stunned by what I am learning. My naiveté is being grabbed away from me with no ground for me to stand on. I am being expected to understand that my country is on the "wrong side" of the conflict, a conflict I have not ever even heard of before. My whole world view as an American—that my country is a "good guy" who helps other countries—is being called into question.

My lesson in geo-politics continues to unfold relentlessly. I come across a book called *What Price Israel?* by Alfred M. Lilienthal in the university library, and I learn from my Palestinian friends that it is banned in the U.S. When I protest that we don't ban books—that we have freedom of the press—I am informed that while that may be true, the Zionist movement in the U.S. bought every copy published, so it never reached the bookstores of America. My eyes are being opened to how politicians distort the truth to gain advantage. I am alarmed. I begin to feel insecure as an American abroad. I am compelled to turn in my badge as a proud American, and eat the humble pie of seeing my country through the eyes of my friends who have been devastated by choices my countrymen have made. I would take a copy of that book—along with my stories of what happened to Palestine—home to Goucher College in the fall, where I would complete my senior year. There I would discover a shocking disinterest among the Jewish students in knowing the truth about what happened in 1948 as the State of Israel took form. I would soon learn another painful lesson for the innocent (even though now home): to challenge the Israeli story of promised-land Biblical entitlement is to be considered anti-Semitic. To know what really happened—and speak out about it—is to be out of bounds in my own homeland.[1]

My discomfort continues to grow as I meet more people who do not like what my country has done in the world. When I ask my new Iranian friends what makes them so angry at the U.S., I am told about how in 1953 ((just seven years ago) the CIA overthrew a legitimately elected Iranian government that wanted to deprive U.S. oil companies of access to the largest oil reserves in the Middle East. The leader, Mosaddegh, intended to nationalize the oil fields for the benefit of the people of Iran. The Shah of Iran, who was quickly installed as leader after the coup, headed a shadow government imposed on the Iranian people by U.S. imperialism. What? Imperialism? My country? I am confused. I am automatically defensive, and, again, I have my head handed to me. I am defending something that is indefensible. My innocence vanishes. Sometimes we have to learn by being humiliated.

I am exposed for the ignorant American that I am. I am having to realize how defensive I am because of that ignorance. I suddenly remember an experience I had with my friend Don Moxon in London on my way to Beirut. While having a beer together in a pub he said, "The trouble with Americans is they can't take criticism." My immediate response was, "What do you mean they can't take criticism!" I sure bit that bait, and proved how right he was. Now here I am again, confronted with the truth of my new friends' experiences, having to look at my country through the eyes of those we have wronged. My eyes are opened; I would never again turn a blind eye as some do who know the truth and choose to distort it, or believe the cultural myth my history classes have perpetrated of my country as the good Christian hero on the white horse galloping around the world to save people. Now I know we are galloping all right, but mostly to gain for ourselves at the expense of others' liberty and right of self-determination. It is a bitter pill to swallow, one I am still choking on today. Can you taste it?

My world expands until it will never be the same again. I am being welcomed, embraced, and loved by the people of a world so unlike my own. And I love them back. I love the call of the muezzin from the minarets in every neighborhood at 4:30 in the morning. I love the spicy food, the strangely melodic wailing kind of music with drums often accompanying. I love the vastness of the Mediterranean Sea, which I can see when walking between classes on campus. I love the market place, with stalls darkened by archways and tarps overhead protecting from sun and rain, where friendly merchants stand in the street calling out to every passerby to stop in for a cup of tea, or coffee, or hubbly-bubbly (smoking, with the smoke inhaled through water). I love the sense of hospitality for the stranger, so deeply rooted in the tradition of the coffee cup and the open door, and so unlike my own culture that now seems to me overly protective from the approach of strangers.

I love remembering who I was at twenty-one—fearless, open, curious, and adventurous. I played field hockey with Indian and Pakistani men. I climbed to the top of the Great Pyramid in Cairo, and saw the most beautiful building I have ever seen even to this day—the Blue Mosque in Istanbul. I even had a reunion there with a student, Jimmy Nuretin Munis, who had come on an exchange program and stayed in my home in Princeton, N.J., when we were in high school. My world is peopled with friends. My path into the mission field is open, my calling clearer. I am no longer a novice. I have weathered cultural differences, eating, dancing, praying and playing in new ways. I have taken in the strange beauty of Muslim culture, and the equally strange beauty of the icons and incense of Greek Orthodox Christianity. I know more profoundly what it means to be an American. I am more acutely aware of the degree of freedom I have as an American woman, compared to Muslim women whose behavior is so tightly controlled by their culture.

I am also a woman more deeply in love than ever before. I have met my mate. Bruce is smart as a whip (a photographic mind, actually), charming, and handsome as a stallion. He knows how to court and he wears his heart on his sleeve. He is totally present. He is a great dancer and some of my happiest memories are of our time together whirling around the dance floor and bogeying to rock and roll. We are both ripe for the picking, ready for a life partner who shares our deepest passion. We would continue our courtship at home, though separated by  600 miles. We would become engaged a year later when we graduate from college, and marry the following year when we have each completed a year at Princeton Theological Seminary. We have begun our life together, sharing our commitment to the mission of the church, with a flair for adventure in foreign lands.

1.

Arab Palestinian revolts against perceived Jewish intention to form a state in their land had begun in 1929. Even while the US and Great Britain were planning how to absorb the 500,000 displaced persons in Europe following the war, the international Zionist movement was working to divert their resettlement to Palestine to reinforce the necessity of a state for the Jewish people. All of this transition was in the context of the Nazi holocaust against the Jewish population of Europe which had killed six million, and a Nazi massacre in the Ukraine that killed 20,000 Jews in two days. The Jewish people desperately needed a safe homeland.

It was the termination of a U.N. mandate on May 14, 1948 that prompted the British withdrawal from Israel. Partition of Palestine into two states was being considered by the UN after the war ended, and a very controversial vote among delegates to a convention to make a recommendation to the General Assembly had passed a recommendation for partition by just six votes, but the UN General Assembly had not yet voted to proceed with partition when Israel raised its flag and declared itself a state at midnight on May 14. Eleven minutes later, President Truman recognized the new state without having informed his Secretary of State or Ambassador Atkins who was at the same time arguing on the floor of the General Assembly against partition.

Seven Hundred thousand Arabs (Lilienthal says one million) were displaced in the process of creating the state of Israel—which has over the ensuing 66 years grown to four million. Many attempts have been made to resolve this dilemma of justice for both groups of people, and to this day no solution has won the support of both groups. Despite strong pressure for a peaceful two-state solution in both populations, the stalemate has left an Israeli militarized occupation of land designated by the U.N. to be a Palestinian state, including what President Jimmy Carter characterized as an apartheid system of control of the Palestinian people, and continuing expansion of Israeli "settlements" (read: cities of 20-50,000) in Palestinian territory contrary to the U.N. mandate and deemed illegal by the International Criminal Court. Israel claims this occupation is necessary for security.

For a detailed account of the creation of the state of Israel from the point of view of an American anti-Zionist Jew, read What Price Israel? By Alfred M. Lilienthal (copyright 2003 by Infinity Publishing Company. Available from info@buybooksontheweb.com 877-BUY BOOK.) This edition is the fiftieth anniversary edition of the original published in 1953, just five years after the creation of Israel. It includes seven pages of endorsements reflecting the importance of Lilienthal's contribution in spite of relentless personal attack from American Zionists over the fifty years.

II
Venturing Into Mission

To live our lives fully,
To work wholeheartedly,
To refuse directly what we cannot swallow,
To accept the mystery in all matters of meaning -
This is the ultimate adventure.
The pursuit of certainty and predictability
is our caution speaking.
Freedom is the prize, safety is the price.
What is required is faith more than fact,
and will more than skill.

Peter Block, The Answer to How is Yes

6

Missionary In the Making: Ghana
1962

"You can't do that!" my mother laments when I tell her I am going to Ghana in West Africa for the summer following my graduation from college. Again our worlds collide, and again I am going out of bounds––her bounds. I wonder if she really thinks the world is flat, and that if you go to Africa you fall off the edge? I don't think to ask her more about what her concerns are, or try to understand her better. I'm twenty-two, I'm in a hurry, and I've already bought the ticket. I am also newly engaged to Bruce Boston. The diamond he gave me is soon put away in a safety deposit box until my return. I am following my star, and the synchronicities are in play again, as they always seem to be when one is open, ready, and focused.

One of the trainers for our J.Y.A. program, Henry Boucher, had done a seminary year abroad in Ghana under the same Presbyterian program, and he had put me in touch with several missionary families there. I wrote to each of them explaining my intention to pursue that calling, and my desire to visit them, join them, and experience the field first hand. The American and Scottish missionaries all responded positively, and one even agreed to meet me at the Accra airport. That's all the information I need. I offer to show the letters to Mom, but she rejects my offer. She is not open to being persuaded and neither am I. Where is her curiosity? Where is mine?

How old were you when you stopped asking your Mother for permission to do something big, like leave home for good? In hindsight, I see it now as an important transition, and one most parents are not ready for, but I don't even notice that that is what I am doing. I hadn't even discussed my plans with her. I have simply taken one share of I.B.M. stock which my grandmother gave me at my high school graduation, and for $500 have purchased a round-trip ticket to Accra, Ghana. I have also enrolled in my second World Council of Churches work camp in the tiny village of Agbosome, where twenty-five Americans would join an equal number of Africans from Ghana, Nigeria, Togoland and Cameroon. This world is truly at my fingertips. I am hungry for adventure and the church is glad to provide it. Nothing fazes me about getting on an airplane and heading for West Africa. Maybe moving those six times as a child and having to make new connections quickly has given me a skill for life that stands me in good stead in these circumstances. Having no expectations also makes leaving easy. Just to be there and be a part of what is happening is enough to satisfy me.

I spend the first two weeks in Agbosome near the Atlantic coast and the border with Togoland (now called Togo), where the work camp is being held. The village has one main dirt road lined on both sides by round mud huts with thatched roofs. I  can walk from one end to the other in about ten minutes. Palm trees are the only vegetation. People move slowly, mostly on foot and carrying a load of some kind on their head or back. I am immersed in the simplest way of life I have ever experienced. There is no need to rush; no one is going very far. The village is surrounded by agricultural fields, where everyone spends their time as far as I can see. There are just a few stores with toothbrushes, combs, and other things made of plastic imported from China. There is a beer parlor with outside tables, which only men seem to patronize. It seems busy all day long, which surprises me. I later learn that men's and women's work in cultivating the fields is clearly delineated. Men do the hard work of breaking up the soil at the beginning of planting; then they rest the duration of the season while the women plant, weed, harvest, and take the produce to market.

We live in an elementary school located at the end of the main road on the edge of town. It is made entirely of concrete, with straw mattresses on the floor for sleeping. With fifty people to integrate, it is hard to form community. Food is a force that keeps us separated by ethnic pallets. When the Ghanaians cook they put red pepper in all the food, which makes it just about inedible to the Americans. Believe me, I tried. Likewise, when the Americans cook, they put more salt in the food than Ghanaians can tolerate, so pretty much everyone is unhappy. This dilemma could be such an opportunity for negotiation if anyone had had that skill, but unfortunately no one does.

We are laying a foundation for a church. Our days consist mostly of digging, filling wheel barrows, and moving dirt. The Africans sing as they work, with a relaxed way of playfully moving through a work day. We Americans provide a nose to the grindstone get-it-done work ethic that leaves us exhausted in the hot African sun. We don't have much fun along the way, with our fierce focus on results. In addition to the food barrier, there is also a language barrier as many of the African women have not been to school. The group is too large to handle these big differences without someone giving leadership to the process. We are left to our own devices, and that pretty much amounts to everyone retreating to the group they feel safe with. It is a challenge to reach across that divide, but that is why I am here.

I befriend a middle-aged Nigerian Episcopal priest named Daniel who always wears his clerical collar, even when we work in the hot sun for hours. We spend every evening in each other's company, talking politics and the Church. I am alarmed to learn that he lives daily with threats to his life and that of his congregation. Christians in northern Nigeria are being persecuted by the Muslim society there. I have never before encountered stories of random killings, house-burnings, and animal slaughter in order to eliminate food supplies—all motivated by hate and prejudice. Daniel's faith and his future are being sorely tested, yet he has a radiant countenance and sense of humor that illuminates his faith. I wonder if my faith would stand up to that kind of threat. I reflect—maybe for the first time—on how safe my life has always felt, and how Americans treat "others" in my culture by denigrating the poor, redlining real estate, and isolating the homeless, disabled, and mentally challenged. Surely I am unconsciously enjoying all the privileges of a white, middle class, educated, dominant group and benefiting from ignoring the plight of the less fortunate. This is a sober awakening for me, happening so far from home through the stories of a victim.

One day, all the Americans go away from the base on a field trip. I decide to stay back and be with the African women. Unbeknownst to me, some of the women—all much younger than I—go into the American women's luggage and find their bathing suits. They put the suits on, giggling the whole time with a spicy blend of delight and naughtiness, and we head for the ocean, a half-hour walk from the school. My ethics of private property are being trumped by the African sense of communal property. To them, what they are doing isn't stealing; it is sharing. The women also dress me up in one of their sarongs and make my hair into corn rows (tiny braids all over my head). I look like a skinned cat with my hair plastered tight to my head. They look like bathing beauties! What a cross-cultural bonanza this outing is, and it would remain a secret to all those whose bathing suits participated while they were off having an African experience. I'm glad I have my camera that day, and the pictures to show that this outing really happened. Given that I choose to keep their secret, my loyalties have clearly shifted from my own people to these new friends in whose land I am a guest.

I feel like a kid who discovers her parents playing Santa, and decides not to report the discovery in order to perpetuate the playful, happy myth. I am protecting something very vulnerable and special. I am inside an experience that cannot be explained or shared. It is about African women getting to pretend they are in a culture where they can enjoy their beauty and sexuality without being seen as prostitutes. They are experiencing a hit of liberation, albeit pretend, but it feels powerful. I am grateful that they trust me enough to include me in their adventure. I wonder what would have happened if we'd all been able to talk about it. I am left with my assumptions. I choose to keep the secret because we haven't done very well around the food issues.

At the end of camp, Henry and Sue Boson meet me in their VW bug and drive me 100 miles north to their village, Manyaka-poinore. It sounds like a song to me. They are a young American couple, probably in their late twenties (no children yet, and clearly still in love). They live in an elegant but simple two-story wooden structure that exudes the history of Protestant mission in this place for a hundred years. All the wooden walls are dark with age. The late evening and early morning sounds of roosters, donkeys and mourning doves tell me I am far from familiar environs. Physically set apart from the village by a few miles—which means they use their car daily to move around—seems to tell another story of cultural separateness that I find strange. Henry and Sue are both teachers in the local elementary school, where I join them for the next two weeks. This village of maybe 500 people is still unaccustomed to seeing white people, so whenever we drive through the dirt, one-lane main road, lined as usual with mud huts topped with thatched roofs, children race behind the car shouting "Brofunio! Brofunio!" meaning "White person! White person!" This is my first experience of being in a minority. It feels strange to realize I have a skin color, and that it is defining my identity. While I am aware of being in an utterly unfamiliar culture myself, I have not realized until hearing the children that I am also a stranger. Oh the tricks our perceptions can play on us!

I spend two weeks with this missionary family teaching English in the school every day, and being part of their family every evening. I teach the children to sing "White Coral Bells" in a round. I listen daily to the waist-high drums that are still used for communication with the next village. I watch the women dancing to their own singing, and they teach me how their shoulders go one way and their hips move the other way—very hard for the inexperienced—as they joyfully pull me further into their world. With their laughing faces and bright colored clothing, they generate all their entertainment in community, a seemingly lost art in my culture. The warmth and openness of these villagers confirms my choice to pursue missionary work. The connection I feel, in spite of us not "knowing" each other, makes the Universal Church come alive for me.

After two weeks, the Bosons travel 300 miles north to a missionary conference, and they take me along. There I connect—as pre-arranged—with Tom Colvin, a middle-aged Scottish missionary who gladly takes me home with him another 200 miles to northern Ghana for another two weeks. He lives in Tamale, which is a Muslim area. In addition to the same huts, dirt roads and animals in the streets, there are muezzin calling at dawn and women with their heads covered. Tom is a builder, and his wife, Patsy, is a nurse in the local hospital. Their home is simpler—made from local mud bricks—and located on the very edge of the village but integrated into the community in a way that the Boson's home was not. I wonder if being this remote made early missionaries more dependent on the village for survival than those closer to the coast. I feel at home in the quiet but generous way Patsy and Tom invite me into their home and into their world. They are the first Iona-trained missionaries I meet (there will be more), originating from an island off the coast of Scotland that is known for training missionaries in a radical understanding of mission that differentiates it from the more traditional missionaries of the 19th century. I can see that their mission is to serve and bear witness, but not convert. That feels so right to me. I am breathing in how to do ministry.

My time here is less structured, so I mostly hang out with people and visit Tom's projects. He builds wells, schools, and hospitals--anything that is needed. His joy in his work is contagious. Patsy's work at the hospital is with birthing mothers. Women here only come to the hospital if they are in trouble, so Patsy is constantly dealing with emergencies. Tom and she both speak the local dialect—a must for the success of their ministry. I am daily reminded of how at home I take the work of nurses and engineers for granted, while here I see them as life-saving and life-changing. Having a well that sustains through floods and droughts here changes the whole experience of survival.

The gentleness of the people reflects the mood of their domestic animals who wander the streets by day and sleep in pens attached to the huts at night. Living in direct contact with such large animals—mostly cows, donkeys, and pigs—is a lesson for me about food and sustainability; these villagers live in relationship with their food supply. It is also a lesson about simplicity and community. Everyone watches out for the animals. They are an integral part of the village. Their presence permeates the feel of the place.

I open to wonder and beauty as I walk the streets, listen to the drums and the muezzin's call, and stare into the eyes of animals up close. Every woman seems to have a suckling baby on her body, and a bundle of some kind on her head. The sarong she wraps around her underarms also serves as a diaper, allowing her to simply release the bottom edge holding the baby's body when the babe starts to urinate, allowing the rest of the urine to fall to the ground just like all the other animals. Children happily play with hand-made toys while animals move boxes, soil, and people. At some point I realize that this way of life is more the norm for humans the world over than the lifestyle I am accustomed to. And it doesn't seem all that hard. There is something soft about it. The pace is kind. The expectations are simple.

Tom and Patsy serve and share in quiet but meaningful ways as part of the community. I see that true ministry is not about preaching the Gospel, but about living it by bridging differences of faith, culture and lifestyle with love and respect. Sometimes that love is just plain service—assisting with an operation, or building a school. Surely here God is a verb. Two years hence, as a Frontier Intern in Malawi, I would be trained in the consciousness of being a Christian presence in a non-Christian world. I would remember the simple lessons Tom and Patsy demonstrated here in Northern Ghana. My life is unfolding just as I have hoped, and more teachers are being given to me as I open further to my calling.

When it is time to leave, the plan is for me to fly from Tamale back to Accra, a distance of about 600 miles. Tom takes me to the local airport, where there is one twin engine plane sitting idle in an open field. There we are told that the pilot is not available to fly that day. I panic. My return flight to the U.S. is the next day. But Tom doesn't panic. He knows this country and he knows these people. After all, he is a builder in an undeveloped land. He knows about options and make-shift solutions. This situation is probably normal for him. We simply drive to the only gas station in town to wait for the next carload of folks driving south, who will inevitably come here before heading out. We only have to wait half an hour, and because Tom knows everyone in town and speaks the language, I am assured a ride.

The car that pulls up to the pump is already full from my point of view, but in this society there is always room for one more—praise be to Allah! No one in the car speaks English.

Mom and Dad sit in the front of the 1950s gray Chevy. Mom has on her typically stunning headdress of colorful fabric wrapped around her head and reaching a foot above her forehead. There are two children in the back seat with me. All I remember of the ten hour ride through semi-desert savannah is singing "Where is Thumbkin?" over and over as the children laugh and try to look behind my back. Music is such a sure way to connect across language barriers. I am being carried by kindness, even though I can't see the faces of my benefactors riding in the front seats. I just sit in the gracefulness of these people—their generosity, and their trust in the goodness of a stranger. Once again I find myself pondering how a similar situation in my home country would unfold. Would strangers agree to take someone from a foreign land when their car is already full, and they will be travelling 400 miles? Would you? Would I? We all deserve to meet people capable of that trust when we are in trouble.

That evening we pull up at a wooden door ten feet high embedded in a mud wall. We ring the large bell that hangs outside. I don't even know I am about to enter a Swiss mission station. Tom has called ahead and they are expecting me. I sleep that night on clean, white sheets, safe in the embrace of English speaking foreigners. It is a strange but comforting place to spend my last night in Ghana. Once again, I feel held in the lap of the Universal Church, and pulled even more deeply into my calling to be this Church, to do this work, to be part of the Body of Christ in God's world. The next morning, these kind Swiss missionaries take me to their local airport, which actually has a runway and a tower as well as an empty seat on a plane to Accra. I feel my angel's wings flapping around me. I see her in the smiles of the missionaries of my wayside inn as they wave me away. I arrive at the right airport four hours before my flight home.

Flying back over the Atlantic, I know I am on the right path for me. I am carrying the joy of connection across borders and across history. I have followed a trail laid down by Henry Bucher, a person I had only known for a few days two years before. The same spirit of calling that led him to do a seminary year abroad had created the opening for me to step into. I know for sure now I am being led where I need to go by who I will meet. I don't know yet that the Tom Colvin I met in Tamale had been in Malawi for many years before coming to Ghana, and that two years hence I would find myself working in Malawi as a missionary, once again following Tom's footsteps. I am being woven into a web of connection—the morphogenic field of the Universal Church—not because of my planning, but because of my saying "Yes" to doors that are opening as I follow my heart. My acorn already has its radar out for the next synchronicity, which I now have learned to expect.

I thought culture shock was something that happens when you go to a foreign land, but I now realize it also happens in reverse. The culture shock I experience upon my return from Ghana is intense. I keep listening for the muezzin to call. I miss being around large animals roaming lazily through the streets, slowing everything to their pace. I miss the joyful, spontaneous singing and dancing that punctuated every day and every gathering. I miss looking into the sea of black faces and feeling welcome. I miss the red dirt and the vista of a savannah landscape. I miss the date and coconut palms and the young boys who scamper up their trunks barefoot to grab their fruit. I miss the church services with nursing babies at the breast and toddlers playing at their parents' feet, with sticks and stones their only toys. I miss eating corn maize with my bare hands and getting used to the red pepper in the meager chicken stew.

The American music I hear lacks the primal throb of the drums. The food seems bland and so ordinary. Women's clothing seems subdued, modest, and quiet, such a contrast to the bold liveliness of primary colors against black, glistening bare skin. I miss the infant suckling as a mother walks with a bundle of wood balancing on her head. All the cars seem so unremarkable in their coming and going, without wild beasts wandering beside them and bicycles weaving in and out among them. Traffic lights seem strangely mechanistic, controlling the movement of everything like some wizard behind a screen. Now back in my familiar town, nothing seems that familiar anymore. The town hasn't changed in my absence, but the lens through which I look has. It is indeed home, yet my home has grown to hold so much more. The whole world—and its people—have now become my home.

I am returning to a fiancé who has missed me, reunion with my sparkling new diamond ring, and entry into Princeton Theological Seminary. During the next year before our wedding, I would give that ring back, afraid that if Bruce doesn't want to do with his life what I know I want, I won't be able to follow my dream if I marry him. He reassures me that he understands my intention and asks me to trust him. I do. We marry the following June and spend a year at the Lawrence Road Presbyterian Church in Trenton, N.J. with Bruce assisting in leading Sunday worship and both of us facilitating the Junior and Senior High Youth Fellowships. We have begun our ministry together. We would leave a year later for Malawi as "Frontier Interns," again following the lead of Margaret Flory's innovative vision for the mission of the church.

Speaking Truth to Power: Malawi, Central Africa
1964

I am packing for an assignment that has only a question for the job description: "What is the role of a Christian in nation-building?" This is my next chance to go out of bounds, to do something no one in my family or friendship circle has ever done—go to work in Africa. The time has finally come to step fully into my calling to the mission field of the Universal Church. With a Master's degree in Christian Education under my belt, a wedding ring on my finger (the diamond back into storage again), Margaret Flory at our backs, and Bruce by my side, we head out across the Atlantic to the Rift Valley in Central Africa, near the place of the earliest origins of humankind. Having been involved with Margaret's projects before, we trust her vision and the web of connections she has woven over many years of work all over the world. It seems I am destined to weave through the manifestations of her mind, as this wonder-working woman creates new programs to help the Church keep pace with how its mission is changing in an increasingly diverse, yet interconnected world. It seems as if Margaret has laid out a path for me to follow; all I had to do was say "Yes," and step up. My acorn has been dancing to Margaret's tune for quite a while. Thankfully, my husband of one year is a willing companion.

Bruce and I had followed Margaret's lead to attend the World Student Christian Federation Conference, with thousands in attendance, at Ohio State University in December of 1963. The conference that year was designed around the eight frontiers Margaret had outlined for the future mission of the Church, which would shape our coming ministry. They included the fields of Technology, New Nationalism, East Meets West, Uprooted and Displaced People, Racism, The University World, and Militant Non-Christian Religions. The question before us at the conference was "How does the Gospel of Jesus Christ speak to people in these situations?" We didn't know then that we would be taking a further step into Margaret's Frontier Internship program, and find ourselves landing in the tiny country of Malawi just two months after this former British colony had gained its independence. We would be lab technicians for the theologians, who want to explore how the mission of the church is being changed by the eruption of new nations in Africa. Our assignment would be to make connections, listen, watch, and join whatever is happening in the economic capital city, Blantyre, where the African Presbyterian Church, our sponsor, is headquartered. We would write monthly reports back to the main office in New York City on what we perceive to be the moving of the Holy Spirit in this milieu, and how that might change the mission of the Church there.

We arrive in September, eager to get involved, but with little sense of where to begin. Blantyre, a small but bustling city of maybe 50,000, is to be our home. The main street is lined with one-story stucco buildings and filled with the usual traffic of cars, taxis, bicycles and scooters. There is a large, four square block open market that becomes the source of our food supply for the duration of our visit, with very little packaged food imported from elsewhere. We are told there is one elevator in the whole country. It is in the American embassy, the only two-story building. Our host, Bambo Pengalaka of the Church of Central Africa Presbyterian, had intended that we would live in the largest mission compound in the country, along with the long-term Scottish missionary families stationed in Blantyre. It is a community unto itself, with six homes surrounding the largest church in the country. It also has the largest lavender jacaranda tree I have ever seen, twice as big as the house it stands beside.

Because we intend to be non-traditional missionaries, more connected to local people and their lifestyles, we choose instead to live in a large African township called Soche, which is on the edge of Blantyre and home to about 1,000 Africans. The only other white person there is a Peace Corp volunteer. We occupy a four room, one-story house made entirely of concrete, with a tin roof. We have cold running water, an electric two- burner hot-plate, and a small refrigerator. We set our own monthly salary, commensurate with those we live around. It is $22 US per month for the two of us. We ride a 750cc Harley motorcycle (after six exhausting months of riding bikes everywhere), and have a lit-tle dachshund puppy we name "Pong'ono," which is Chinyanja (the local language) for "just a little bit." Our next-door neigh-bors roar with laughter at that name, the same way we do when we learn that their black lab is named "Police Station." So much for picking names in languages other than your own! The two questions our African neighbors ask us as they get used to hav-ing foreigners in their midst are, "Why don't you have servants?" and "Why don't you have any children?" We don't have servants because our commitment is to live at the same level of income as the people we are working with, and besides, we wouldn't know how to have servants anyway. We don't have children because we have access to birth control, which our neighbors probably have no knowledge of, and we are intentionally waiting until we complete this venture in our lives to start a family.

We connect regularly with a web of Scottish missionaries— all of whom have been in Malawi for more than a decade—who also harken from Iona. These men, who are accompanied by their families, are not preachers. Like Tom and Joyce in Ghana, they are builders, plumbers, and teachers. They have all participated in the ten year struggle for Malawi's independence, supporting the families of men imprisoned for their political involvement, and running secret messages from the leaders to those on the outside. These are the long-termers; we are the new kids on the block, and the only Americans among them. They welcome us, and fill us with stories of the 150 years of the mission station, the varieties of their ministries, and the building of the Blantyre Church, which is an exact replica of a church in Blantyre, Scotland. All the other churches we will visit are built with mud walls and a tin roof. This church is three stories high, built with bricks adorned with pineapples, cows, and other marks of the local craftsmen. It even has an organ, which I would sneak in to play when no one is there because the church is always open.

Barely a month after our arrival, we find ourselves in a hot bed of rebellion. The sixty-year old Prime Minister, Hastings Kamuzu Banda, who had returned from forty years in exile in London to fill the post, has fired one of the thirty-year old cabinet ministers who had helped lead the revolt against England. The rest of the cabinet resigns in protest, and together they go underground. Roadblocks spring up, and preventative detention begins (which means we will arrest you before you have a chance to do anything we don't like)—things we Americans have never experienced before. Another eye-popper is that the radio, newspaper, army and police are all controlled by the government, which is now a heavy handed dictatorship bound to stay in control. We have to listen daily to the British Overseas Broadcasting radio station to find out the truth of what is happening in Malawi.

Over the next eighteen months we practice our assignment to be witnesses, not leaders. We are here to watch, listen, ask questions and ponder the changes together. Our assigned question is always in the background as we witness the suppression of the revolutionary fervor of our first few months in Malawi. Fear of reprisal does breed silence. We have made inroads with the young people who have completed secondary school but lack the resources to continue their education. They are a generation in limbo. They are too well educated to return to ancestral villages and be farmers, but the urban scene does not offer employment at their level of education. We have created a drop-in center in the township where we live, and we put on weekend work camps to give those youth focus and community. We are also active in eleven secondary schools teaching Bible classes and leading discussion programs as a way of connecting with the youth. We host an Easter weekend camp where we construct a life-size cross and literally carry it up a mountain side and plant it in the ground for an Easter dawn service.

As we stretch to meet their needs, we are also trying to address our question: what do they think about nation-building? This generation had not been the fighters for independence. They are the inheritors of it. They worry about their own futures, not their country's future. How to find a job and earn money in order to have economic freedom and opportunity are their most important concerns. These young people, for the most part, are growing up without the support of their families. There are no resources to send them on for more training. Often their families live in a distant village where they own land and farm. To these young people, farming is a backward existence, and their future is a blank slate.

We create a safe harbor for them, a place to belong and to learn from each other, as so many youth have to do when societies are in transition and they can't follow the way of their elders. We listen. We watch. Political freedom is not the focus of their attention as it had been for the previous generation. More dictatorship is so ordinary, and the freedom that is being lost is still so new. Their reality is much more personal. I think of Maslow's hierarchy of human needs, with food, shelter and safety the first priorities, and self-actualization at the top. We have to be concerned with where they are from one day to the next, and walk beside them as they make their choices.

I flash on a memory of a group sitting in our living room in Soche and I am trying to explain the international dateline and why we have time zones. I take a shade off a standing lamp and use an orange to show the earth rotating while it travels around the sun (the lamp.) They are mystified;, and we all wonder why it is important for them to understand anyway. I don't remember how we even got on that subject, but it is an example of the many tangents we went on together as our very different worlds met and we wondered about the future. Rarely did we touch on the subject that had been our assignment in coming to Malawi—what the theologians back in the ivory towers of the U.S.A. wanted to understand. Our ministry, like Tom and Joyce, was one of being-with, befriending, and sharing our life experiences as we open to the presence of Spirit among us, which more often showed up in smiles, laughter, and a helping hand than in discussions about nation-building.

One day a coup erupts unexpectedly, and the rebels are caught. The Prime Minister goes to Parliament to seek the death penalty by public hanging. This is prohibited by the law adopted from England at the time of independence. We pick up the morning newspaper later that week, and a front page story tells of a parliamentarian who stood up following the Prime Minister's proposal, and added that these rebels should not only be executed, but skinned and hung in the national museum for all future generations to see what happens to anyone rebelling against this regime.

When I put down that newspaper, my life would never be the same again. With no forethought as to strategy or consequences, we know we have to do something. For eighteen months we have held to the discipline of our training that we are not here to lead but to follow; that we are to be a Christian witness in a non-Christian world (the new model for missionary work in the 1960s, adapting to liberation struggles happening world-wide.) In the next moment, the only truth we know is that if the Universal Church means anything, we are its feet, heart, and voice in this place. To do nothing in the face of this tragic turn of events would be to nullify any reason for our being here as a representative of that Church. We also know that, given the upsurge in preventive detention, we can take chances that a Malawian cannot. Being Americans will protect us, or so we think.

We take action with immediate clarity. We call the Parliament in the capital city of Zomba, ask for the office of that politician, whose name is Kapwiti Banda, and make an appointment. Do we consult with any of our colleagues in Blantyre, or our New York office? No. The urgency to speak our truth is stronger than any consideration of reason or consequence. The next day we take a bus thirty miles to the capital. We find our way to the very British-looking brick building with its slightly intimidating grand staircase mounting up to an overbearing entrance. We inquire after the office we want, and find our way to the door. A middle-aged African in a western business suit and tie welcomes us with a big smile, unconcerned about why we might be here. We politely receive his welcome, sit down on wooden chairs across from his prodigious desk, and proceed to say "We have come to talk with you about the moral responsibility of politicians." Yes indeed, the purpose of our coming to Malawi crystallizes in that moment: What is the role of Christians in nation-building?

An hour later, we have exhausted our repertoire of ways to explore this topic. It is a wonder, as I reflect on this experience, that this man was willing to spend so much time with these young, foreign upstarts. Who did we think we were? The only comment of his that I remember is "You missionaries have misled us in a lot of ways in the past. This is an African problem, and we will deal with it in an African way."

Ten years later, I would find myself participating in a study group on Gandhi's strategies of nonviolence, and hear for the first time his teaching about "Speaking truth to power." I then had words for what had happened to us that day in Malawi. Another ten years after that, I would learn from Arnold Mindell (Process Work training in Portland, OR) about "time spirits" that he believes grab individuals and catapult them into history in ways beyond their own imagining. Perhaps we didn't even have a choice? We spoke our truth with no regrets. We were way out of bounds, but we didn't know it. What we did seemed so right at the time.

The next day, African friends come searching for us in the market where we are shopping to tell us that we have been given twenty-four hours to leave the country. They heard it announced over the radio. We are being deported on a trumped up charge given to the U.S. State Department that Mrs. Boston had led a student protest on the capital city protesting public hanging. Would that I had! As we pack to leave, the radio blares out that any Africans found associating with the Bostons will be severely dealt with. Nevertheless, our friends come quietly one-by-one to the back door to bid us farewell. One says, "Someday the Church here will be able to say 'We did something.'" Bambo Sangaya seems forlorn and quiet as he bids us farewell at the airport. Surely he is going to have to pick up the pieces of the fall-out from this turn of events. We never hear from him again. We are also very sad to so abruptly leave our missionary friends, our neighbors in Soche, and our work with the young people. We have shared so much of ourselves with them—and they with us.

As we fly above Malawi in our hasty departure, I am having my first lesson in how history gets written–brave acts, false reports, and unintended consequences. We decide in the short flight between Blantyre and Nairobi, Kenya that we do not want to return to the U.S.A. We know there are Frontier Interns in Kenya who had been in our training. We decide to de-plane in Nairobi and try to find them. Personnel from the State Department and our New York office are on hand at J.F.K. airport to meet the plane we are supposed to be on that day. We are temporarily nowhere to be found, much to our parents' alarm. Sometimes when you are grabbed by the Holy Spirit, you shatter others' expectations in your wake. We do connect with our friends because they heard about us on the radio and were hoping to hear from us. When we call them from the airport, their response is, "Great! We'll be right there to get you." We spend the next two weeks in Kenya seeking a visa to stay, which is denied due to diplomatic relations with Malawi. Meantime I see the bluest skies and the reddest dirt I have ever seen. We also have an encounter with a group of adolescent boys wearing loincloths, carrying spears, and having smeared red clay all over their bodies. They are crossing the road just as we pass, so we pull over. They are on their rite of passage walkabout, and can't return to the tribe until they have each killed a lion. They speak perfect English, having been to a Christian mission school, so I can ask my burning question: "Are there enough wild lions to go around?" the answer, with much laughter, is "Yes, madam."

Our New York office sends us a telegram saying "Proceed to Geneva; seek European assignment." Reluctantly we call the airlines and book passage. I feel like a true jet-setter now. On to Geneva, Switzerland we go, where we will spend the next eight months completing our contracted time by working at the World Council of Churches (W.C.C.). We transition from speaking Chinyanja behind our little house in an African township to participating within the biggest bureaucracy the Protestant Church has ever created, in a bustling multi-lingual metropolis of Europe.

As serendipity would have it, on our journey to Geneva we have an overnight layover in Rome. We find ourselves standing on the curb outside our hotel about 9 p.m. with a map and two hours to see the city. A limousine pulls up where we are standing and a window lowers. A man in a Stetson hat and overcoat smiles at us and says, "Can I help you?" He seems nice enough—and generous—so we tell him our predicament with so little time and not knowing where to start. He offers to drive us around. We haven't got any riches he could swindle, and besides he doesn't look like he needs anything, so we get in the car. He drives us around the Coliseum, the ancient forum, fountains, and St. Peter's basilica—Rome in a nutshell! Then he invites us back to his Renaissance palace! We drive into his brick-lain courtyard with a lit up fountain in the center. It is now about midnight and we are entranced by our host's charm and generosity. Not only is he an art collector, but the walls of his living room are covered with framed photographs of him shaking hands with the royalty of the world. He is an international philanthropist. We promise to send him contact information for the artist of some amazing African nativity frescos we saw in Nairobi. His driver takes us back to our hotel about 2 a.m. and we drift into sleep in utter amazement at our good fortune.

We are leaving one hotbed of political intrigue for another. Our assignment has us living in a student center for graduate students at the University of Geneva (directed by an American missionary employed by our Presbyterian church just as in Beirut) and working in the Youth Department of the World Council of Churches. Being in this center puts us shoulder to shoulder with students around our age and from mostly communist countries. Their opinions of the U.S.—with our newly escalating war in Vietnam—would heap mountains of sarcastic criticism on our country, a country we have been disconnected from for almost two years. I reel from the brunt of it, yet listen, ponder, and stay open to what these very savvy students who are supposed to be my "enemy" have to say. Thanks to my initiation in Beirut, I am better at controlling my defensiveness and more able to listen with true curiosity to these French, Yugoslavian, Polish, Romanian, Jamaican, Pakistani, Russian and Chinese scholars. They smirk about how the war won't end soon because the stock market is up. I don't understand the relationship between the two. I stare at magazines in the student lounge with covers featuring hundreds of Chinese children shouting "Down with America!" and puzzle over why they hate us so much. I am on a fast learning curve for sure.

I befriend a Yugoslavian woman, Vishnya, who has lived on a state commune before her husband came to Geneva to study economics. She is the first person who tells me she believes Kennedy was killed by my government. She says everyone in Europe believes his assassination was a conspiracy. I get caught again. I stand my ground and deny it. I am still inside the hypnotic trance of patriotism. But once again, I am shaken into realizing I don't really know the truth. I have just believed what the media has said, with no critical awareness of who my government really is. My rough edges are being honed for bigger work in the world. These friends with the outsider perspective are training me to question my childhood image of who my country is, and to see the reality of imperialism operating in Vietnam as well as the Soviet occupation of Eastern Europe.

I haven't seen my mother for two years. She and her second husband, Brad, want to come to Europe and meet us in Spain. When I ask her if she would like to come and visit us in Geneva, her reply is. "I'm not ready for that." She has been receiving our reports back to the New York office. She knows we are hobnobbing with Communists and learning from them. This is too far out of bounds for her. So we meet them in Spain. Her first words to me upon disembarking from our plane are, "What's all that black gluck on your eyes?" I guess I had adopted some of the lifestyle of Geneva—eye make-up—along with speaking French again, which I hadn't done since high school. The two years had changed my appearance as well as my consciousness. I had hoped for more gladness at being reunited after such a long and relatively harrowing experience for both of us, but there is something utterly familiar about the lack of warmth and acceptance.

Bruce and I would spend eight months on the staff of the Youth Department working on a document called "Youth in

God's World." I find this undertaking quite perplexing, as I can't see how we can talk about the youth of Malawi and the youth of New York City in the same document, or who would read it, or how it would change any lives. You can see my activist bent showing up in spades. Bruce, however, loves the assignment as it sends him to the university library to research the Bible in Greek and Hebrew, seeking passages that support the task. Our different experiences with this project reveal that our ways of serving are becoming divergent. It is beginning to feel like when I bloom, he wilts; and when he blooms, I wilt. When he would return to Princeton to finish his doctorate, he would move in the direction of being a theologian rather than a minister as had been our original plan. We are now marching to different drumbeats, a harbinger of changes to come.

As we finish our time in Geneva, it is the summer of 1966 and we are returning to a country burning with its own rebellion against a government that is drafting more and more young men to go to war 12,000 miles away in Vietnam. How different this experience of protest would be from what we had seen in Malawi, with freedom of the press, habeas corpus protection, nonviolent protests coast to coast, and conscientious objector status in place. I have a new relationship to governments now. I have a conscience that is more educated, and the courage to back it up. We return to our ministry at the Lawrence Road Presbyterian Church, with Bruce assisting in the pulpit and I as Director of Christian Education. The next year would be stormy, with the drumbeats of war dominating the evening news and protests growing. As we are pulled farther into that fray, we would leave our ministry as the leader of the governing body objects to our participation in anti-war marches and tells the minister "It's them or me." The Universal Church still speaks to us of standing against violence no matter where we are, as does that question that sent us on our journey to begin with: "What is the role of Christians in nation-building?" We would have a steep learning curve for the next nine years, combatting our own country's in-stitutionalized violence as the Vietnam War dominates our lives, continuing to meet the challenge to speak truth to power that began the day we picked up that newspaper in Malawi.

Gifts from the Sea:
Parent Effectiveness Training
1972

Sometimes a random walk on the beach yields an unexpected gift from the sea—a perfectly formed shimmering shell, or a smooth stone dazzling with specs of mica—that you want to scoop up and take home to treasure. I am hungry for such a gift, longing for something to cross my path that would anchor me deeper in the meaning and purpose of my own life. When we returned from Malawi and the Frontier Internship experience, I had fulfilled my adolescent dream of being a missionary. I had internalized the spirit of service and deeply enjoyed the mystique of an utterly foreign culture. I was now ready to be home and engaging in my calling where I truly belong. I traded in my credentials as a jet-setter for motherhood. I spent the next five years birthing three sons and being in a completely different and compelling service that left no time for thinking beyond bottles and bedtimes. While Bruce was completing his Ph.D. in Theology at the seminary, my world was defined by food, diapers, play, clean-up, baths, stories, more clean-up, and other women with babies. My own life, or any sense of mission, was a blur.

On a whim, I join an intriguing eight-week class being offered in our church basement called Parent Effectiveness Training (P.E.T.) I have no inkling that just such a surprising gift has swept up in front of me, and as I pick it up I am crossing a threshold into an arena that would become the centerpiece of my professional career. My intention is to be a good parent, but I have no strategy or framework for handling conflict beyond my father's fiery temper thundering through the house when he was mad, or my mother's look of disgust and emotional withdrawal to show her disapproval. There had been no negotiating when differences arose. If I insisted on something that was important to me but a problem for my parents, the message I got was that I was bad, disobedient, and only thinking about myself. Ouch! That parental shaming – so common in our culture – is exactly what makes us all so afraid of conflict. I am no exception.

If you have ever been a parent, you no doubt know that point of exasperation when you say something like, "Stop crying!" You find yourself demanding that the child stop feeling what they are feeling because you have run out of patience and want something settled to your liking. Did you ever consider that your behavior is a desperate grab for power, and in that moment you are making your need more important than your child's? I hadn't ever seen it that way. That is one of the first lessons of P.E.T., and it is a pretty humbling realization. But what is the alternative? Isn't it a parent's job to control children, to make them behave? I am about to be introduced to a strategy for handling differences that would protect children from adult domination, that would give them a voice, and empower them to believe that—when there is a conflict of needs—their needs matter, too. Nothing about this teaching is familiar in 1972.

P.E.T. is a toolbox for the parenting trade, with a skill for every conceivable impasse in communication, whether with children, spouses, in-laws, colleagues, or neighbors. What a treasure chest! Having this tool box means that whatever the differences, I have a tool to keep both people in the interaction long enough to come up with a next step that satisfies both. At the heart of the matter is the meeting of needs, and the understanding that most arguments are not about needs, but about strategies for trying to meet them. When those strategies can be negotiated—that is, sharing the power to decide what happens—limitless possibilities become available, especially if you are willing to hold the other person's best interest at heart. That means you will only settle for a solution that meets both parties' needs. I also learn to stop calling impasses "conflicts," and instead call them "differences," which implies a level playing field in the realm of needs. Differences are much less threatening, and don't imply that anyone has done something wrong or bad.

The teacher, whose name is lost to my memory but whose presence lives on in me, tells us how his family with four teenagers holds family meetings in the dining room. They make flip charts for each problem someone wants to address. Then they identify needs trying to be met by all the parties involved, brainstorm possible solutions, circle the solution chosen to see if it works, and list a date at which time the family will check back to see if the problem is solved or if it needs to be revisited. He says the flip charts stay up on the dining room wall until the problem is solved. I know in that moment that I want a family that cares about each person's needs like that. That level of respect and the willingness to do the work needed to create it are skills I want to bring home.

I am excited! The value system underlying these skills is congruent with the Gospel I have been in service to my whole adult life—love your neighbor as yourself. That means your needs matter to me, even if we are having differences. This training takes the "right/wrong" argument out of an interaction; it implies equal importance to both party's needs, Why not choose to negotiate? Why not choose to share power in deciding what happens? I come out of that first class on fire with enthusiasm, eager to dive into the challenge of putting these skills into action. I know I have found the best preparation for parenthood I could ever have. For men in our culture at that time—who are accustomed to being the "decider"—the idea of sharing power feels like giving up power. Sadly, my husband is among those men who look on the whole enterprise of P.E.T. as one of questionable value. Sharing power is not his job; being in charge is. I would get no support from him.

Undeterred, I go on a treasure hunt for clues as to how to play this new game of communication. I put a penny jar on the kitchen table. When my five year old son Aaron asks me what that is for, I explain that every time I use one of my new skills I will put a penny in. Every time I forget and use one of the "roadblocks," I will take a penny out. The roadblocks—twelve of them—are the typical ways we scold, blame, threaten, analyze, or lecture the other person when we don't like what they are doing and want them to do it our way. Boy does he learn that lesson fast! Within a day, Aaron gleefully announces, "You have to take a penny out of the jar, Mom, you yelled at me!" He is right. I thank him for being on my team to help me learn to lead with my needs and a request instead of obliterating his needs with a demand.

My request becomes an invitation to negotiate. "Hey kids (three of them under six), when I come upstairs with a full laundry basket, I need to be able to walk through your room to put clothes away without falling over toys, so I would like you to clean up your room." Answer, "We can make you a path!" That's not the solution I prefer, but does it meet my need for safety? Yes. Can I live with it for the sake of sharing power in deciding what happens? Yes. Are the kids learning that their needs matter too, and they can help solve my problem? Yes. I would never have thought of that solution myself. We are in the realm of limitless possibilities. The gifts from the sea- inspirations born of invitation and creativity—are awash at our feet.

The children's bedtime resistance is transformed one night when, instead of demanding that they get ready for bed by putting on their pajamas, I ask them why they always complain about it. Aaron explains that he doesn't like having to change into cold clothes in the morning. Hum. What is my need? To get them out of dirty clothes. Their need? To be comfortable in the morning. Possibilities? Again they come up with the workable solution. They will take off their dirty clothes, put on clean clothes, and sleep in them instead of pajamas. When I think of how jumbled their clothes are in their drawers anyway, sleeping in their clothes is no different, so I agree because it is a solution that meets both party's needs. That solution works fine until their grandmother comes to visit, and she asks where their pajamas are. I dig to the bottom of their drawers and find them.

Have you noticed what you can learn when you take the time to listen to children when they are resisting your strategy for getting what you need ("Do it my way!")? One day I am standing at the foot of the stairs and yell up to the kids, "Come on, it's time to go." They don't come right away, so I yell again, "Let's go! Hurry up! What are you doing?" Now I am interpreting their behavior to mean they aren't listening to me. They aren't minding me. Back comes Aaron's voice, "Kyle can't find his shoe and I'm helping him look for it." In that moment my whole energy changes from frustration to respect and appreciation. From that day on, I realize that when I meet resistance, what I need is more information. I can learn to be curious about what need the other is trying to meet by refusing to meet my need in the moment. It doesn't mean the other person doesn't care. It means something more important to them is happening, and it behooves me to find out what that is.

One day when my middle son Nathan is eight, I call down from a second-story ladder, "We have to leave in ten minutes to go get your brother at camp." Nathan replies, "I don't want to go." "I don't have time to find someone," I mindlessly bark back. Nathan simply goes inside the house, asks a housemate if he is going to be home, comes back out and announces, "Alan is home, Mom, so I can stay." Nathan knows he has options besides the first one I propose, which meets my need but not his. Thirty years later, I would be present when Nathan's son Bodhi, then three, is whining about something. Nathan just calmly inquires, "What do you need, Bodhi?" What? A three year old being asked that question? Would he even know how to talk about his needs? Bodhi is quiet for about ten seconds, with a frown on his face. He is going inside which is where we have to go to answer that question. "I need help," comes his answer. In this simple and non-blaming interaction, I recognize that the wisdom of P.E.T.—finding out what need another is trying to meet by their behavior—has passed to the next generation.

Six months after putting my toe into this water, I take the instructor licensing training at a hotel in New York City with over one hundred people. P.E.T. is sweeping the country. As I begin teaching these skills, I am drawn deeper into the dynamics of family life, which eventually would lead me to a career in family therapy. Sometimes family patterns are stronger than good communication can manage, and students have to know how to support themselves when their important needs are not being met or considered. I talk about the "Politics of 'I Matter,'" using the skills to show women how to honor their own needs even when they conflict with others, and how important it is to show self-respect in order to gain respect from others. One student comments, "Sandra, this course is about so much more than just communication." Another says, "Once I realized conflict is not about my self-worth, I can be in any conflict." I know what I am teaching is as life-changing for my students as it has been for me.

There is a skill in P.E.T. called "The Non-Negotiable Stand" for situations when we need to say "No." It is for those times when your own needs over-ride all other considerations, such as going to church regularly or paying bills on time. You don't want to negotiate whether or not to do that in order to meet another's needs. It is a skill to say "No" while fully acknowledging the consequences to the other of their need not being met, and negotiating how to honor those unmet needs at another time so they aren't ignored or devalued in the relationship.

One day I get a call from the school nurse telling me that my son Aaron, now ten, is refusing to take the TB test required for him to be in school. She says if he doesn't comply, I will have to take him to our family doctor. I go to the school, try to convince him to cooperate with no success, and simply hold him down while the nurse pricks his arm with the tiny syringe. This is my non-negotiable stand. But I know what I have done: I have met my need for him to stay in public school (without me paying a doctor's fee) at the expense of his need for safety and control of his own body. So I offer him the chance to leave school for the rest of the day and get ice cream on the way home. That restores the power balance (who decides what happens) that I have usurped in the relationship. Years later, I would hear someone ask the famous child psychologist Bruno Bettelheim about bribing children to do what you want. He replies: "Does it work?" When the answer is "Yes," he says, "Then why call it bribery? Why not call it making a smooth transition from one activity to another?" Sharing power in deciding what happens creates happy and trusting relationships.

At the heart of P.E.T. is the ability to listen to the other person's needs and feelings even when they conflict with your own, without becoming defensive or lapsing into arguing. Another training that helped me learn to do that is Re-evaluation Co-counseling. In this training I learn how to give unbiased attention to another's feelings without an agenda of my own. This practice becomes another foundation for my future work as a therapist. From this experience I begin studying family therapy to better understand the dynamics that people bring to class. I add a whole new dimension to my curriculum: "Differentiation of Self in Family of Origin" (Murray Bowen). This skill is one of standing your ground when differences arise while also staying emotionally present and connected to the other's experience. This skill means not trying to "win" by making the other person wrong, or retreating like a person who gives up on meeting their own needs in order to get out of a conflict.

Many students find this skill life-changing. They learn to say,

"I see it differently," without arguing the rightness of their position or needing to make the other person wrong. It is now safe to be themselves, want what they want, tolerate differences, and still belong. From that place of internal safety, they can even bring curiosity to the interaction and add, "Tell me more about why you see it that way, because I see it differently." Internalizing this skill of differentiation helps me understand my own mother with much more compassion when she needs to distance from me because she has no other strategy for confronting differences. Because I understand why she does that, and what one could do instead, I am able to help many others navigate a painful impasse with their parent or spouse. I am also able to stay in relationship with my mother, not taking her tactics personally or catching the ball of blame when she throws it. It is a life-long challenge to build the agency of inner authority that allows us to stand our ground when confronted with external authority that expects compliance.

One of my personal victories with my mother comes on a day I am visiting at her home in Florida with my son Nathan, who is eight. She comes into my bedroom where I am napping. Nathan has just come in moments before and is sitting on the edge of the bed. "I suppose you don't want to come into the living room and have a drink with us. You always have something more important going on." She turns and leaves. Nathan says, "Mom, what did you do wrong?" It is so validating to have a witness to this age-old dynamic between my mother and me–that I have somehow disappointed her but with no discussion of issues or a chance for me to explore our differences. I never know what I am doing wrong except to be different from her (in this case, drinking is not part of my lifestyle).

But this time I know my assignment. I don't catch the ball (though tempted to argue that taking a nap is the epitome of having nothing else going on...). I hear the disguised request behind her defensive accusation and respond to that. I can bend in this situation for the sake of connection. I am not religious about not drinking, it's just a preference that I decide to forgo in this instance. I get up, comb my hair, go out into the living room and ask for a rum and coke. That is the end of it. There is no further discussion. I am numb to how much her distancing tactics hurt—no doubt that ole "I don't care if you don't like me" defense is operating. But the telltale feelings come whenever I encounter a friend who has a close, loving relationship with her mother and talks about it. At first I feel envious, and then lonely. Deep down under my high-functioning personality I do feel like a motherless child.

I have work to do with my brother Sam as well. I have spent most of my life avoiding him. At a family farewell dinner before I left for Beirut, after a few glasses of wine, he pushed his chair back and announced, "I used to lay on my bed and think of ways to kill you." My mother's predictable response is, "Oh Sam, don't say things like that." But I knew the truth of what he was saying, and I recognize her denial, which I have accepted as the norm and which has left me with no protection from his abuse throughout my childhood and adolescence. I feel validated in this moment for my years of fear and hurt. I feel some relief that he dares—under the influence—to own his menacing attitude towards me. But mostly I feel sad—sad for me that I never had a brother I could enjoy, sad for him that he is trapped inside those feelings, and sad that our family is still dealing with this painful dynamic.

Now fifteen years later with the P.E.T. skills for support, I am able to ask myself not what kind of brother he is to me, but what kind of sister do I want to be to him? This is real differentiation work. I have always wanted acceptance and inclusion from my brother, which made me feel like his victim. All he had to do was refuse to give me what I wanted and I felt powerless. Through my study of The Buddha's teaching on grasping and aversion, I could now see how I created my own suffering by wanting something from him that he was unwilling to give. I can now make the choice to be the sister I want to be. I choose to stop reacting. I am no longer afraid of his story about me. I now have a firm grasp on my own inner authority of who I am, and I am no longer vulnerable to his rejection. My actions are motivated by what I want to give, not by what I want to receive.

I begin calling him on his birthday to wish him well and inquire how he is doing. He is baffled at first—disarmed. Gradually, over the years, he is no longer surprised by my call. Each time our conversation lasts a little longer. We hit a big impasse the year he sells our deceased mother's house and doesn't even tell me, having secretly gotten the deed signed over to himself by a senile surviving spouse. When I ask for my share, the old venom erupts again—how dare I challenge his control! I breathe, listen, and stand my ground without reacting to his attacks. I am requesting what I want without being attached to whether or not I get it. I acknowledge his perception of entitlement and his outrage at my challenge, and then I add, "And I would like my share." My biggest challenge is not about getting money and a fair share, but about overcoming my fear of his abusiveness. Can I keep my inner authority and serenity as I weather his predictable attack on my character? "You're not going to get any because you don't deserve any," he carries on, "You hurt our mother every time you had contact with her!" I am mystified by this characterization and my mind immediately floods with memories of times I felt thwarted by her, but I don't go there. I stay focused on Sam and what he wants me to understand about him. Like a good martial artist, I am determined to not be his target, while not contradicting or arguing with him either. Focusing on my skills helps me not get hooked by my feelings about what he is saying about me. I simply feedback what he says so he feels understood, and then repeat my request.

After a forty minute phone call that ends surprisingly with him saying, "I'll think about it," we write letters that cross in the mail. Mine says, "We have six children between us who are watching to see how people in this family treat each other, and whether we can expect a fair share of the resources among us. I hope we can show them they can expect fairness." His to me says, "You have always had a penchant for agitation and now that you see an opportunity for personal gain (emphasis mine), you have aimed it at me." He concludes with "I don't owe you a penny, and don't call me on the phone anymore." I am amazed. I see for the first time how he perceives himself as my victim. It is, to me, a clear example of projection. After all, who exactly is getting the personal gain? Instead of challenging him, knowing now that he is not capable of negotiation, I feel compassion for his state of being. I let go. My victory is in refusing to be intimidated by his abusiveness, not in what I get from him. It is a personal victory. I feel like I just earned my Ph.D. in communication skill. When I am no longer afraid of his insults and character assault, that behavior begins to lose its power. It gradually disappears from our relationship.

That next fall, Sam's wife and daughter make a trip to visit me and to "see the autumn colors." The morning after their arrival, I ask Connie if I can talk to her about what is happening between Sam and me, and she replies, "That's why we came." She and her daughter proceed to commiserate with me and tell me their stories of Sam's obsession with money and the ways they have had to protect themselves. I see now that, while I have lost any chance of an inheritance, I have gained the emotional support of the other women in our family—a much more valuable outcome to me. A year later I make a trip to Florida to visit them. During the visit, I find myself mysteriously drawn to taking a ride on the tourist boat that Sam captains that goes out into Sarasota Bay to watch the sunset. This request surprises the family, but they are willing to go along. The next evening, a ways into the hour-long trip, I again feel led to get up from the place where the family is enjoying a beer and make my way to the cockpit. I am not thinking as I move toward him. He is alone, and I slide into the one seat beside him. We both watch the peaceful sunset in silence. There is nothing that needs to be said. After about twenty minutes, I leave and return to the family. All I know is I am at peace with myself, my brother, and my world. This episode is one of the most important experiences of transformation in my life.

Continuing to explore the application of these skills, I spend the next ten years as a trainer in conflict resolution for Movement For a New Society. Participants in our year-long program come from many countries to learn strategies for nonviolent direct action campaigns. I call this training "The Language of Nonviolence." We all have the values of nonviolence, but when push came to shove in a confrontation and tensions are high, old habits can take over our communication. The skills for parenting are a perfect fit for this new arena. When I participate in a march to stop the building of the Seabrook Nuclear Power plant in 1979, I pass a property owner who is standing in his front yard just a few feet from where we are marching by. He is shouting, "Get out of our town!" I decide to stop and engage him. I listen to his concerns—how many jobs this plant will bring, and how upsetting it is to have thousands of out-of-towners marching through his neighborhood as if we owned the place. He is so taken aback by my attention, the next thing he says is, "Why are you here, anyway?" Now there is an opening to honestly talk about our differences. I have a chance to tell him why we don't want our country going for nuclear energy with all its devastating environmental and health risks. No one is persuaded to change their minds, but we both feel listened to. Sometimes just managing our differences is all we can do, but to do that with respect and connection is a skill.

In 1999, as I am looking for teachers to expand my skill base, I follow a lead to Arnold Mindell in Portland, Oregon. I join his five week training program in multi-cultural conflict resolution. Our group of sixty participants represents twenty-seven countries and eighteen U.S. states. Mindell is a Taoist and a quantum physicist who believes in the deep unifying patterns of energy that exist under apparent chaos in the universe. He convenes groups of 300 at a time made up of polarized communities who are killing each other in places like South Africa, Kosovo, and Northern Ireland. He and his team of forty-two facilitators (of which I am aspiring to be one) hold the space for each party to be heard and understood over six days. He calls this arena "World Work." I am shocked by the level of abusive language, accusation, blaming and rage that Mindell tolerates. The word "difference" that I am now accustomed to using instead of "conflict" does not contain the degree of energy present in these exchanges; it is indeed conflict, with all the innuendos of right and wrong I have worked so hard to train students to avoid. I just about have my head handed to me for being an American whose country has violated the trust and democratic process of so many countries represented here. Even an Australian tells me he would never make an agreement with an American.

I have never put my toe into this kind of water, where righteousness and murderous rage are the norm. Mindell shows me that in the heat of differences such as these—political, historical, and life-threatening—the skills I am teaching are not useful. My skills are meant for relationships with a high degree of commitment. People who have been violated do not want their conflict resolved. They are identified with their conflict; they want to be understood without being contradicted or asked to consider the needs or truths of the other parties in their conflict. I watch as the facilitators move close to whomever is ranting at a microphone, and tell that person when they finish, "If that had happened to me, I would feel the same way you do." Over and over, no matter which side a person is on. Over and over. The same message. No processing, just compassion. Gradually the container becomes safe enough for someone to open to the Tao and everything changes.

Mindell has no strategy other than to walk into the center of a group and say, "So what's happening here?" With his bald head, big ears, and blue jeans hanging on his ninety-five pound frame, he reminds me of Yoda from Star Wars—the wise elder who isn't in a hurry. I ask him after a week of watching the fur fly following his question, "Arnie, when you walk out there, what are you trusting?" "Mystery" is his answer. Over the course of the five weeks I watch the Tao—"the way things work"—happen. I watch as people from Serbia cry out "You killed my father!" and the retort from the Kosovars comes, "You killed my grandfather and burned our village!" Back and forth, back and forth the rage goes in a dizzying frenzy of unleashed emotion. Suddenly the rage of wounding is spent. There is a break down into a well of grief—sobbing—followed by a prolonged silence. Here the exhausted cry for justice is replaced with vulnerability, compassion, and human connection. Our common humanity is revealed. In this sacred space "my pain" becomes "the pain" (Stephen Levine). Lines of separation dissolve. As we watch this happen—not often, but enough times—we begin to trust that deep patterning beneath the chaos. We can't know when or how the necessary break down will come, but that it will come. Mindell tells us, "The Tao is like an underground river. It fills any channel that is open, but it comes when it will." When we can trust the Tao, we can allow the labor pains of chaos.

Watching Mindell in action with his team of facilitators changes my relationship to conflict. Conflict, he teaches, is not a failure in relationships; it is to be expected—normal. "After all," he says, "Nature reveals itself in polar opposites non-stop. We can try to resolve it, but another will pop up soon after, and then another." He says the only purpose of conflict is "to learn, to love, and to grow." I would eventually translate that perspective into my curriculum as the "personal victory." I would ask my students, "How did you create understanding?" and "What did you learn?" I bow to Arnold Mindell as one of my greatest teachers, who took me into the realm of the Tao—the way things work. I did decide that being a facilitator in that arena was not for me. I prefer to work with family relationships and the perhaps simpler dynamics where that higher degree of investment in resolving or managing differences is present. As I take this experience into my therapist and trainer role, I now understand that creating understanding—not resolving conflict—is the main goal of communication. Often the conflicts that bring a couple or a parent and child into therapy simply dissolve when understanding arises.

Why do I call this work with communication "Gifts from the Sea?" Finding this work seemed like a random gift that swept unexpectedly up on my shore just where I was walking as a young mother. Each skill I learned was a treasure I wanted to take home and keep. There would be more gifts. I would study "Nonviolent Communication" with Marshall Rosenberg, Inner Bonding with Margaret Paul, "The Work" with Byron Katie, healing shame with John Bradshaw, Harville Hendricks and so many more. The sea is also a metaphor for that source of limitless possibilities—indeed, the gift of life itself—we must turn to as we learn to navigate differences with respect instead of control. This skill-set has given me tangible, important skills to offer, and a platform for carrying them into the world. As feminism took root in our culture, men—who had been scarce in the first decade of my teaching career—began to be bolder participants as they gradually came to understand that sharing power in relationships with partners and children was better for them as well.

Many confided to me that they might still be in their marriages if they had acquired these skills sooner.

Eventually I would develop my own materials, integrating the work of my most important teachers and creating my own model. I would take the skills into community groups, classrooms, teachers' meetings, agency staff trainings, church groups, board meetings, women's empowerment trainings, couples therapy, and abroad to Canada, Switzerland, Russia and Uganda. In 2000 I would start The Conscious Communication Institute and, over the next five years, train thirty-five teachers. I would write my first book, *Aiming Your Mind: Skills and Strategies for Conscious Communication,* as well as a teacher's manual. I would produce a video, *What Do You Say When You Don't Agree?*   P.E.T. is another venue for me where God becomes a verb. It is love in action. I could never have known when I stepped into that church basement at thirty-two that I would still be teaching the same skills at seventy-three, while having so many adventures in learning along the way.

9

Finding What You Don't Know You Are Looking For: Movement for a New Society
1972

Have you ever turned the page of a magazine and seen an ad for a faraway destination that you had never thought of visiting, only to find yourself going to the computer to google it, and beginning to plan how you would get there? Maybe your attraction was a new car, an adult education class at your local community college, an art class, a cooking class, or a dog in a shelter needing a home. Whatever it was, the experience was the same—feeling surprised, delighted, and eager. Let me tell you how that happened to me.

Bruce and I have been part of a self-identified "theological team" of graduates from Princeton Theological Seminary for two years since moving to Philadelphia. Indeed, the reason we moved here was to be part of this team of six. Bruce had finished his course work for a Ph.D. in Theology, and I was getting my Ph.D. in motherhood with three boys under six. We were leading workshops on putting Christianity into action and taught university courses at Temple and Penn. One day in the mail, an invitation comes to be resource people for a weekend program at a peace camp sponsored by the Fellowship of Reconciliation, the War Resisters' League, and other groups we had never heard of. Just like that surprising ad in a magazine, this invitation is intriguing. Having no personal computers in 1972, we can't google these groups, so we have to trust our gut and go see what is happening there. We are hoping for a fun summer weekend away, and the invitation says, "Two dollars a day, dogs and kids welcome, camping, workshops, and speakers on peace and justice." Right up our alley. So we pack up our kids and camping gear, travel two hours on a Friday afternoon to a Catholic novitiate training center in Northern New Jersey, and come upon an encampment of hundreds. The license plates in the parking lot are from many neighboring states.

We pitch our tent on the lawn overlooking a small lake in the midst of a forest. Inside the dormitory-like training center, people of all ages show up in the food line. It is the 70s, and the vegetarian food is now the norm in radical circles. There is a carnival atmosphere of commotion, with book tables, film postings, bulletin boards with all kinds of info about actions taking place up and down the East coast, and listings of countless workshops being held throughout the weekend and into the rest of the summer. After dinner, the kids find the lake and are in the water before any talk of bathing suits or bedtimes can happen. The evening is spent singing with guitars around a bonfire, and watching the night sky with smiling, happy strangers. We are at a center for training priests, but I can't tell the priests from everyone else. It seems like no one is in charge, but somehow over 100 people get fed and bedded down.

On Saturday, we are on a panel about Paulo Freire's strategies for organizing for change (*Pedagogy of the Oppressed*). The energy of the crowd is intense, focused, and excited. It seems as if we are all there to foment revolution. Well, maybe most of us. I notice my husband doesn't catch the vibe as much as I do. For him, this would be a one day event, and then he would go back to his familiar life as a scholar, writing his thesis on the revolutions of the 20th Century. For me, something is waking up in the company of these people of the Catholic Left. Dorothy Day—founder of soup kitchens and rehab farms for urban alcoholics—is here, as are Fathers Dan and Phil Berrigan and Sister

Liz McAlister, clerics who have poured their own blood on draft files to thwart the Vietnam War machine. I am surprised by my hunger for their stories and their lifestyle. They live for their witness to their Christian understanding of justice. Their spirituality informs their politics, and their politics informs their spirituality.

Singing, poetry, skinny dipping, and rock-and-roll dancing weave in and out of workshops and presentations by people on the front lines of struggles for justice, infusing the gathering with the perfect blend of contemplation, stories of daring deeds, and play. These are my kind of people. They generate immediate community with deep connection and a strong sense of purpose. Compared to the relatively simple household life of a nuclear family, this gathering feels dynamic, magical and compelling. I have found what I didn't know I was looking for—a community that speaks to a yearning I had lost touch with through my years of mothering. The sense of mission that I had laid down when we returned from Malawi is being rekindled. I want to be a part of what I see happening in this place.

I return here with our three kids—ages two, three, and five—week after week through the rest of the summer, while my husband enjoys the quiet at home to write his thesis. One weekend, the resource panel is comprised of a few members of Movement for a New Society (M.N.S.), an urban commune located in my city. All they do the whole evening is lead singing. They tell their stories of political struggle through the songs we sing. The melodies and messages of "How Can I Keep from Singing," "I Shall Be Released," and "Woke Up This Morning with My Mind Stayed on Freedom" dance through my being. Some of the songs I know, some are new. I bubble with joy in their presence that night, and I know I want more. I am delighted that they are a network of communal houses located just a half an hour from my neighborhood in Philadelphia.

A new chapter in my life is opening; I feel it before I have words to name it. My acorn has found her kindred spirits. Every day brings eager anticipation of what I would learn or whom I would meet next. When the camp weekends end with the close of August, I begin joining the M.N.S. community activities in West Philadelphia. I attend a Quaker Meeting on Sunday evenings, followed by a potluck dinner and singing. Over dinner, eighteen-year-old P.J. Hoffman from St. Paul, Minnesota and I talk about how to create that new society. George and Lillian Willoughby, already in their sixties, tell stories of forming a food coop in the basement of the first M.N.S. house. Dick Taylor shares his story of using canoes to blockade the Baltimore harbor to stop arms shipments to Vietnam. The shared vision, passion, and fun of these gatherings is compelling.

I join a Re-evaluation Co-Counseling class, where I learn how to take responsibility for my feelings, working with a reciprocal listening partner to reach more clarity in my thinking and actions. I join a macro-analysis seminar, an eighteen-week leaderless curriculum of study created by a collective of M.N.S. members to educate ourselves on analysis, vision, and strategy for nonviolent, direct action to create social change. What had begun in 1971 as a collective of twelve Quaker activists with four communal houses called The Life Center has grown this fall to a community of eighty people living in twelve communal houses. It would eventually grow to 120 members and twenty households, all within a ten square block neighborhood. By January, I move in as a member.

I invite Bruce to come with me. I do not want following my passion to cost me my marriage. However, he is still rooted in the path of the institutional church, while my ministry has changed. M.N.S. feels like my church now. While Quakerism, one of the founding principles of M.N.S., is based in Christianity historically, its practice is to listen to the inner guidance of spirit. This tradition considers everyone a minister, and no one is *the* minister. That shared leadership appeals more to me now than the traditional meaning of minister. Bruce's reaction to M.N.S. is, "I'm under-impressed. You don't take your politics to the street." "Really?" I query, "Where do you take them?" "I don't know, but not the street" is his answer. This conversation is pivotal for me as we seek to reconcile our differences. I feel powerless to change what is happening between us. With M.N.S. as the most immediate catalyst, this is the defining moment for where our nine-year marriage has arrived.

Our paths are diverging, with all the pain, angst, and logistics that separation would entail. Our three sons will now have to grow up in this dilemma of differences—not in our core values, but in how we want to express them in the world. For me, living responsibly and with purpose must be put into action in community. Bruce sees it differently; his way is that of the scholar and theologian, and so we come apart, not for lack of love, but for lack of a common vision for our lives. That diamond ring would go back into storage for the third and last time, yet again not belonging where I am going. It had somehow become a symbol for our different paths, beginning when I first gave it back nine years ago—before we married—with my doubts about our common future.

We frame our change as freeing each other to become more fully who we really are. I honor his choice not to join; he honors my choice to follow my truth. This transition is a roller coaster ride. The highs of anticipation and resonance I feel with the community are matched in intensity with the sadness I feel about our marriage not having the resilience to survive these changes, and the undeniable guilt I feel as the one forcing unwanted change on the other four people in my family. When I first tell Bruce what I want to do, I ask for a six month sabbatical from the family in order to go and see if this community is indeed what I think it is. His response is, "If you think you're taking the kids, you're mistaken." I can't imagine my future without my children, but I have to go and see.

I join a household in The Life Center, but I come home every Friday afternoon, do five loads of wash, a big grocery shopping, take the kids to the park, go to church together Sunday morning, 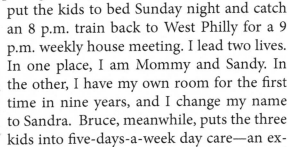 put the kids to bed Sunday night and catch an 8 p.m. train back to West Philly for a 9 p.m. weekly house meeting. I lead two lives. In one place, I am Mommy and Sandy. In the other, I have my own room for the first time in nine years, and I change my name to Sandra. Bruce, meanwhile, puts the three kids into five-days-a-week day care—an expense I never thought we could afford—and takes in a boarder who barters for cooking and child care. Bruce isn't about to take on what I had left to be done.

One month into this experiment I receive a visit from our pastor in Germantown where we live. I tell her about the guilt I am dealing with, and how deeply I feel conflicted about what is right for me and the consequences to my family. I am also having to let go of my identity as someone who does not break her vows. Jean affirms that there are good kinds of guilt and bad kinds. Mine is the good kind. I *am* causing hurt. But, she queries, haven't I also been hurt in the relationship? Don't we all inevitably hurt the people we love? Isn't that part of how Life unfolds and change happens? We make vows, she points out, but when we change as people, the vows are like shoes that no longer fit. Without truthfulness, the vows no longer serve their purpose.

I search for the grounding that allows me to be sorry for the pain I am causing, and feel it along with my loved ones, while also making the choice I need and want for my life. I am battling with the age-old message to women that they should always be the one who put others first. I struggle to stop the judgments and know that what I am doing is loving because it is my truth, and that is the essence of authentic relationship. I make my way out into that field Rumi talks about—beyond right and wrong—

where, he says, "I'll meet you there." Bruce does eventually let go and meet me there. I call one day in tears two months into this trial time, knowing I do not want to go back to the marriage, but knowing I cannot leave without the children. Bruce now agrees there are other options.

I will be forever grateful for his willingness to let change happen that would cost him being able to have his kids grow up in his home. He does tell me he thinks that what I am doing is the most selfish thing I could ever do. He is right. His words sting, but there is no defense. His parents don't speak to me for four years, and his sister writes me a scathing letter of incrimination for my choice. Her words, "Your community is three children too late" are seared in my memory of that time. Part of nonviolence discipline is the willingness to accept the consequences of one's actions no matter how painful. I would learn that lesson every minute of every day as we pack up our household that following summer. Bruce moves to Reston, Virginia to pursue a career as a writer. I move into a Life Center house with the kids, and we begin a family routine of visits every third weekend, alternating who travels.

We would continue over the ensuing forty years to keep the integrity of family—a divorced family—by spending every Christmas together until our grown sons had families of their own. Now we spend every Thanksgiving together. Continuing to be a part of each other's lives and building on our strong bond as co-parents (which includes Bruce's new life partner, Jean), while liberating ourselves from a marriage that no longer served our lives, has been one of the greatest lessons for me of what is possible when you follow your heart and also stay emotionally connected. Just this year, Bruce called me to acknowledge what would have been our 50th wedding anniversary. It was not unusual for us to express appreciation for the other, but this time was special. I realized during the conversation that I felt we had kept the vows we made to each other so long ago. We are still in each other's lives, very much a family, and we've got each other's back. When I posed this thought to Bruce, his response was, "I think you're right." It was a tender, beautiful moment of healing, gratitude and forgiveness.

I would spend the next ten years in this M.N.S. community, which becomes an international training center for social change activists from around the world. People come from India, England, Japan, Germany, Australia, Uganda, and most of the United States to participate in a year-long training program, live in one of our houses for one or two years, and then return to their homes. In addition to training activists in the skills of campaign-building (long-range strategies), we have twelve different collectives working on promoting social change across the country and the world. I am a member of The Churchmouse Collective. We would lead workshops in twelve states on economic justice  and the American lifestyle, advocating a return to simple living for both individuals and the church as an institution that espouses social justice. Other collectives work for the liberation of Namibia from South Africa, divestment from the South African apartheid system, and the Macro-analysis Seminar which sends its study plan to college campuses nation-wide and later morphs into the New Society Press that to this day publishes books about Nonviolence. We have Neighborhood Watch groups, and identity groups such as W.O.W.—Wonderful Older Women—who give us "speak-outs" on the oppression of old people. We have working class support groups, gay liberation support groups, and spirituality sharing groups. One summer, we run a three-week training specifically for a group from Germany, who return to start the Green Party that later becomes a leading force in Germany's Parliament.

We function like the congregation of a church. We sing vigorously at every monthly Network Meeting where the members of all the collectives come together to report on their projects and ask for support from the whole community. We live in twenty communal houses in a ten block area of West Philadelphia. We are most known in social change circles for our attention to process. We know that to create the society we want, we have to be a movement that people stay involved with their whole lives. For that to happen, people need to know that their point of view is important and will have influence. They need to participate in deciding what happens. They need respect for differences from the group norms. If someone feels strongly enough to block consensus on a decision (a Quaker practice), they are responsible for returning the next month with an alternative proposal that they have worked out with the people with whom they disagreed.

We have a leaderless model; everyone is considered a leader. Facilitation and agenda building are jobs that rotate. Decisions are made by consensus (also learned from the Quakers). A very particular Clearness Committee process, from the Quakers as well, is used whenever an important decision has to be made by an individual or a group, such as membership in a communal house. If too many hands are in the air wanting to comment at a meeting, the co-facilitators will instruct everyone to turn to someone near them and each have two minutes to say what is on their mind about what is happening in the meeting. They understand that people mostly need the experience of being heard, not necessarily by everyone. When tensions heighten, a facilitator might call for a moment of silence. I love how careful and respectful our process is, and the communication skills I am beginning to teach harmonize fully with these skills of facilitation.

I have found a home and a chosen family. I grow in skill,

consciousness and commitment. M.N.S. eventually spreads to twenty-five cities across the U.S., with annual network meetings in the middle of the country. We become a tribe. Dispersed in 1987, we are still a community, holding reunions for mutual support and inspiration, writing books, teaching in colleges, running food coops, showing up on national news commentaries, even running for governor (in Massachusetts for the Green Party), and facilitating the inevitable funerals. The Internet keeps us abreast of each other's actions, musings and milestones, as we continue to celebrate the great contribution we made to the social change movements of the last three decades of the 20th century. There will be more stories about my experience raising my three sons in an M.N.S. communal house in the chapter that follows.

Parenting in Community
1973-82

"Who's on kids?" I hear nine year old Aaron calling as the front door of our communal house bursts open and the kids come careening into the kitchen after school for a snack. Its 3:30 p.m. on a weekday, and the energy in the whole house changes from adults quietly talking in meetings, to shouting between the three floors, balls bouncing off walls, and skateboards rolling down the front hallway. "Who's my special time with today?" asks Kyle, knowing that one of the six adults in the house would be planning to do something with just him for a little while, and hear about how his day was at school. If it's my day "on kids," I am in the kitchen with a snack ready and have the answer to Kyle's question. If it is not my day, I may be in a meeting at another house and not be home for another hour or two. I know the kids are in good hands and will be well cared for in my absence. It is such a joy to have the freedom of movement in my life that communal living affords. I so appreciate the other five adults I live with who have taken on the assignment of raising these kids with me. Our shared commitment calls into question the habitual frame of "my kids." Yes, I am their Mom, but they also have a village; the boys are "our kids," and we are all stronger for that.

"What is it like to raise your kids in a commune?" asks my twenty-two year old honorary granddaughter, Carmen, who has come to spend a weekend with me to help me pull my memoir together. Carmen has been part of my chosen family since she was born and her mother—a dear M.N.S. friend—asked me to be a grandmother to her three children. Saying "yes" was a natural continuation of the co-parenting that had supported me so well through my child-rearing years. "Did your kids like it? Did you agree on discipline and rules of conduct?" Carmen queries. I reflect on what a steep learning curve it was for all of us who ventured together into this unexplored realm of co-parenting. Although we are a web of twenty households with 120 members, most of us had never done anything like communal living before. College dorms might have been similar, but in those days they were not unisex, and we didn't have to deal with money, food, or housekeeping with each other. None of us had been raised communally, or had ever thought of helping to raise someone else's kids. We have twelve children among us.

Half of our houses are owned by a member, the other half are being rented. I had initially joined one of the rented houses, but after a year I was able to purchase one in the center of our web on a quiet one-way street just a block from the trolley line. Each of the houses in The Life Center has a name. Our name is "Rainbow" after Pete Seeger's song, "Rainbow Race." Nearby is "Nashville," "Trollheim" (one member is from Norway), "The Crossing," The Gathering," "Daybreak," "Sunflower, "and "Youngest Daughter" (from the Tarot, I think). We live on a two-block long one-way street where our kids play stick ball between cars parked on both sides. Almost everyone living in the houses is participating in one or more of the twelve collectives working

for social change. Most are also involved in Re-evaluation Co-Counseling, the personal growth training I mentioned previously.

Let me introduce my sons. Aaron loves being the oldest. He makes the rules and his brothers follow his lead. He loves all kinds of sports and pushes himself to be the best he can be. He leads the pack of neighborhood kids with fairness and inclusion. When I'm trying to tell a bedtime story and his brothers get distracted, he will say, "Shh. Listen to Mom. She's talking." A class in pottery-making at the Y is his downfall. Aaron does not like failure, and gives up quickly when he can't master something that requires patience and practice. He would grow up to be the captain of his football team in high school as well as college, and be voted into his alma mater's Hall of Fame. Wherever he works as an adult, he becomes the manager of other employees and runs the business like a football team. The early signs of his success—a combination of focus, passion and discipline—are there to see. To this day when he calls me up he will identify himself with "This is your first-born son calling."

Nathan is not the typical middle child. He never frets over feeling at a disadvantage. He simply goes out of the triangle and makes his own set of friends. He is perennially cheerful, abundant in friends and athletic prowess. His 4th grade teacher explains to me that he lets Nathan wander around the classroom because he seems to learn better when he can listen in as the teacher explains something to another student. His challenge with dyslexia (not diagnosed at the time) creates a lot of frustration with school, so he sets his sights on adventure instead, and would end up making his career in outdoor, experiential learning where he thrives. Nathan wants freedom to do things his own way. He will become the Director of a Youth-at-Risk Program and use Nature as his classroom for teaching disadvantaged kids to focus and care about their future.

Kyle is shy and quiet, but he has a near-photogenic mind like his father. He beats all the adults in the house at "Memory." His stack of "wins" is three times as high as mine. His third-grade teacher tells me that he qualifies for an advanced placement class but she feels strongly that he needs to stay with the regular class in order to improve his social skills. Kyle always seems okay with being last among his brothers. He never has to make his own set of friends because there is already so much going on he can just join. He is a loyal follower, and bonds so strongly with his oldest brother that he drags his sleeping bag into Aaron's room and sleeps on the floor next to his bed for years. All his watching and going with the flow leads him into the field of social work. His quiet confidence in meeting any challenge takes him through the ranks into leadership as a Program Director for his foster care agency.

The kids are enrolled in the local public schools, where Aaron is one of six white kids in a class of thirty-six in the fifth grade. Cambodian and Vietnamese refugee children are among their friends, as are blacks and Hispanics. Open classrooms are the latest trend, so the boys are all in multi-grade classes where older kids teach younger kids math and reading along with the teacher. We also live a trolley ride away from the Phillies' baseball stadium, and that is a frequent destination for the four of us. I cringe now to think that I would let the kids roam all over that stadium with 12,000 spectators and not be the least bit concerned about their safety.

Three pillars of our experiment in co-parenting communally are Parent Effectiveness Training, Co-Counseling, and the Clearness Process. I brought the first with me when I came to this community with my relatively new skill set in negotiating needs. No such skills had existed in our nuclear families when we were growing up. Parents made the rules, and kids were punished if they didn't obey. When my three sons—now nine, seven and six—join "Rainbow," we have regular Sunday night house meetings to address whatever problems anyone, including the kids, want addressed. We teach the children how to facilitate, build an agenda, and use negotiation skills. They learn, along with the adults, the difference between needs and solutions. They learn creative, non-judgmental brain-storming of possible solutions. They learn to follow up and be sure a problem is solved after agreements are made. I have succeeded in having my dining room wall full of flip charts.

After the kids' house meeting, we team each kid up with an adult, and every team does one of the house chores for the week. With music blaring and everyone working, the house gets clean in half an hour. We end the night with ice cream (each week one person gets to pick the flavor), and then whoever is "on kids" puts the kids to bed before we start the adult house meeting. The kids, now in their forties, will tell you today that they hated those house meetings because it was something they were made to do. But my oldest son, with three kids of his own, has regular "family nights" on Sundays where they play games and talk about things.

My mother, during her one visit over the ten years I lived there, commented that I was living like the Queen of Sheba with all these other people doing "my work." In our quest for gender equality, my work had become "our work." I will always wonder why she could not understand and value something that was so liberating for me. That mystery lies at the heart of our relationship. I am now partnering with adults who all take turns washing the dishes. Everyone puts the kids to bed. Everyone takes out the trash in turn. I had one house job (washing the kitchen floor), one night to cook for the nine of us, and one night "on kids." I have my own life back. I have as much free time to study, join collectives working on social change projects, and go out with friends as non-parents do. This is what the new society we want is going to look like. Whichever adult is "on kids" for that day helps with homework, and gives baths, stories and backrubs all around.

A particular challenge comes from the kids who demand stories that are made up rather than read. I mostly base my stories on a series popularized by Marlo Thomas called "Free to Be Me" in which Atalanta and John—who are best friends—go off and have separate adventures—where they each do brave and smart things—then come home and tell each other all about what they have done. It is a series meant to pull American children's literature away from the Dick and Jane stories, where they are always together and Dick is always leading. One housemate in particular, Adam, has the best series of all based on a bumbling early adolescent boy—reminiscent of the Little Abner cartoon character—named "Gumbo." Gumbo is socially awkward, trying to learn about sex and girls (a great way to introduce sex education), while dealing with scary peer groups and disapproving parents. Adam's stories are so full of laughter that adults who aren't on kids might stop what they are doing if they are home and come listen.

The second pillar of our community, Co-Counseling, is a process of learning how to take responsibility for your feelings, instead of unconsciously expressing "distress" and "chronic patterns" of defense or low self-esteem to those around you when you are upset. We learn to "discharge" those feelings by crying, shivering, yawning, laughing, or screaming in a safe, non-judgmental, contracted setting, as in "Can you give me five minutes of attention?" Almost every adult we live with practices these skills, and supports the kids in doing the same. When they would get into power struggles with each other, or feel frustrated over something unfair, we would say, "I'm just going to hold you until you feel better." They will tell you today that they hated it when we did this, but they would discharge their feelings and eventually get below their anger, cry for the hurt they were really feeling, and then go off to play again, clear of distress.

In our household it is normal to hear pounding, wailing and muffled screams coming from behind closed doors as people discharge their pent up feelings with their co-counselor. One day, after I had a painful encounter with another adult and am crying in the laundry room, Nathan, who is nine, comes in. He puts his hand on my back and says, "It's OK to cry, Mom." I cherish this memory of being so held and loved by my son. My boys are learning to be comfortable with feelings, both their own and others'. Today—thirty years later—they are all empathic, patient, kind fathers who know how to get close and stay connected through trouble with their own kids.

The third pillar, the Clearness Process, is used both for people who want to join M.N.S., and for those wanting to join our communal house. This process is one of discernment in what we are looking for in a housemate, and what the candidate is looking for in community. When I first came to the community as a single parent, I had just hoped other adults would help me with my huge responsibilities. I asked if others could cover the boys for just the times I needed to be away. Within six months, that typical nuclear family culture transformed, and so did our clearness process for new housemates. Now if you want to live with us, you have to value what you can learn from the privilege of living with children. We all participate in this two-way exploration of whether or not the new candidate is a good fit. We have a chance to explain how we intend to nurture the children, what our agreements are as adults about how expectations, breeches, and discipline are handled, as well as how we expect each adult to invest time and creativity with the children.

Adults who join our household agree to participate in having a half-hour of "special time" with a designated kid each day sometime after school, and one night a week "on kids." These commitments are possible because one of the norms in M.N.S. is that no one has a full time job in order to free our time up to do social change work. We also have designated "godparents" outside the house to take the kids away from "the pack" and have another adult friend in the wider M.N.S. community.

When there is a fifty-two day teachers' strike in Philadelphia one fall, we set up home schooling in our dining room. We teach all twelve of our kids how the plumbing, heating and electrical systems of the house work. We have them do math using the various meters, compare quantities of usage, and figure out bill-ing. We take them to City Hall to observe the debates in the City Council on the strike. Then we come home and they role-play the council members, school board, teachers union, and parents. After a few weeks, they go to the council meeting by themselves on the trolley, and report back what they hear and see (after pay-ing a visit to William Penn on the top of City Hall.) It is amazing to me in retrospect to realize what trust we had in them moving on their own in the fourth largest city in the country. It was their playground!

The boys ride on the shoulders of the men into demonstra-tions, and we have many camping trips, including across the country to M.N.S. gatherings in Colorado, Michigan and Kan-sas. When Three Mile Island blows in 1979 just twenty miles from us, the boys are evacuated to New York City with two of our housemates, while I and others stay to help organize against nuclear power. When there isn't an after school sports program in the local elementary school, two of the men and I start a little league and drag equipment in grocery carts to a local field for practice—something I would never have attempted on my own.

We don't always get it right. One lesbian separatist housemate shocks me when she tells me I should give the boys to gay men to raise and put my energy into raising girls—not very support-ive. Food is one of our biggest challenges. A shift overnight from meat, French fries and white bread to homemade whole wheat bread and vegetarian dishes of rice and veggies never really takes with the boys. Aaron comments, "How come your food is all brown and green?" I have to compromise on the bread because the kids balk at taking sandwiches to school that are brown. We buy one loaf of Wonder Bread, take it home and divide it into three packets with their names on them. That bread is only to be used for school lunches. I also have to compromise around dinner. At 5:30 p.m., I get out cottage cheese, applesauce (a great combo), nuts and raisins, yogurt, and PB&J. That is their supper in case they don't like what is served by the chef that night. Our solution meets my need for nutrition, and meets their need for familiar food they like. I want them to have some power around this change in lifestyle.

One day, when the boys are visiting their father in Virginia, I discover two holes in the walls of a rec room we have built in the basement, obviously made by skateboards ramming into them. One hole would have been shocking enough, but two holes means they didn't stop what they were doing after the first hole was made. I am livid! I stomp upstairs and grab the phone to call the boys and blast them for such carelessness and destruction. Robert, a housemate, catches me in the act and inquires calmly what I am up to. When I tell him—with steam coming out of my ears—he gently but firmly says, "Would you like me to handle this?" I can see in his eyes how determined he is to interrupt my distress. I yield, and stand there amazed as he very calmly calls the boys in Virginia, explains what has happened, and tells them that we expect them to take responsibility for their damage when they return. He is loving, respectful, and clear. They respond in kind. How different their experience would have been if no one had way-laid this flaming, indignant mother.

So how did it go, Carmen wants to know? Sometimes the bedtime stories are so good the other adults show up to listen. Sometimes the games being played in the living room are so animated, we have to stop what we are doing to go see what is happening and join in. I remember a bike trip across the Ben Franklin Bridge into New Jersey with eight year old Kyle bringing up the rear, and Nathan and Aaron out in front of twenty bikers. I remember neighborhood "Monster" games, when all the kids and as many adults played off our front porch, hiding in bushes up and down the street, chasing through alleys, backyards and church parking lots, adults against the kids in a mad chase to capture.

When Aaron reaches the 4th grade, I start a day-off-a-month

from school for each of my kids. It is a special time away from the brothers, the routine, and the "pack." It is a day when that kid can plan what he wants to do and I follow. I am motivated to start this practice after a workshop I attend in which I am asked to create two pie charts. One shows how I actually use my time, and the other shows how I would ideally like to use my time. The slot allocated to "the kids" shows me that I see them as one activity, not the three unique people they each are. I realize I am missing the experience of knowing each one well. In my second chart, I have time for "the kids" and time for each one. I see in a new light how important and how precious that singularity is, since there is only a small window of time left when they will want to spend special time with just me.

We go to the library, play tennis, go to the pinball arcade (arrgh), eat at MacDonald's (arrgh again), and then to a movie of their choice (Bruce Lee if possible). It is a stretch for me to enter fully into the world of a pre-adolescent boy. We skip along the tops of stone walls, and down the sidewalk of Broad Street in Center City. It is also a day I check their shoes for holes or tightness, and their clothes for mending or passing on. It is a time for intimacy, for specialness, for being friends. One day, when Aaron is twelve, he asks if it is OK with me if he does his day off with our housemate, Jerry, instead of me. I am a little chagrined that maybe my time is up, and they would have more fun with a man for a playmate, but I am happy that Jerry is willing to do it. Spending three Tuesdays a month with a kid for a whole day has been a major undertaking. I guess I deserve to graduate, too. Community makes this possible.

Differences are the big challenge in our household, and they aren't always able to be resolved—even in the New Society. One episode happens with a dearly loved gay man, Firefly, who one day declares that he won't continue to live in Rainbow unless the house is land trusted so there is no inequality of ownership. I am shocked out of my unconscious classism, seeing nothing wrong with the present arrangement. The quandary for me as the owner is that I am raising three kids in a community with no long-term commitment. People stay until they feel it is time to go. They leave and we have to find replacements to make the economics work. Also, I have seen another single parent in our community have to leave a household when things didn't work out, and I am not willing to be the one who would have to do that. I am leaning on my privilege as a homeowner. It is an unequal situation. We call in a mediator from another household, and listen deeply to each person's needs and feelings. In the end, Firefly moves out. I help him move and we have stayed friends for thirty years. He now owns his own home.

My assessment of our ten years of communal living is that the kids received better attention, inspiration, care, and modelling of life skills than they would ever have gotten in a nuclear family with a full time working dad and an exhausted maintenance-of-life mother. The kids saw their dad every three weeks. At first I would travel down with the boys or he would come up for a weekend. We continued to share space as a family on those weekends. Later, we put them on the express bus from Philly to D.C. As the boys grew up, they each had a year living with their dad, and we finally moved away from the city when they reached middle school age. Nathan wrote his college application essay on living communally and allowing strangers to become family. That is one of the greatest testimonies for me of what it meant to the boys. When Nathan turned twenty-one, it was Robert (of the skateboard holes) who helped him facilitate a men's circle while I, turning fifty on the same day, had my women's circle. It is Jerry and Robert who are there for Nathan when he has to transition through a painful divorce at forty. The tribe we are a part of still lives in our hearts, and shows up on our doorstep when we need them.

A New Spiritual Quest
1974

I am thirty-three and I am finally ready to shed the cloak of religion. I have lived out my adolescent dream of becoming a missionary. The two years as a Frontier Intern in Malawi, Central Africa has been a spiritual quest of sorts, to put my whole self into service living the Gospel of Jesus Christ as best I could. That dream bloomed, and now has faded. My short time with M.N.S. has offered me the silence of Quakerism, a sense of presence without words. The working for justice in community—with its accompanying song, prayer, play and celebration—is my church now. My calling is changing from within and without.

When did my beliefs about religion change? Was it when I went to talk to my pastor about changing the sexist hymns extolling "Sons of men and angels sing, glory to our new born King" and he refused? Was it when six Episcopal bishops interrupted the ordination service for the first nine women bishops with their ancient protest that none of Jesus' disciples were women and the apostolic lineage would be destroyed if women are admitted? Was it the Catholic Church refusing women access to birth control, abortion, or divorce, perpetuating as God's law the treatment of women as property? Enough. I'm out! This nasty mix of religion and sexism no longer speaks the Gospel to me.

Women are telling a new story, a feminist story, a message of original blessing replacing the old one of original sin. The sacredness of life, as honored by the Goddess-worshipping cultures of the 30,000 years preceding the emergence of Patriarchy, is becoming my central focus of worship. I need a new spiritual quest that will answer new questions. Is there a God I can feel loved, affirmed, and lifted up by? Does She have to be feminine to be authentic to me? Is there a tradition of faith that has integrity for me? Is there a community of believers that will be a safe spiritual home for me, where I can share communion and grow through inspiration and conscious, inclusive leadership? I am now in transition. I leave the Church the same year I leave my marriage. A compelling catalyst for this change is reading Mary Daly's *Beyond God the Father*, in which she likens women leaving Patriarchy to the Israelites leaving Egypt. The Israelites have to wander forty years in the desert, being led only with manna by day and fire by night—representing the presence of Spirit— before they can enter the Promised Land. The generation that had been slaves has to die. The next generation will be able to open to the new. I, too, need to wander far away from organized religion. I need to go out of bounds. The slave in me needs to die.

I want no words, no answers. I want quiet where I can hear my own voice and open to Spirit. I find a vacant room in another communal house where I go every morning after the kids leave for school. I read, meditate, and journal. I invite chosen friends to visit and I interview them about what they believe and why. I ask questions like "How does your faith sustain you?" "Do you ever consider leaving it behind and moving beyond what you have always known?" "Do you dare to go out of bounds?" To my surprise, my friends are eager to come. They have the same questions, and few answers. It seems that among my peers, wandering is the new norm. As Starhawk's book *Dreaming the Dark* foretold, we are "dreaming the dark," opening to the truth of our own experience as the touchstone for our faith. We are questioning any external authority. We even call ourselves the Movement for a New Society. We collectively feel a disconnect from our culture and the ways we have been raised. We are claiming the possibility of a new way to live together that none of us have known before. We are sharing our own stories and writing a Gospel of "Good News" from the ground of our own Being.

I am drawn to stories of Lilith who, it is told, lived outside the Garden of Eden, away from the rules of forbidden fruit and a punishing god. I am drawn to the goddess Diana, who lived alone in the forest with her bow and arrow for protection. I resonate with her rebellious freedom from the patriarchal harnessing of women's power. Athena, goddess of law—her own law—speaks to me. I love Sappho's words, with her island of lesbians writing erotic poetry that the Crusaders sought to destroy entirely because it was so out of bounds from their reality of women as helpmates to man. Some fragments of Sappho's poetry survived that holocaust to show the radiant beauty of women in community—safe from Patriarchy's reach—serving and adoring each other. When I read her poetry, my spirit grows fiery. The good Christian in me is giving way to an erotic pagan grounded in the holiness of all creation. *Dreaming the Dark* shows me a blend of spirituality and politics I can embrace with my whole being, with the equality of male and female living from experience rather than from dogma. It is a spirituality that begins in me rather than in books and preachers.

During this time I felt led to re-articulate King David's beloved Twenty-third Psalm as a means of claiming my new spiritual path:

> The hand of the Great Mother rocks the cradle of my soul,
> I shall not want.
> She shows me how to lie down in green pastures.
> She leads me beside the still waters.
> She restores my soul.
> Yea, though I walk through the valley of the shadow of death,

I will not fear,
For She is with me.
Her song and her touch, they comfort me.
She blesses my whole being with her kiss.
She prepares a table before me in the presence of my
limitations.
My cup overflows.
Surely, goodness and mercy shall surround and fill me
all the days of my life,
And I will dwell in the heart of the Mother forever.

During one of these visits a male friend, an Evangelical Christian, asks me, "What's the matter with bowing down to the Creator of the Universe?" My reply clarifies for me where my wandering is taking me, "Men need to learn to bow down; women need to learn to stand up. I'm glad to have Jesus walk beside me, but I am not following him." I realize anew that nothing has changed in my relationship with Jesus but the context. His teachings and His way of being in the world live in every cell of my body. I am walking with him, but not worshipping him. I do feel a loss in this process. It is a loss of being in the continuity of history, in the communion of saints, an identity that has given such momentum to my early adulthood. When I hear Martin Luther King calling on the traditions of Scripture—"I have SEEN *the* Promised Land"—knowing so many recognize fully what he is referring to, I feel lonely. I feel sad to be separated from that belonging. That is, however, the price of going out of bounds.

At twenty-nine, I had taken a training in Transcendental Meditation and begun a daily twenty minute practice. This is not a religion, but a means of finding a relationship to my own mind. Learning to watch my thoughts rather than energize them with thinking taught me to know the one who is observing the thoughts. This very practice is, I believe, what enables me now to observe my Christian beliefs as beliefs, as thoughts that I have the freedom to disengage from. This practice of meditation also supports the spirit of wandering I am embracing. When the mind quiets, there is only stillness, emptiness, being without doing. Just as quantum physics shows that what appears as empty space is in fact pulsing with dynamic energy—the quantum soup—so it is that mental stillness is also pulsing with aliveness. That very aliveness is at the center of my new spirituality. I am also drawn to aspects of Buddhist practice such as non-attachment and beginner's mind, which teach me to release my mind from having to make meanings out of everything. I savor my experience, yet I continue to resist the Buddhist teachings of right speech and right livelihood—a right way to do and be. I still crave the freedom to name "right" for myself.

Starhawk has come into my life as the teacher at a weekend for women near my home. One hundred and fifty women show up. Starhawk is an author turned political activist (or vice versa?) She describes herself to us as "a good Jewish princess who grew up to be a witch." Her Master's thesis was on the Wiccan practices of the European Middle Ages, the remnants of a vibrant pagan tradition that has persisted through the onslaught of Christianity. She now passes those practices on to us contemporary witch-identified women. We learn to raise our arms outstretched to the rising sun, to new beginnings, to inspiration, with thanks and petition to Spirit which is present in the physical world around us. As I follow her teachings, I begin feeling a sense of worship again. I begin to see the natural world as sacred, as nurturing and sustaining me. I begin to feel a connection to the sacred feminine, the aliveness and presence of The Great Mother who had been at the center of pagan worship for 30,000 years before patriarchal religion arose with sword in hand to stamp it out, replacing her worship with the message that women were the cause of original sin and Man's suffering.

Now I am entering a belief system that fits my experience. Starhawk teaches us to chant:

"Where there's fear, there is power.
  Passion is the revealer.
  The wheel goes around and around.
  When you're ready it will carry you through."

I am being drawn into a vortex of life, death, and rebirth. She teaches us the sacredness of the four elements that constitute life itself: earth, air fire and water. She teaches us to stand within a wheel with one of the elements in each of four directions. All of life's challenges and blessings are held within this wheel of experience that keeps turning and turning, from endings to new beginnings. In turning to the East, I breathe in the sacred gift of life which is air, opening to change, inspiration and new beginnings. Turning to the South, I feel the fire in my veins, in my belly, in my mind, my feet, and my hands. I rejoice in play and passion. In turning to the West, I feel into the element of water with its energy of change, loss, and letting go-- all that sinks below the horizon yet is never gone. Facing the North, I honor the Earth as Mother, as sacred home, as teacher of how to walk on the Earth in a sacred way. I learn to claim mastery, sitting in maturity and accomplishment, but not permanently, for the North is also a place of waiting and watching for new beginnings arising in the East.

The Wheel inevitably turns and we find ourselves awakening (by choice or by ordeal) to a new reality that demands change, growth, letting go, and acquiring new skills. I realize how this wheel has unfolded so clearly in what happened to my marriage. I did not decide to abandon my marriage vows; they changed as I lived into the Wheel, as the organic web of people, experiences, ideas and challenges changed the shoreline in my life. My horizons changed. My sense of who I was had evolved from the dedicated missionary to the dedicated housewife with three children, to the dedicated wanderer and social change activist living in an urban commune. The Sacred Wheel holds it all.

So now I find myself again in the East, opening to new possibilities. I have learned more about making peace with change and practicing acceptance as a lesson. This choice to follow the Wheel around the four directions is not about answered prayer delivering me from unwanted dilemmas. It is about not resisting change, seeing it in the wider context of this Wheel going round and round through my life, giving me the lessons I need in order to mature and open to Spirit. Change is built into Nature. It is in the original contract with all of life. It includes disease, lost jobs, homes and relationships, trees shedding their fruit and leaves, and one species eating another. Fundamentally, the Wheel and its four directions are about saying thank you for Life.

God, for me, is now no longer a father to pray to. God is an event to live into and embody. God happens when we move toward each other and all of creation with love, compassion, joy, sorrow, and question. God is a communal experience. God happens in inspiration and in overcoming ordeal or oppression. God happens in song, poetry, and art. Judgment Day, for me, has been replaced with singing Hallelujah!

Rumi wrote,

"Come, come, come, come, ...
though you have broken your vow a thousand times,
come yet again, come, come."

Perhaps the Wheel itself demands the breaking of vows as we move from not-knowing to challenge, to resolution and new beginnings. Somehow the breaking of vows fits with wandering, with going out of bounds, but never going outside that Wheel. The Wheel is about journeying with Spirit. My wandering has become a Pilgrimage. Could it be that acceptance of change is the Promised Land the Pilgrim seeks? I am still wandering, but the slave in me has died.

A Citizen Is Born:
My First Civil Disobedience
1976

I am driving north on the freeway out of Philadelphia on a cloudy Sunday afternoon in March, heading for trouble. I have now left my naive loyalty to my country. I have left my marriage. I have left the church of my childhood. Going out of bounds feels normal to me now. It is where I find my truth. It is where I thrive. Today I will add another dimension to the truth of my being; I will go outside the law of this land. I am about to undertake my first act of civil disobedience. Ever since I met the Berrigan

Sandra Boston: 'You're asking you students to be crucified in pursuit of an illusion.'

brothers at the Oak Ridge Peace Camp in 1972, I see intentionally getting arrested as a badge of courage—not the social disgrace my mother would see. What I will do this afternoon will be a conscious choice to break a law that is protecting something that I perceive to be an a dangerous and morally irresponsible way of generating electricity—nuclear power.

I am ready to take unto myself the authority as a citizen in a democracy to declare what is moral, ethical, and responsible, and not leave that up to the powers that be. I want to use this action as an opportunity to educate the public about the issue I want addressed—the significant danger to human health and the environment of radiation leaking from these plants without public knowledge of that danger. It is time to speak truth to power again, but this time with full knowledge of what I am doing and the M.N.S. community of allies at my back.

Mary Bye, my ally, is with me in the car. She is an anti-nuclear activist older than I by twenty years. She is a wiry, fiery Crone with that tell-tale "no nonsense" look that reassures me—the novice—that we will succeed in our plot. We are on our way to the Visitors Center of our local nuclear power plant, Three Mile Island, in Harrisburg, PA., which is also home to colorful farm-land and grazing cows. I will wear an old fashioned, ordinary tan trench coat in order to hide the lock and chain I will carry with me. Mary will do the same in case we are separated or dis-covered before our deed is done. We have planned this action for weeks, as part of a nation-wide campaign to wake Ameri-cans up to the peril of nuclear power plants. Any serious acci-dent could release enough radiation to cause permanent evacu-ation of towns and cities in a 150 mile radius. The nuclear waste that is stored at the plant site—with no technology or plan for its disposal—is lethal for 450,000 years and has no safe place to be stored. Americans are mindlessly piling up this waste at 109 plants in our nation with no thought for the safety of future gen-erations, who will have to guard the remnants of our lifestyle with their lives. This is unconscionable to me.

After a forty-five minute drive, we pull into the visitor's lot and park. My adrenalin is revved up, hovering below the sur-face with anticipation. Mary's confident stride reassures me as we enter the Visitor's Center with a steady stream of others and begin to mill around the spacious and well-lit display room with its bigger-than-life photos of the pristine inner workings of the nuclear reactor. We blend in with the sixty or so other visitors who are there seeking an interesting Sunday afternoon experience. On the hour, we all enter the auditorium, fill the rows of cushy theater-like chairs, and wait to view the film that will tout the grand benefits of this supposedly clean energy. During the movie, in the dark, Mary and I quietly shed our disguise and chain ourselves to our chairs, which are screwed to the floor. Mary is in row three on the left of the auditorium. I am in row twelve on the right.

We wait in the dark as the film tells its proud story of technology's wonder. As I contemplate what will be my first arrest, I feel a mixture of fear and excitement. I am eager to face whatever challenges arise, whether legal or how the public chooses to respond to us. I flash on a paraphrase from Audre Lourde who said: when my purpose is clear, it is less important that I am afraid.[1] This imminent action will be my initiation into a new relationship to my country, my voice as a citizen, and my legacy for future generations. My truth is my citizenship in action. As I see it, this choice to generate radioactive waste that will be a terrible and dangerous burden to all future generations is unethical, immoral, and unjustifiable. We have other means of generating electricity—solar, wind and hydro— that don't require planning for permanent evacuation. I want to take an action that matches my outrage and fully expresses my truth that we deserve a safe and clean way to meet our energy needs as a society. I say "No" to this life-threatening form of energy production. My fear is no match for my determination and clarity of purpose.

When the lights come on at the end of the movie, and the power plant representatives invite questions, we rise and begin to pronounce the dangers of nuclear power to all who will listen. We call for the plant to be shut down in the name of safety, sanity, and our responsibility to future generations to leave them a livable environment. What happens next? The company representatives empty the hall. No one speaks to us. All the other guests file out as they are told. I am disappointed that there is not any show of support.

We sit in the dark hall until the police come. I have hidden the key to my lock in my panty hose, so the police have to get a tool to snap a link of chain to free me. We are released without charges, a strategy on their part to avoid attracting any attention to the episode that might get the newspapers asking questions they don't want discussed in public. We as activists would experience this frequently in the coming years as our actions would escalate and the powers that be would learn that by not pressing charges they could avoid confrontational court cases with expert witnesses blabbing information to the press that they do not want known. So all my psychological preparation is for naught, but my career as a nonviolent, civil disobedience activist is inaugurated.

Nonviolence as a strategy for creating change has been called "The Force More Powerful."[2] People willing to stand their ground while neither retreating nor resisting in the presence of adversaries creates the most possibility for peaceful change—the changing of minds. When we don't threaten an adversary, they are free to listen. Nonviolence is a life-long commitment. Our training says "You don't lose till you quit." That implies that we may not get the outcome we are seeking on the first or second or hundredth try, but it is a force that over time others who see it in action will want to join. It builds social power toward a tipping point of change that can never be predicted, but in hindsight always arrives. I would join that force again at Seabrook, New Hampshire in 1979 with 2300 who would be arrested, and 1,700 locked up in an armory for two weeks to protest the building of that nuclear power plant. I would join 236 women at Seneca, New York, as we climb the fence surrounding the largest arsenal of nuclear weapons on the planet to demand their dismantling. I would join others in my home town as part of a national Pledge of Resistance campaign to halt our government's funding of war against the Sandinistas of Nicaragua. I would join with 136 allies to stand against re-licensing the forty-year-old nuclear power plant that is just eleven miles from my home, endangering all of New England with the threat of permanent evacuation. And I will stand again, and again, and again, whenever the Truthforce demands it. "And what do you mean by the Truthforce?" Gandhi was asked when he first used that term to describe what motivated his actions. "That which meets the most human needs," he replied.

Just three years after this action, on March 28, 1979, Three Mile Island would experience the worst nuclear accident in U.S. history, causing the release of 40,000 gallons of radioactive water released into the Susquehanna River and the evacuation of 140,000 pregnant women and pre-school children from the area. This accident would take ten years to clean up and cause the loss of credibility with the public which would usher in the cancellation of building any more nuclear power plants in the U.S. until 2013. Obama and his 'all of the above" energy policy once again is providing government guaranteed loans to begin building them again.

Subsequently, Chernobyl in April of 1986 would cause permanent evacuation of that area of Ukraine, and in March 2011, Fukushima would shock the world with the meltdown of two reactors, causing permanent evacuation of over two million people and sending radioactive waste into the Pacific Ocean that will likely make its way around the world. "When will we ever learn? When will we ever learn?"

---

1. Full quote from Audre Lourde reads:
   "When I dare to be powerful—
   to use my strength in the service of my vision,
   then it becomes less and less important
   whether I am afraid."

2. *A Force More Powerful* is a 1999 feature-length documentary film and a 2000 PBS series written and directed by Steve York about nonviolent resistance movements around the world

Joining Lesbian Liberation
1974

I am sitting alone under a favorite Maple tree in a park near my home. It's a warm, spring day. The grass is a fresh green, daffodils and tulips are in bloom, and the sun is dancing pleasure on my skin as I lean back against the trunk, eyes closed. All seems well on the surface as I drink in solitude, but there is a restlessness within. I have raced through the decade of my thirties living a radical life focused on external projects like ending nuclear power and divesting in South Africa to bring down apartheid. After years of living inside the roles of wife and mother, longing for a lost part of myself, I have transformed those roles by embracing a new community, lifestyle and home. As I turn forty, another transition is stirring impatiently in my inner being, and I am not in any way prepared for the tumultuous change it will bring to every significant relationship in my life.

I have been a single parent with three young boys seeking a love relationship with men in my new M.N.S. community for the past seven years. I am a package deal: love me, love my kids. I don't feel any resonance with this reality in my significant others. One, two, three lovers later, I am coming to the sobering conclusion that the men I am involving myself with seem to have a self-absorption that leaves me out. Decisions that affect me, like time available to spend together, are made without including me. I notice that I am busily considering their needs and well-being and it is not reciprocated. I never feel the give and take is equal. My children are never as central to the relationship as I hope they will be. When the men feel it is time to move on, they are unable or unwilling to talk about it. They seem to have a way of shifting into fifth gear and being gone with no need for mutual understanding or consideration of my feelings. It is just a done deal.

I have now been around that barn enough times to realize that I am settling for my own second fiddle status in exchange for love, sex, and belonging. I remember saying to myself, "I'm done trying to find what I am looking for in relationships with men." I am no longer willing to hope or believe that they can understand what equality means to a woman. I am in nowhere land, determined to never turn back, yet not seeing anything recognizable as a new direction. I don't know if my sexuality will ever open to include women. In the beautiful solitude of the moment, the rightness of my choice satisfies my longing for connection. I am connecting with my own truth, my own needs, and choosing a boundary that supports me.

The decade of the seventies is jam-packed with weekend-long women's music festivals and Saturday night concerts featuring our own rock and folk stars in a burgeoning women's culture. I have my first experience of women-only dances, with women shedding their tops and dancing bare-breasted in large numbers. Something tribal is being unleashed. It is a kind of raw sexuality that is celebratory and collective, not aimed at any one person or relationship. It is pure fun! Now I find myself joining in the fray on the dance floor and screaming with delight at the concerts. Songs like, "The Woman in your Life is You" with Alice Dobkins, "Hiking Boot Mama" with Holly Near, and one about a crush on a gym teacher with Meg Christian are on the tip of my tongue and boring into my very being. These singers are powerful women, leading a revolution in identity consciousness akin to the "Black is Beautiful" movement for blacks in the '60s. We women need to hear songs of liberation for our bodies as our own, our sexuality as our own, our choices of lifestyle as our own, and that is just what this generation of songwriters is giving us—on steroids! All of our new choices about our bodies and our sexuality seem out of bounds, but we are changing where that line is drawn.

My soul feels like it has found home, a new kind of home for a new part of me. I join an eighty-women choir called Anna Crusis, led by a sassy lesbian named Cathy Roma. Unbeknownst to me, at least half the women in the choir are in love with her. Her spunky style of directing, her obvious joy in being out in front, and her flirtatious manner are all mesmerizing. Unsuspecting, I fall under that same attraction and find myself relishing just staring at her, which is totally appropriate under the circumstances. In hindsight, falling in love with a super-heroine is a safe way to begin opening to the new possibilities I am hunting for.

A pivotal event is my first experience of going to a women's bar in Center City, Philadelphia. Following a new friend from the choir up the winding staircase at the back of a regular bar to a second floor loft is like entering a movie set. The small room, featuring a bar, a tiny dance floor, and tables, is packed with women of all ages, races and sizes who are dressed to the nines for sex appeal, bantering over wine glasses while music is blaring. A mirror covering the back wall exaggerates the steaming, tantalizing ambiance. There is a mystique of delicious danger to the scene as taboos are being smashed, ground under foot by black-booted dykes coming on to eager "fems" with–yes–gay abandon. I am way out of my own bounds, yet I feel drawn to the company of these women who seem so at home in this place.

This bar scene is an initiation. Something new is stirring in me—an exhilaration evoked by the energy in this place that demands a response. It commands participation. I am surprised by how easy it is to join in the dancing and playing sexy with the friends I have come with, especially one of them. Cathy is a twelve-string guitar-toting, motorcycle dyke with a black cowboy hat. She has a radiant smile and an enticing sparkle in her eyes. She pulls me into a strong embrace as we dance, our breasts pressed together so hard it is clearly an invitation for more.

Where is the line here? Am I just playing at being a lesbian? Am I becoming one without ever deciding? Am I letting the gay women pull me over to their side of some equation I can only imagine but never define? All I know is I like this sexy, bold, exciting energy and I want to play. Later that night, after hours of dancing and flirting, Cathy ventures, "Are you sure this is what you want?" She knows—and I know—that straight women use gay women all the time to "try it out" and then go back to men. "Yes," I hear myself say. It is news to me, but there it is—a declaration of a turn in the road, a claiming of the goodness I am feeling about what is happening. No, I'm not in love. We both know that. I am infatuated, lured by the archetypal temptress, but oh. does it turn me on! All my lights are green.

I feel like I have been let into a secret pact, a strange sorority that has different criteria for joining than the typical college clubs. There is an undercurrent of "Bad Girl" that is delicious. It reminds me of the bumper sticker that has caught my eye and seems to define what is happening to me: *Good Girls Go To Heaven; Bad Girls Go Anywhere They Want!* Yes, indeed, I am now one of them. Seduction is fun. I never again have to worry about whether that sexual attraction to women switch will turn on. All my engines are firing.

What I don't anticipate in that heady night of wonder and intrigue is the ending that is happening outside my awareness. I am leaving the safe haven of heterosexuality where I have never had to worry about being accepted, only about being picked. I have never had to be concerned about the impact of my sexual identity on my three sons. I certainly never anticipated the look on my mother's face a year later when I would tell her about Cathy moving in with me and us planning our future together.

Nor did I anticipate my mother disinheriting me with the comment, "Your father would never have approved of who you have become." It seems that—once again—I am dishing up something unpalatable for her.

When I tell my boys that Cathy and I are partners and she is moving in, they don't bat an eye. They are already living with a gay male couple and a heterosexual couple. A lesbian couple completes the picture. One night at dinner, in the middle of the meal, Nathan, who is now ten, asks, "Robert, when you and Jerry make love, do you make love to him first, or does he make love to you?" There is a stunned silence all  around the table as Robert continues chewing his food. When he has swallowed, he smoothly replies, "Sometimes I make love to Jerry first. Sometimes he makes love to me." No further comment. Everyone goes on eating as if nothing out of the ordinary just happened. I am incredulous at Robert's grace and at Nathan's comfort with bringing up such a subject at the dinner table. This is indeed a New Society.

So there you have it, the beginning of a new sexual identity that is an ending of the old, familiar, inherited one. I feel like a pioneer heading west, knowing I would never return to the safe haven of roots and normalcy. Ahead lay unknown territory, with new friends, new possibilities, and a new trust in myself.

Women Warriors at Seneca
1983

Did you ever jump out from the sidelines and join in a parade? You are happily watching the parade go by, but then something grabs you—maybe someone you know, or a sign someone is carrying that speaks truth to you—and you want to be a part of what is happening. Well, news that 2,000 women are gathering in New York State to march on the largest repository of nuclear weapons on the planet grabs me! OMG, 2,000 women going out of bounds together! I start singing, "I want to be in that number, when the saints go marching in!" It's the summer of 1983, and I am going to jump into that parade. My country is deploying cruise missiles to our bases in England as a first strike defense against Russia. Did I just say "first strike" and "defense" in the same sentence? That is how weird the thinking about nuclear weapons has become after forty years of cold war between our countries. The women of Greenham Commons, England, have been camping outside that military base for seven years in protest against their nuclear weapons. What if their energy and vision should spread from England to the U.S.A., to Germany, Italy and Japan?

Well it has! Now we American women are taking up the challenge. An organizing collective has purchased a farm in Romulus, NY that abuts a military base that holds those nuclear weapons. We are coming from every corner of the country, ready to join our sisters world-wide in saying "No" to the insanity these weapons represent. Everyone knows we can't ever use them. The other side would retaliate, and the mutual devastation would kill civilization as we know it, as well as the very environment that sustains our whole planet. These weapons epitomize male arrogance and power gone amuck. The women are coming!

I find three friends who feel the same magnetic pull. We pack my old Toyota station wagon with camping gear and hit the road for the thirteen-hour drive from Greenfield, M.A. to Romulus. It is a week before the big action set for August 1st. We arrive at a typical two-story white farmhouse by the side of a country road a few miles outside of town. Nothing else is typical of a rural community. A clothesline spanning the grassy front yard holds 100 pillow cases, each one decorated with a symbol of life- flowers, children, trees, sunrises, music, gardens, etc. A young woman with a clipboard in hand and wearing shorts, a baggy button-down faded shirt, and hiking boots meets us as we turn in the driveway. She records our identification and points us toward the parking lot. Ahead of us is a huge, two-story red barn. On the side facing the road is a mural of women taking action with banners, tools, and children. Beyond the barn there are multi-colored tents as far as you can see. This place is pulsing with energy.

We find the outhouse, then hit the chow line under a big open-air tent, and sit on the ground for our first meal of rice, stir-fries and salad. A woman sitting near us, Sue from Ithaca, N.Y., explains how the pillow cases came to be strung across the front lawn.

"Local people are calling us communists," she explained. "Some campers thought we should fly the American flag to show that we are patriotic Americans. Others in the camp opposed that, feeling it is chauvinistic and not in alignment with what the camp stands for."

"Wow," I respond. "A full blown controversy. I wish I could have been present for the process that yielded in a compromise everyone could live with."

"It took what seemed like endless hours into the night. We're not sure we would find our way through this one," Sue continues.

She then tells us how they arrived at a solution. One of the pillow cases would fly the American flag, but it would be surrounded by all the other symbols of what the camp stands for. What a beautiful story to be greeted with our first night.

This farm is a village. Posted on a large communal bulletin board are meal schedules, work teams, chore sign- ups, child care systems and schools to run. There are workshops offered on topics from organic gardening to nonviolence and civil disobedience training. There are strategy sessions late into the night and daily vigils at the main gate to the army base. There is swimming at a local waterhole, yoga classes, and singing late into the night around bonfires. It's late July and hot. Hats and water bottles are basic gear, as are our own eating utensils carried in net bags so we can hang them on bushes to dry after we wash them in the communal kitchen. It seems our ability to create a village is in our DNA. No one has to tell others what to do. No one is in charge. We are all in charge. Creativity and initiative are in full swing. We're having fun and we're serious about our mission. Names seem less important than ideas and schemes. My body is bustling with delight. My two-person tent, surrounded by hundreds of others of all colors and sizes, is home to my soul as well as my body. There's no place else I'd rather be than hunkered down amidst this mighty energy of women rising.

The next day, I make the twenty-minute walk up to the main gate of the military base where we go in shifts to keep a constant presence. I have never been next to a military base before. All the personnel are in uniforms and carrying weapons. They wear heavy boots and all have crew cuts. They don't smile. The rigidity of their bodies mirrors the rigidity of the steel link fence which announces the presence of authority and command. I see a woman doing Tai Chi near the gate and hear a young soldier lean out with a worried look saying, "Please don't cast a spell on me!" My first thought: we are the witches returning and he feels it. My second  thought: the witch burnings of the Inquisition era are in all our psyches. Whenever women go out of bounds, they will be labeled. They will be in trouble with the Patriarchy. That trouble is here. Even though we are committed to nonviolence, it doesn't mean the soldiers we encounter daily are.

A group of four women sits in the road in front of the closed gate with their arms around each other's shoulders. They are meditating or praying as the soldiers with their rifles look on. An eighteen-wheeler arrives at the gate. The gate swings open. The women don't move. The truck driver lays on his horn. No movement. The soldier disappears inside a building to make a phone call. For a brief while, the women are in charge. They have the power. It is short-lived. It is symbolic. It matters. It is a moment of conscience, of witness, of the presence of the sacred commitment we feel to the Earth and Her people. Soon the women are dragged away and the truck enters the base, but the energy in this place is changed. The drama of good and evil is in play. A spell is being cast!

Before me is the army base, with one-story white buildings—probably offices, barracks and training centers—as far as the eye can see in monotonous utilitarian array. There are no trees. The nuclear weapons are invisible, stored below ground in temperature-controlled silos. Reaching high above the buildings is a gray water tower and on it is written "Mission First, People Al-

ways." It seems a strange declaration for one of the most malevo-
lent places on the planet. Later that week, I would be awaken at
dawn by jubilant cries throughout the camp. In the night, one
woman, dressed in black and blackface, climbed the link fence,
snuck into the base with a can of paint, climbed the water tower,
single-handedly wiped out the "Mission First," climbed down
and snuck away undetected. The message on the water tower
would now read "People Always." Words, intentions, and principles are the arena of the confrontation we are here to create.
Again I would feel the impact we are having here on an ener-
getic level that cannot be erased, controlled or thwarted. We
may not be able to stop the missiles from deploying or close this
base, but we can change how it feels to be here. Later that day
we would have a surprise visit from an off-duty officer from the
base bringing us a case of beer—his congratulations for pulling
off such a feat.

Shortly after I arrive, and a week before the big action that
drew us all here, I am asked by the organizers—one of whom
is an ally from M.N.S. in Philly—to train 500 peacekeepers. I
say "Yes." I have done such a training many times before, but
never on this scale. It is an awesome responsibility. The thought
crosses my mind, "What if this very assignment is what I was
born to do?" I am ready. Here is my cause–to protect life and
end violence. Here are my people, 2,000 strong. We are jumping
into a global sisterhood parade! My acorn is spinning like a top
in anticipation.

They ask me if I need anything. "Yes. I need a co-trainer."
The next day they introduce me to Dawn McGuire from Kentucky, who has volunteered, and we go out to breakfast in town
to get acquainted. Over breakfast, I ask her what her experience
is leading nonviolence training. "I've never done it," she reported, much to my amazement. "I thought this would be a good
chance to learn how." Thus begins one of the most passionate,
stormy and bewildering two-year relationships of my life as we

navigate through the trials of August 1st, and then on past the Seneca adventure, through her entry into medical school at Columbia and my graduate study at the University of Connecticut. We do this relationship while living three hours apart and me parenting now fourteen-year-old Kyle as he navigates high school. You just never know when life will do its jig and you find yourself standing in a place you never expected, with a most unlikely partner whom you adore but can't for the life of you figure out how to get along with. But that is another story.

On the morning of the all-camp march to the main gate we gather our throng at the head of our driveway. Directly across this narrow country road from our driveway is a contingent of about forty townspeople with signs saying, "Commie lesbians go sleep with your sisters in Moscow." The animosity behind those words sends a chill down my spine and sharpens my focus. Carlos Castaneda's words, "Every warrior needs a petty tyrant" pop into my mind. The meeting of two forces is what makes history, and here we are, facing each other on this warm, sunny August day surrounded by corn fields and farms, separated by a two-lane country road. Somehow, to these people, if we are against nuclear weapons being deployed to Europe, we are anti-American, which makes us communists. It is a quick lesson in how fear of "The Other" triggers violence in the name of self-defense. It is a good time to know we are grounded in nonviolence and will do nothing to provoke a fight.

We will be warriors of a different kind. The essence of nonviolence is self-control and non-reaction to these provocations. In the peacekeeper training, we rehearsed being harassed in order to find that inner resolve to respond to violence with calm and patience, and to neither resist nor retreat. As we leave the driveway of our farm, we wave, we smile, and we sing.

It is a mile up this country road to the main gate of the base, our destination, but it will take two hours to reach. Rumors have been spreading that all the bullets in the county are sold out.

The local police have called the State police and hold us up until their reinforcements arrive. In the meantime, Congresswoman Bella Abzug—known for her wide-brimmed hats—holds forth with a mighty big voice, both cheering us on and giving the police her "What for?" about the delay. Up ahead, we can see an overpass lined with people and beyond it a sea of people with protest signs across the road. This scene is indeed ominous. The prospect of physical confrontation is frightening. I call for five of my closest M.N.S. allies to come to the front of the march, lock arms, and begin singing. I wish I could remember what we sang, but the details are a blur. All I know is that by the time we reach the bridge that sea of bodies has dispersed. It is as if the Red Sea has parted for our safe passage. There are no police in sight. Is it the singing? Is it our numbers, with banners and drums and sure-footed women as far as the eye can see? Is it angels? Is it the "Force More Powerful" as nonviolence is often called? Whatever the cause, that opening in the road is the closest to a miracle I have ever experienced. We press on.

A link fence that surrounds the base lines our route about ten feet from the road. In negotiations with the army about our plans, the officials made it clear that we could hang things on the fence, but we could not rattle it. When I heard that, I thought, "Oh, they're telling us exactly what would undo them psychically!" That made it a powerful behavior. I imagined 2000 women grabbing that fence and raising such a vibration that the whole army regiment would just get in their vehicles and vacate! But our focus is on the weapons, not the people. The temptation is averted. Instead, as we march forward women hang symbols of what we are here to stand for on the fence—lowers, diapers, photographs of children, cooking utensils, peace symbols—brilliantly transforming a symbol of control into a pulsing symbol of the sacredness of life. I place a picture of my three sons on the fence along with countless others to mark my commitment to a nuclear weapon-free future for them and their children. The fence becomes a work of living art. Once again we are changing how it feels to be in this place. Our determination is matched by our joy in placing our bodies between the vulnerable people of the world and the arsenal of deadly nuclear weapons. From where I stand I can see the water tower with its "People Always" sign, and remember Gandhi's words:" Be the change you want to see."

Our final destination also involves the fence. We have come to commit civil disobedience, to break a law in order to adhere to a higher one. We have come to say, "We do not recognize the law of private property; you cannot erect a fence and do whatever you want on the other side without our consent. We do not give our consent. We will climb your fence and enter your space in order to declare that what you are doing here is a crime against humanity. Nuclear weapons are tools of mass destruction. They represent the intent to attack civilian populations, which explicitly violates the international law to which our country is a signatory. These weapons must be dismantled!"

On this day, August 2, 1983, 246 women climb the fence of this army base. I am one of them. We are acting in concert with our sisters in England, Germany, Italy, Japan and Seattle, WA. A mighty force of feminine energy is wrapping our planet in a spiritual web of peaceful nonviolence. Women are going out of bounds together all over the planet, claiming our right to a peaceful, united world dedicated to life, not death. Gandhi once said, "Full participation is full victory." This day I feel that victory.

With all the details, responsibilities and challenges of this day, I have not prepared myself for the physical challenge of getting over this six foot high fence. Handing my camera to a friend, I mount the back of another friend who offers her body as a perch. The fence is still at my chest height! I am going to have to mentally will myself over it. With toes barely poked into the links and muscles straining, I somehow—perhaps with some divine intervention—scramble up and over, pausing astride the top for a photo, and then am very kindly assisted down on the other side by an MP who has handcuffs ready. Cuffed, led to a tent where we sit on the ground to await our sisters, we are finally loaded onto buses and taken to a detention center to be booked.

While waiting on the bus, amid laughter, more singing, and a familiar sense of adventure and purpose—kind of reminiscent of my elementary school bus ride at the end of a school day—I am aware of a nagging pain in my wrists. The plastic cuffs are too tight and they are pinching my flesh. Is this degree of discomfort an accident, or intentional on the part of my jailer? Is this predictable pain their way of showing us who really is in control? There is no answer. What is real is the pain. I drop my awareness down, down into the pain, and my helplessness to change it. That simple pain takes me deeper still into the pain in my heart. I find the pain I feel about my country being the biggest perpetrator of death and destruction the planet has ever known. I feel the helplessness of the victims of our bombs. I feel the pain of all the injustice in our world. Gradually tears arise, as I come into the core of my being on this bus, and feel my love for this suffering world. The bondage of my wrists is like the bondage to fear that drives our inhumanity. How right it seems to be in jail, in handcuffs, with my sisters of peace.

Now we are inside the beast, inside the base, face to face with the agents of war. It is about 9:30 at night; I am tired and hungry. As we sit on the concrete floor of a long, narrow hallway with cinder block walls waiting to be booked, I feel our strength in numbers. We are not afraid, just as Audre Lourde said. We are calm. We are in the right place at the right time. We are embodying Gandhi's "Truthforce." Our victory that day is over our own fear of reprisal and our socialization to be good, law-abiding citizens who stand on the sidelines and tolerate the parade of war. Our victory is in moving out of our ordinary lives—going out of bounds together—and claiming a new world, the world we want.

I am released later that night, and walk back down the now quiet country road, gently lit by ancient stars. The fence still holds its gifts of love, and the barn and array of pillow cases anchor home for this weary warrior. Crawling into my tent, I am a-glow in a feeling of connection. I am in touch with my expanding sense of self that now reaches beyond patriotism to global citizenship. I feel my caring for all the people of the world, and my decisive rejection of the policies of my own government. I sleep that night in the arms of sisterhood and in the strength of our resolve.

I return to Greenfield changed by that resolve. The farmhouse collective would continue to occupy the adjoining land to the base for another five years and be a hub of actions, training and consciousness-raising for a whole new generation of women, one of whom would follow me to Greenfield three years later to be in the 2nd cycle of a training program for women that I would create. My focus for that training would be on women choosing to live the life they want to live—with all the risks as well as rewards that choice would bring—instead of the one prescribed for them by their culture, gender, class, government and families of origin. We would be warriors for a new world where women's voices, values and aspirations would shape the course of history. "You may say I'm a dreamer, but I'm not the only one..." Yes, indeed, I always have been a dreamer, always will be. There's no turning back now.

Claiming Power, Birthing Freedom:
The Pilgrim Warrior Training
1983

"What do you want to create for the lives of women, Sandra?" Jerry asks me as I sit with six of my M.N.S. allies in my living room drinking cups of tea and enjoying a warm feeling of tribal connection. It is May, 1985, and we are holding a "Clearness Committee" for me as I face a shift in my professional focus. This is a Quaker tradition, a process for inviting feedback on important decisions, which we have used with each other for ten years whenever it was called for.

"I want a network of vibrant, powerful women who know the future of this planet is in their hands and who feel capable and eager to create the world they want," I answer. "I want to support women to heal themselves from their earliest hurts and cultural messages that robbed them of their beauty, intelligence, creativity and confidence. I want to work with women who are living from the inside out, speaking and walking in their truth and connected through their inner guidance to a wisdom far beyond their personal life experience." I can't stop; the visions keep flooding forth. "I want us to be daughters of the Great Mother, serving Her and all Her creation with a balance of abundance and vulnerability." There is more I have never heard myself say before: "I want us to walk with fear as our ally, transforming it into power, and taking the risks that are necessary to shape the stories that will be told about our times."

Why is Jerry asking me this question? For years I have

worked with families and taken myriad trainings informally. I have recently completed a Master's in Social Work and become a licensed social worker. I am applying for a position as director of a Women's Center at UMass, Amherst. Until now, everything I have done, from where I lived, to how I ate, to how I raised my three children, from who I slept with, to what I did with my skills has been out of the ordinary. At forty-five, I surprise myself by taking a turn in the road and deciding to attempt a career path through respectable channels. Strange but true, a new part of me is pushing forward, wanting recognition in "the system," the place where you fit in, live a normal life, and gain esteem for accomplishment. I want a chance to explore that other road in the proverbial fork that I passed up for adventure so long ago.

Even though I had left the Philadelphia community three years before, I still have allies near-by. Two have come from Amherst, (just twenty minutes away) and the other four from Boston (two hours away.)

"I want to see you training women to be leaders for social change," says Robert.

"You have ten years of experience doing that, and you're really good at what you do," Jerry comments. He worked with me in M.N.S. as we trained social change agents from around the world in nonviolent direct action skills.

"You're at the top of the skills ladder as a trainer, Sandra. Lots of people can direct a women's center. Not many can do what you can as a trainer," adds Dakota.

I know in my heart they are right, but I know, too, that if I am offered the job, I will take it. After years of doing everything in collectives, a dormant part of me wants the sense of power in being chosen and being in charge, not to mention the $40,000 salary. I have worked in two women's agencies in Philly dealing with rape and domestic violence, and I have worked two years with a similar agency in Greenfield. I have the credentials. Reaching for this job feels like a rite of passage, the fulfillment of an adult developmental task, achieving rank in the world of work. It is the natural counterbalance to my radical lifestyle. Maybe I am having a midlife crisis?

As it turns out, I am not offered the job. What arises in the ensuing empty space will become the centerpiece of my career as a women's empowerment trainer. Perhaps my friends are in cahoots with my acorn, because as I begin to follow the vision which arose in response to Jerry's query, my acorn is now pushing out with clarity and urgency. I have all that I need. As I write this, I suddenly remember what the young Sandra wrote thirty years ago as she imagined her future

"Up I jumped to be on His way…
Never to finish but only to start,
Not seeing the end, but knowing her heart."

Continuity with that original intent is with me as I delve into my experience as a trainer and begin to craft a program for

women that will reach deep into their vision for their lives, their community, and their world, and will hone the skills and intentions needed to bring those visions to life.

Like an artist standing before a blank canvas, I wait expectantly to see what will arise to fill this new space. I know the process of change has to be grounded in life experience, and in facing the inner barriers to full empowerment. It isn't enough to want a better world. Women need to heal their own internalized self-doubt, self-depreciation, and pent up rage from all the ways they have been held back by rules about a woman's place in society. I will gather together the most powerful experiences that moved me forward in my own life and weave them into an eight day progression. A future participant would one day blurt out, "Yeah, but you didn't do them all in eight days, Sandra!" It would be intense—demanding—and out of bounds as usual.

Two weeks later I invite twelve women friends to meet in my living room on a Sunday afternoon to hear my plans and give me feedback.

"I want to do this!" Prudy declares. "How many women do you need? I'll find them."

The Pilgrim Warrior Training is born two weeks later, and will fill my days for the next eleven years as I take forty-two cycles of women through an eight-day process, and take myself through a daunting explosion of creativity. My experience as a trainer is deeply rooted in experiential learning thanks to my years in M.N.S. That early entrepreneur in me—with her summer day camp—is eager for another round at bat. The lessons from the wind are in my belly. Most of all, the decision to take this step feels right. I am in alignment with my calling to bring women to that same fork in the road that I have just passed (again), and support them in saying "Yes" to their deepest calling. This mission becomes my ministry, my church, and my spiritual community.

"Why did you have to pick two of the most Patriarchal words to define your program, Sandra?" a close ally asks me. I don't have an answer. These words were given to me. I didn't think them up or even choose them. This journey into the authentic self, it seems to me, will make women Pilgrims. Like the ancient ones archetypically journeying toward the Holy City, these women will be leaving the home of the Patriarch—the rule of the fathers with their norms and sanctions—and journeying toward the life they want to be living, sourced from dreams, bold creativity and courage. I hadn't seen myself as a Pilgrim until now, but this is what I have been doing for the last ten years of my life. Leaving my marriage with three small children to care for, I was listening to my soul. I had to battle the voices in my own head that told me putting my own needs ahead of my family was selfish. Crossing that threshold, I followed my heart to a community of people who shared a vision for how to create a more egalitarian world that included the maintenance level of life. Because of that gender-neutral lifestyle, I was free as an adult, as a mother, as a woman, to take my place in the scheme of things with the same power, influence and time available to serve the vision as those without children. I had the courage needed to let go of knowing the outcome which that transition required. I didn't know if it would work out to be a good decision. I have had to trust Spirit and find a web of allies to support my changes—I didn't make it alone. I know the ingredients of success. I believe I can lead other women through their challenges, whatever they are.

Holly Near—one of the leaders of the women's music movement of the 1970s—wrote a song about war with this line: The greatest warriors are the ones who work for peace." That line brought me the word "warrior." Women need to find that warrior archetype within themselves if they are to succeed in leaving Patriarchy as Mary Daly had described in *Beyond God the Father.* They have to be prepared to meet the ground where it rises under their feet, and face the storm of criticism and discouragement that will come when they challenge the status quo of female socialization and go out of bounds. The change I am imaging will be defined by new boundaries, new ways of saying "No," as we move beyond others' expectations of who we are, or what we can do or be. There will be a new "Yes" to our autonomy, coming from listening to our own inner guidance rather than responding to what others need or want from us. It will be a warriorship of the soul, searching for the truth of our Being, for what we took birth to understand and create. I feel clear and confident. I trust the presence and guidance of Spirit. My acorn is giving a standing ovation. My M.N.S. friends are delighted, and they have my back.

We Pilgrim Warriors head for the woods, to a cabin in a state forest with no running water or electricity. We will sleep on the ground in tents, collect spring water, and listen to the owls and coyotes at night. We will live in the rhythms of our greatest teacher, Nature. As I begin working with the women who have found their way to this training, I become a student as well as a teacher. I continually hone the curriculum to focus deeper and deeper into the labyrinth of internalized negative self-image planted there by our socialization in a culture that does not see women as equal. I realize with each new group that any external changes in the world are only going to come to the degree that change happens within. We need our whole selves to move energy in the world. We can't be held back by fear of inadequacy or fear of rejection. We need a new community to anchor our changes, a community that sees each of us as powerful and important and that wants our gifts and visions.

I design the training to go daily to a new "edge," a place where women typically give up their power in order to be safe or belong. If we can't go past these edges, we can't be pilgrims or warriors. Every one of these places of fear are also places of sorrow, where the authentic self has been threatened, even suffocated. Changing these stories is not something we can do alone. We respect each woman's vulnerability, while also holding her feet to the fire, calling her to move beyond her fear and into her beautiful, powerful, truth-speaking self.

We begin by exploring our fear of joining a new group. Women are scared to have to admit how unsafe they feel in a new group with memories of fifth grade exclusion still haunting them. We use a process called Spectrums where women take a position between point A and B indicating their level of comfort with each new difference we invite. They are scared to have anyone know their sexual preference if it isn't the socially accepted one (which changes, incidentally, over the eleven years of the program), or know if they are rich because of an inheritance, or poor because of class background. We need to break down these barriers of silence in order to build trustworthy community for the challenges ahead. On the very first day, each woman is asked to step toward the group and ask for acceptance in which ever realm of difference she feels threatened because of past wounding. Tears come as each woman finds within herself the willingness to trust the group with her vulnerable but willing self.

We can't find our courage until we truly need it, so on the second day we use a high ropes course to learn the inner pathway to calling it forth. Having to stand on a cable thirty feet above the ground and reach for a vertical support line that is out of reach is terrifying even though you know you are "on belay," which means someone on the ground has you in a rope and carabineer system that will not allow you to fall. I call up to each woman in turn: "What do you want your courage for? What do you want? Reach for it!" The moment she lunges for that cord and begins to cross the twenty-five foot cable, the pathway to that courage opens up. Now it can be hers whenever she need it, and surely she will.

On the third day, we use psychodrama to reclaim our authentic selves from the grip of our family of origin, with all the adaptations to that system we have made that compromise our truth-telling voice. I ask each woman in turn, "On your path, what is it you meet that stops you, throws you into confusion, and makes you feel powerless?" As a woman begins to tell her story, which almost always involves voices in her family of origin, members of the group stand up, take their cue from her story, and reenact the old story. She can then meet the challenge to make a new ending to that old story, one that allows her to stay connected to

her truth and take the heat of the oppressive energy that threatened her need to belong so long ago. Instead of "Let me go!" we hear "I'm free!" The authority to claim freedom has moved from needing to get it from another to a willingness to create it from within. As she stands in her power, there is a tremendous release of energy that brings transformation to everyone in the room. An age-old battle is over.

We end each piece of work by singing a song by Sarah Pirtle:

"There's a hand pulling you on,
There's a hand pulling you on,
Loving you weak,
Loving you strong,
There's a hand pulling you on."[1]

By far the most challenging "edge" is when we risk the ordeal of naming what each woman's fair share of the total cost of the training is by talking about class, money, and differences in our life opportunities and support systems. (This process, called "Cost-Sharing," had been developed by M.N.S. to address the difference in resources by which people were able to travel to our annual national gatherings.) Each woman has paid a $500 deposit to attend the training, but she doesn't know what her total cost will be; the women know this edge is coming. This is the day these women have to face how ashamed they feel if they are not be able to pay an equal share, or how mortified they are that they might be expected to pay for the whole training themselves because they are wealthy. We share stories of scarcity thinking and tell each other of the shame, guilt and other negative attitudes towards ourselves and others associated with money, and explore how these attitudes work to separate us and create mistrust. We see how we have all been organized into cooperating with a system of beliefs—that you are good and successful if you have money, and bad or a failure if you don't—that we are here to challenge. When asked at the end of our exploration "Which class would you like to be in?" the answer is always, "None!"

So the question of the day is, "What does economic justice look like among the women in this group?" This is the day someone will likely consider packing up their tent and heading for a safe haven. "I can't do this. I'm terrified." "Explore the fear, Sarah. Stay with it. Don't resist it. Let the fear speak," I tell her. More often than not there is a family taboo about money that she is being expected to violate in this situation, but it's often unconscious so she truly does not know why she is so afraid. Sometimes women remember fierce fighting about money between their parents, or a misfortune that changed the family's status and caused great shame or panic. "I feel so alone," one woman shares, "as if I will be an outcast if I tell the truth about our situation to anyone outside the family." I sit with her as she works through the feelings and perceptions that flood her being. She will cry until the shame or fear of judgment is all cried out. It is like wringing a saturated sponge dry. It is deep healing work.

Each woman makes an initial pledge toward the total cost and receives feedback about whether the group members think it is too much, too little, or just right based on her reported present resources. "I can pay my fair share," states Liz, but the group gives her feedback that she would be stretching much farther than anyone else and that doesn't feel right. Phyllis says, "I suppose I can pay for the whole training myself if that's what people want." She has a big inheritance. "No, we don't want you to do that, because it would deprive the rest of us of contributing according to our means." Both women are having to learn to trust a group to think well about them in a very vulnerable situation. That is why we are here.

Things like health conditions, shared living expenses with a partner or roommate, parental support, amount of education, kind of vehicle and situation of housing are all taken into account. This task challenges all of our internalized classism, revealing the estrangement between classes that is mostly unconscious in our culture until such a challenge as this brings the fears to the surface. The pledging will go back and forth, changing as understanding and acceptance of differences deepens, until everyone is satisfied with what they are pledging to pay.

This process only succeeds when all the other edges have been met and transformed. The women need all their courage, and their willingness to tell the truth and hear the truth without the old feelings of self-doubt or shame interfering in order to reach our goal. It is liberating to dump those old beliefs and habits about money and privilege that keep us unsafe and separated from true community. One participant summarizes, "This was the most terrifying part of the training, and the one I grew in the most. It was an empowering experience to get out of my guilt about money and see it as energy to be shared, something that doesn't mean anything about me as a person. When I can let go of all the meanings attached to "my" money, I feel freer and more giving than I've ever felt before." Completing this assignment is an achievement and a transformation for each woman. It is a new society in the making.

Now we are ready to begin to focus our energy out into the world again, to explore our new-found possibilities and set our intention continuing our pilgrimage toward the Holy City of our authentic life. The women make shields for their warriorship by painting their personal symbols of power—trees, animals, flowers, spirals, drums, hearts, or the four directions—on white tee shirts. They go solo into the forest overnight to connect with Spirit, be still, and listen for guidance, while graduates return to the all-night fire to drum the heartbeat of Mother Earth, connecting each solo quester to the web of community. Out of their solitude, they begin to focus their response to the calling they are hearing to be a healer, a leader, or a transformer. What will be each one's particular gift for the healing of our out-of-balance society?

Finally, each woman holds a Clearness with three others—just as I had done at the beginning of this journey—to name her vision of the changes she wants to make going forward. The group gives her feedback, challenge and support. She in exchange gives focus, passion, and accountability. She makes a commitment to her next step, and agrees to tell another group member when she has accomplished it. At our fire circle on the last evening, each woman wears her shield, declares her intentions for her life and her contribution to healing our world, and receives the blessings of her sisters for her sacred journey. I celebrate each woman in her bigness and her beauty. Each of those faces around the fire is forever etched in my heart.

In between each session we swim naked in a near-by waterfall, sunbathing on rocks and frolicking in the mud deep in the forest. We fill water jugs from a spring near the cabin. We start each morning at 7 a.m. by meditating and then calling in the four directions. We sing back to the bird perched a-top a four-story pine tree standing like a guardian beside our little two-room cabin. We have a night hike without flashlights to learn to be one with the forest and the night sky. Drumming and chanting around the fire at night, we immerse ourselves in ritual. We make puppy piles and share massage. There is safety to wail and scream, and also to laugh at ourselves. We cry a lot and hold each other through the pain as we cast it off and find new ground under our feet. One perspective candidate told me, "I could never do the Pilgrim Warrior Training." When I asked why, she said, "I could never swim naked in a waterfall." Strange how those edges show up in unexpected places. Here is clear evidence that without community, those edges stop us. With community, all things are possible.

Over the next eleven years, I would lead forty-two groups in four countries, meeting each woman in the turmoil of fear and diving deep to find the courage to meet and transform that fear into power, intention, clarity, and blessing. I see women take off wedding rings, quit jobs, create businesses, pick up and move from the familiar into the unknown. With each change I witness, my own soul journey opens more to the soul of Woman, and to the soul of the world. I see our birthright of freedom and creativity take form again and again. Then I see the women move with responsibility to tend that freedom with vision and courage, and become co-creators of our world. Each woman's journey is a gift to all of us, an inspiration to live the life we deserve. As midwife in these transitions, I find my greatest vocation, my church, my spiritual home. Every cell of my body is shouting "Hallelujah!"

Early in the birthing of this training, I channeled a sacred dance. I say "channeled" because I don't have words to describe how it came to me or through me. It just arrived as I experimented with Erica, a talented M.N.S. dancer friend, one day out in the loft behind my house in Greenfield. We were searching for a way to celebrate the central theme of this training—connection with Spirit. We moved non-verbally, trying out accompanying gestures, as we asked ourselves, "What wants to be expressed?" Here is what came through as we opened to Spirit and held the space together:

> We are all one,
> Sending forth Spirit,
> Astride the path,
> Alone together.
> We are by earth and sky blessed,
> And we are healed, as we let go,
> And we give thanks,
> Receiving what we need,
> Return to love,
> Blessed be.

This prayer became our way of ending every sacred circle in the training. It became the Pilgrim Warrior prayer. It now holds over 400 women in a web of love, connected to the Earth as home and Spirit as guide. It holds all of what my calling has become. It is the final testimony of my life as I contemplate what will be said of this one precious life when the time comes to give it back to the Spirit from which it came.

And what of my other visions for my life work? In the midst of continuing to lead this training, offer psychotherapy, and teach communication skills, I will once again grab the mantle of adventure and head out on another assignment to create the world in which I want to live.

---

1.   "Here's a Hand" by Sarah Pirtle ©1984 Discovery Center Music. Sarah Wollstonecraft Pirtle sings the song this way, "Here's a hand pulling you on. . . loving you scared, loving you strong, here's a hand pulling you on." It is song #12 in *Better To-gether*, a collection of 40 songs. www.sarahpirtle.com

Visiting a Revolution: Nicaragua
1987

I seem to be drawn to places where history is being made. The 1970s is a decade of revolution all over the planet, and Nicaragua is caught up in it. From 1974-79, the Nicaraguans have three insurrections against their U.S.-backed dictator, Somoza. They are led by the Sandinistas, who named themselves after Sandino, the hero of an insurrection in 1929. They are the party of the poor. A nun I would meet there would tell me that of the thirteen countries she had worked in, none served the poor as the Sandinistas did. Because of this anti-capitalist intention, the U.S. government has determined that they are communists, and is therefore determined to prevent them from succeeding. To that end, my government is funding the remnants of Somoza's army, called The Contra, who are ravaging rural areas, killing people and destroying the new infrastructure—health clinics, schools, coops—that are bettering the lives of the people. In 1985, I have joined a national solidarity movement called The Pledge of Resistance, whose 15,000 members have pledged to do civil disobedience across the U.S. simultaneously if Congress votes to continue giving aid to The Contra.

In the midst of this political struggle, in solidarity with the liberation movement in Nicaragua, a woman from Boston initiates a program called The Nica School. Her intention is to link up North American solidarity activists with a Nicaraguan organization called The Mothers of the Heroes and Martyrs, and bring the activists down to see the revolution first hand. They would lend solidarity to the Nicaraguans' struggle to keep their hard-won freedom, and return home with stories and experiences to further the movement in both places. I am a prime candidate.

I believe in solidarity and here is an opportunity to put my values into action. I want to join my voice with those suffering under my government's persecution and call out for their right to self-determination. I am inspired by the story of Ben Linder, a twenty-three year old American who was killed by the Contras while helping to build a dam in northern Nicaragua. His family put "*Internationalista*" (meaning one who identifies with all countries) on his tombstone. I want to be an *internacionalista,* too. Never having studied Spanish in high school, I buy tapes and books before I leave and begin learning the language. I wish someone had told me as I began that the best way to learn a new language is by simply learning verbs. If people get the gist of what you want, they can fill in the rest. Trying to wake up an under utilized part of my brain at forty-seven is a huge under-taking, one that would bring me to tears by the second week of living with a family where only the seventeen-year-old speaks English and she is only home very late in the evening.

That acorn of mine has already packed her bags. Always hungering for adventure, especially political ones, I rally my local support network to gather school supplies (two suitcases full), get my visa and shots, and head south, undaunted by threats of on-going war. My eighteen-year-old son, Nathan, wants to accompany me, but his father's response, "No son of mine is going into a war zone" squelches that plan.

I land in mid-afternoon into the hot, steamy climate of the capital city, Managua, in the center of the country. I am met by a guide, Manuel, a roly-poly guy with a Santa-like presence, accentuated by his bushy mustache and round belly. His broad smile and skip to his step put me right at home. He takes me by taxi to the local bus station where I board a public bus packed to the gills with people and stuff. There is barely room for my feet under the seat in front of me. My suitcase full of supplies ends up on the roof. I wonder if I will ever get it back without a claim check of any kind. I watch the sun set over mountains in the distance as we bump along the pothole-pocked two-lane highway away from any signs of civilization.

Esteli is my destination, a city of about 120,000, and a four hour bus ride north of Managua. That night I join thirty-six other students from the U.S., Germany, Canada, England and Japan—all much younger than I. We are all gathered in one classroom of the school as the families file in and sit at the desks. Our names are called out one by one and our Nicaraguan families are called to pick up their student. I am assigned to the family of sixty-year-old Alejandra Picado, who lives a ten minute walk from the school with her husband and two of her twelve children. Alejandra is short and stout, with long, greying-black hair pulled straight back from her face and reaching to the middle of her back. She wears a plain skirt and blouse, with no color. No jewelry. No fuss of any kind. Simple plastic sandals, probably from China, protect her feet. I follow her home down cobble stoned streets with the houses all joined together, featuring only front doors to distinguish them. I mumble "No comprende" as she carries on in Spanish as if she is being understood. Maybe she is used to my level of ignorance of her language—she has hosted thirteen Nica students before me. In any case, she makes me feel at home and I am quickly put to bed in my own little room off the inner courtyard of their home. I barely notice my surroundings as my body craves the release of sleep.

The next morning it is apparent to all that I am not going to be a good conversation partner. Alejandra again seems to brush it off and continue her offering of friendship and connection. She is a woman with a mission. She feeds me an ample serving of rice and beans at a small wooden table in the kitchen next to her crackling wood stove. Little do I know that this will be my

meal, three times a day for the next
five weeks. As I look around my new
home, all the rooms, including the
single bathroom and separate shower, open into the courtyard, which is
as big again as the whole house and
full of chickens, vegetable plants,
a blooming tree, broken bicycles,
stacks of bricks and tile, and one pig.
The neighborhood we live in is identified by a medical clinic, Obando
Choa, and that becomes my landmark as I learn to navigate through
the town to the school every day.

The Nica School is a two-story stucco building with classrooms on both levels, all opening onto a courtyard with benches
and gardens. It is airy and sunny all the time, and much cooler as
we have travelled into the mountains to get here. I attend Spanish class from 8 a.m. to noon five mornings a week where—in
spite of all my self-styled efforts—I am placed in the beginner's
class. Daily I go home for lunch, walking through a park with
old growth trees shading benches filled with people chatting,
and then through an open-air market jam-packed with carts full
of vegetables and fruit. After lunch I return to the school to go
on a field trip to meet revolutionaries in action, and see many of
the manifestations of this government in service to the poor in
the Esteli area.

What I see in this war-torn country is stunning. People are
excited, proud, and engaged. Everywhere we go, what is happening is new—new roads, new schools, and new factories. The
whole society is in high gear. The sense of care and satisfaction
is palpable. It is like one big college campus with thousands of
courses to choose from and everyone studying! This is a country, a society, a culture in transition, in the process of liberation.

While evidence of poverty is everywhere—shacks with tin roofs, people carrying large bundles on their carts, heads, and donkeys, dirt roads, few stores—there is a happiness that hides the hardships. While the daily news is relentlessly devastating from the more rural areas where the Contra are wreaking their havoc, the momentum of liberation seems unstoppable.

This is a revolution still in the oral history stage. When I ask someone what happened, I get their story about what happened to them right in the place where I am standing. They tell of relentless daily decisions to take life-threatening risks for uncertain gains. They tell of arbitrary, unpredictable twists of events that converge to create unimagined possibilities for victory. Now they are in power, yet atrocities continue: fifteen coop workers killed one day, a vehicle with five technical advisors blown up the next day, a helicopter downed with eleven soldiers the next. Twenty-three hundred have been killed by Contra attacks in the first three months of this year. I have come to witness this war for the future of these people, to know the truth of my own country's involvement in undermining the success of this revolution, and to tell the story to all who have ears to hear.

Let me take you along on a typical day of my routine. I have settled into a bedroom vacated for my use in Alejandra's home (someone of the four family members is surely doubling up.) It is barely 9'x 6'. My suitcase fits under the bed. It's another early morning in Esteli, Nicaragua. The roosters have begun crowing. Stirring, I know not to open my eyes yet because it won't be light out. The roosters only crow to each other for a little while, as if they are doing what everyone expects of them, and then they too go back to sleep for a little while longer. After some time, I hear a radio. This is the actual beginning of the day. Soon another is heard on top of the first, and then, as I now expect, the one in the room right next to my head goes on. Even though I still don't open my eyes, for I don't have to be anywhere for another three hours, the daily symphony has begun. Now I am aware of the pig oinking hungrily just outside my bedroom door, the chickens clucking, and voices greeting and questioning in the family courtyard that the door of my bedroom leads to. I roll over and peek to see if it is daylight yet. No, just dawning greyness. But soon I hear horseshoes on the cobbled street, and the roar of a large truck shifting into second gear. Then the shrill pounding of the blacksmith across the street adds to the cacophony. Now I know it is a quarter to six. His rhythms are as regular as a clock, and this is the one sound that does not blend into the others. I begin to wake up.

Daylight is now visible through the cracks between the boards of my bedroom wall and door, and through the empty nail holes in the tin roof above my bed. The shower runs as one of the daughters gets ready to leave for school, which begins at 7 a.m. Her name is Belia and she is seventeen. I think about her for a moment: happy, eager to go to school, growing up in the midst of a revolution. Nine years ago there were no free public schools. What was she doing when she was six, seven, and eight and should have been starting school? There was war in the streets. Her older sisters and brothers were hidden away doing dangerous things everyone was afraid to talk about. Now she walks freely in the streets, finishing her secondary education, expecting to go on to university, reaping the fruits of revolutionary struggle.

After a while, the second shower of the day starts. This is Xiamara. She is eighteen. She has to be at work by 8 a.m. She is a bookkeeper for the public communications system. She works eight hours, comes home for supper, goes out again to school for her final year of secondary school, and then at 8 p.m. she goes to another school for secretarial training. She comes home at 11 p.m. This routine is required by the now- rising expectations for a better life, especially for girls. Her mother tells me that when Xiamara was seven she ran messages between the safe homes where Sandinista soldiers were hiding during the insurrection in their town. Now she seems so much like the teenagers back home, fixing her hair, changing clothes, borrowing make-up, talking about her boyfriend, watching soap operas on TV, and reacting with boredom and impatience when the Sandinista announcements come on the TV. It seems she has forgotten about the war. While surrounded by the hardships of dramatic changes going on in her society, she greedily gobbles up the opportunities created by these changes–free health care, free electricity and water, a guaranteed food supply–without reflection. She lives freedom without awe. That deeper realization of what has been achieved is in her mother's eyes.

Just as my thoughts move to the mother, I hear the crack of wood splitting, and I know she is starting her fire for the day. When she has done that, she will put the coffee on to boil and boil and boil, and then take her plastic sack and head out to the neighborhood bakery to buy bread for breakfast. I ponder the life of Alejandra Picado, this sixty year old woman who bore twelve children with a man who is now just a shadow in the house. He is here, part of the history of what happened to families who lived through three insurrections. As Alejandra tells me, her sons got involved with the Sandinistas; then the daughters. Then she, the mother, who was at first just afraid for her children, began to listen to them, and felt herself being changed. Opening up to the possibility that the young people could succeed and finally yielding to that hope, she began taking one step after another—hiding her son's friend, carrying a message to someone in hiding in another safe house, then hiding the radio which had become forbidden. Fights began with her husband because he was afraid that if she kept the radio the National Guard would find it and kill all of them. She not only protected the radio from his fear, but took in more young fighters who had to hide to stay alive.

She fed them. She began to sell food from her house to cover up for all the food being consumed there, to cover up for all the suspicious comings and goings and muffled sounds that could be heard late at night through the adjoining walls. Her husband wanted her to stop. Stop? Turn back? Abandon the young people who have now gone too far to ever live a normal life again? She knew what she must do, even while she knew the future was in the hands of the young people. She would feed, shelter, pray, cover, sell, cook, watch. She would meet the National Guard soldiers on the street outside her house and walk towards them as if there were nothing she was hiding. Children and old people, madres just like her, were being shot in the streets. She stepped between the bombs and bullets and continued feeding and sheltering, as her children made bombs, flags, and leaflets by night and fought in the streets and mountains by day. Sometimes she went for weeks and months not knowing if her sons were all right. One fateful day, there was a picture in the paper of dead Sandinista guerillas. She thought one was her son. Letters from him had stopped coming. Other family and friends said no, they didn't think it was him. No news.

Alejandra comes back with the bread and it is my time for the shower now. I catch a glimpse of her short, plump but straight-backed body standing on a brick step in front of the stove to stir a pot over her fire. I remember the ending of that story. His body was tied to a car and dragged, then tied together with a buddy and set on fire. She was called to come and identify the body. She said no, it wasn't her son, and left him there with the enemy in order to protect the other boys hiding in her safe home. By then, all the young fighting men were her sons, and after all, he was dead and they were alive. It was simply what a mother did. It was revolution, and they were going all the way, one step at a time, not knowing what would ever turn the tide in their favor, but trusting and living in solidarity, risking everything. Everything. No chance to bury the dead. More sons would fall, but the force would move forward.

Then one prearranged night, 30,000 people in the capital city left their homes in the middle of the night—an exodus of Biblical proportions—and marched eighteen miles to the next city. The National Guard was so spooked, they suspected the Sandinistas of hiding among the throng so they followed the river of people. The Sandinistas took the capital at dawn without a shot. The dictator, Somoza, fled in defeat. An exodus had once again brought liberation. As Alejandra told me this story, she said "When it's your time, I hope you fight before your children have to fight for you." I breathed in this legacy, the pain of the price of revolution, and how precious the rewards are.

I am in the shower now. There is a concrete floor, covered with mold. The water is slightly cold. It could be worse, but it's still hard to put my head all the way under. I ponder the privilege of a hot shower back home in my clean tile tub. One thing the revolution has meant is that people who never had running water or electricity before, have it now and it's free. Amazing! Well, the government says it helps increase production, and besides, if they charged for it, most folks couldn't afford it. Just for a moment, I flash back on all the rate hike fights I've taken part in, and the fight against nuclear power that has gone on for years, pitting the rich against everyone else and threatening our environment. I ponder how these power struggles over who controls our quality of life tear at the fabric of our society, keeping us angry and discontent, and rarely resolving in favor of the people. Here the electricity flows freely as a resource for people's lives, seen as a basic necessity for a life of dignity which this government intends for all of its people. Strange thoughts for a morning shower.

As I am starting to dress, I hear Alejandra's radio click on in the kitchen. It's 7 a.m., and the news is on. Picking up that thread of thought—a life of dignity—it seems to me the people here use that word a lot. Since I don't hear that word used much at home, I wonder if it is a poor people's word. The Sandinista government has named fifty-four basic commodities they deem necessary for a life of dignity, including shoes, underwear, toothpaste, and toilet paper, and has guaranteed them at fixed low prices the average Nicaraguan can afford. These prices are not affected by the 700% inflation pummeling this economy under siege. After 400 years of rulers who never thought the poor needed or deserved what the rich took for granted, this revolution is about shoes and toilet paper! And for this they are labeled communists and targeted for attack by the leaders of my country.

Speaking of toilet paper, before we came to Nicaragua, the Nica School organizer told us to bring our own supply for five weeks. Never before have I had to figure out how much toilet paper I would need for five weeks. I always just bought more before I ran out. What if I estimated wrong and ran out? What does one do without toilet paper? And how would I feel if I have my safe supply and no one else in the family has any? Would I share mine? Then it would be gone even sooner. I couldn't possibly carry down enough for me and a family if I'm limited to two pieces of luggage. Suddenly I realize how silly those anxieties were. I'm here now. Yes, they get their monthly allotment of toilet paper, but they don't use it for the toilet. It's special. They use the newspaper, like they always have. I've have to learn to act fast if there is anything in the paper I want to save before it ends up in the bathroom. The toilet paper is kept on a nail behind the kitchen door. The only thing I saw it used for was stuffing into new shoes that were making a blister. Oh yes, I did see the seventeen-year-old daughter help herself to it as she was heading for the bathroom. I guess dignity means something different to her than to her mother.

I come into the kitchen now, ready with my Spanish greet-ings and bracing myself for the strong, sweet coffee. "Buenas dias! Como amaneció? Bien, bien," and she begins to fill me in on the news I have missed. Bishop Obando Bravo is going to be on the Council of Reconciliation to implement the peace ac-cords in Nicaragua. She scowls. She doesn't trust him. She tells me the Catholic hierarchy has always been allied with counter-revolutionary forces. In Latin America, the Gospel is subversive literature because Jesus taught that all people are equal. The rich don't believe this. Alejandra goes on in rapid Spanish now, for-getting who she is talking to, "To be a Christian is to be a revo-lutionary; Christians cannot run away from their revolutions." She knows what is true like a wise owl who listens from the tree without needing to do anything. She continues, "Inside Nicara-gua, he is our enemy, but he is one of us and we know how to handle him."

So the political lessons start with breakfast here. The news continues, reporting that yesterday afternoon, the Contra at-tacked a Department of the Interior vehicle carrying seven tech-nical assistants who were travelling through the northern region visiting agrarian reform projects. Five were killed and the vehi-cle destroyed. She scowls again. I am silent. I know already that most of the fertile land in the northern region cannot be farmed because of Contra violence. Everyone knows who perpetrated this crime, and that the war for independence is still going on daily. Nicaraguans are dying, and valuable resources for building the country are being destroyed. Numbers of victims, percent-ages of lost production, schools closed, or health centers blown up–all this horror stings and pierces, and the pain does not go away. But her back straightens a little more as she stirs her pot and repeats what has become a litany on her lips, "Reagan is evil. Reagan has no heart. We do not know what will happen, but we will never surrender. We will never go back." I ponder what it is like to start her day, every day, with this news, this litany of destruction, of war. This is the revolution I came to see. I am here as it is happening while breakfast is being stirred. I feel the pain too.

The Alcoholics Anonymous prayer suddenly comes to mind: "Lord, grant me the serenity to accept the things I cannot change, the courage to change the things I can, and the wisdom to know the difference." I look at this Nicaraguan mother stirring at her stove, feeding me, the fourteenth North American student she has brought right into the heart of her family and into her personal caring in order to teach me this same lesson. Where did she learn it, this wisdom that leaves her undiminished by loss, strengthened by adversity, yet committed to my well-being and understanding? She is working to change what she can: my consciousness as an American whose government is killing her people. I feel sad and humble in her presence, and grateful for her caring for me in the midst of her own suffering. This is what solidarity feels like.

I have to push through my own guilt to receive the love that is here for me. I see her commitment to live the revolution with no assurance of outcome, but with action that is her own liberation from the rage and grief of a victim of injustice—the taking care of me! This is what I made this journey to understand. I came to see and experience what living a revolution is like. It is here, in this Nicaraguan mother's kitchen, as we listen to the morning news. It is death; it is courage. It is fury; it is patience. It is loss; it is vision of what is being created right through bombs and burned bodies. It is the spiritual strength that grows more powerful with every fallen hero, and everyone who has fallen is a hero here, a flower that will sprout a hundred seeds.

I am touching the heart of the poor of the world, coming into the presence of what Sandino described when he said, "Only the peasant and the worker will go all the way." This is what I want so much to feel in my being and in my network of allies. I think about home and how it is so different from here. The U.S. government is not blowing up vehicles with helpers in them. The violence comes not through attack, but through indifference to poor people's needs, and disinformation that confuses, through rate hikes, housing speculation, and things that feel like personal losses. Groups lead strikes and protests, but people are rarely killed. It's hard to find a hero. It's hard to find the source for spiritual strength to keep on in the presence of an invisible force that is working against justice and—yes—dignity. Well, here I am, and it's happening right now. I am immersed in the heart and soul of these revolutionary people, who are paying the price with dignity and determination, and they have invited me in.

The news continues as we listen together in Spanish. She slowly explains to me that five Latin American presidents have signed the Peace Accords, a plan set forth by Costa Rica to build regional solidarity for peace and development. They have rejected Reagan's plan for control of the region. Reagan is calling all his Latin American ambassadors back to Washington to strategize about how to sabotage the success of this regional plan. We look at each other again, silently hearing what is not said, that of course he will find his ways of scuttling these possibilities for peace. What crumb will he give to those other countries who are so dependent on the U.S. that they will step out of that solidarity with each other and throw their lot in with their own oppressor? Alejandra comments again, "Honduras is poor like we are, but they have no dignity. They take money from the U.S." There is that word again, so central to her analysis. She, who has had two years of schooling, understands the heartbeat of revolution and what is needed to bring down a ruthless dictator, to break the grip of imperialism. She stirs the coffee again. The toilet paper hangs there on the hook. I leave for school, pondering the events that are passing through her life and are now touching mine.

I am becoming personally involved. Here the bloody deeds and peace-slaying plots are part of the pulse of the day. Back home, these deeds are couched in false images and disinformation. I wonder how to find the power and the preciseness to bring the truth of our destructive policy home to a people too tired from their own personal battles to be much involved in anyone else's. How do I tell people who are afraid of communism that our first invasion of Nicaragua happened fifty years before the Soviet Union ever existed? Will Americans think it is a good thing that this new government brought 500,000 people out of illiteracy in the first six months after they took power, ended polio and TB, gave land to 8,000 landless peasants, and brought 600,000 workers into trade unions where they share in decision-making? Will they wonder why Reagan takes satisfaction in paying for the killing of twenty-five people a day to supposedly " bring democracy" to a country which already has its own democratically elected government? Will they be able to let go of the label of "communist" when I tell them there is political pluralism, a mixed economy, and a Constitution that guarantees free elections? Will they change the labels if they know that there are more than twice as many advisors from Western Europe here as from Russia and Cuba together? Will they ever realize we all have something to learn from this tiny nation which has given the world community a model of autonomy for indigenous people within their national government? Will they ever learn that this government, which Reagan describes as terrorizing its own people, has compiled written testimony from 100,000 participants in public forums preceding the writing of their new Constitution? When have facts ever changed anyone's mind?

I pick up my book bag and say my goodbyes, trying a new phrase today, "Le que vaya bien" (go well), and head out the door into the street. Small children stop in their games to follow this gringo and call out the usual, "Tiene lapis?" No harm in asking for a pencil—we foreigners have so many things stuffed in our back packs that we take for granted which are special to these children. I stop and give two pencils away. Then I round the corner and walk past a story-high pile of bricks, a continuing reminder of the twenty-two days of bombing this city suffered after the Sandinista soldiers ran out of ammunition during the second insurrection and had to retreat to the mountains. Somoza retaliated by leveling this city. That was just nine years ago. The bricks remaining where they fell are a memorial to what these people have suffered. Everyone has a pile of recycled materials in their yard, waiting for the day they can afford to use them. Alejandra has the tiles for another floor stacked in her backyard; she can't buy the cement to lay the floor.

I pass the market with large baskets and wooden carts full of fruits and vegetables lining the street. I think about buying a pineapple or a watermelon for the family on my way home and wonder why it is that, in a tropical country flowing with fruit, my host family cannot afford to buy fruit. They eat the same food—rice and beans—three times a day. I've never had to do that. I pass through a park waving hello to the shoe shine boys I met the first week when my Spanish class was sent there to interview them. There's Simon. He is thirteen. He works all day, earns about $2.00, goes home and gives it all to his mother. He goes to school at night. I visited one of those night schools recently. A group of ten people in a neighbor's living room—adults and kids—were gathered together around a young woman about seventeen, who was the teacher and was drawing on the adobe wall of her house with chalk. I marveled again at the newness of education and the mix of generations together in a process where anyone with a sixth grade education becomes a teacher.

Every afternoon, the students at the Nica School have a field trip to experience some aspect of how the Sandinista revolution is manifesting in the lives of ordinary people. Today I visit a factory where workers are making furniture. The workers are given two hours a day of paid time to voluntarily participate in adult

education. Another day we visit a prison where literacy training
is part of the daily routine. One day we are taken to the street
where the bombed out rubble that used to be Somoza's palace in
Esteli is. The space is being cleared and has been designated to
be a new museum for the mothers of heroes and martyrs to tell
the stories of their children's sacrifices, retelling the stories that
continue to fuel the revolution. We spend an afternoon there doing "rojo y negro" (their terms for volunteer labor for the country), moving hunks of earthen bricks out of that space. How just,
it seems, that I—a North American—would be bending my back
and dirtying my hands removing the remnants of the dictator
who was supported by my government to oppress and murder
these brave people. Perhaps some retribution is being offered by
my labor.

As I walk on, I see the old walls of that neighborhood pep-
pered with bullet holes, shops built into half-buildings, and
armed soldiers standing in front of important buildings or riding in trucks through the town. Soldiers, guns, and stories of
sacrifice tell me I am in the midst of a revolution still unfolding.
Later, I will learn that the Contra attacked an agricultural coop
today while I was at school, killing fifteen people and blinding
the cows. Why blinding the cows? Only I, an outsider, would
ask that question. I feel the rage climbing up my spine. Who
do I tell? How do I pass this horror on so I don't have to hold
it alone? Who will be more shocked than I am? How can I get
some distance from all this horror and utter vulnerability? Distance? Sandino's voice flashes through my mind as I walk, "Only
the peasants and the workers will go all the way." This is a sobering thought, as I struggle with my own ability to integrate all of
what a revolution really is.

Soon I will leave this town and return to my own land. I see
Alejandra's face, her mother-eyes glaring, yet calm. She even
smiles at me as she sees me beginning to feel what it is like to
be in this story, to let the horror in and not pull away—to not

lose focus—and to feel the courage and determination evoked by listening to the news. It was a pledge of solidarity that propelled me to come to this land and this struggle. I came to sleep in this home, walk these streets, witness the struggle for self-determination, and join them. Today, looking into Alejandra's face, I know I have understood what solidarity means. "Aquí, no se rinde nada" ("Here, there is no turning back"). I start humming the F.S.L.N. national anthem: "Adelante marchemos compañeros, avancermos a la revolución . . . nuestro pueblos es le dueño de su historia, arquitecto de su liberación" ("Let's go, we are marching friends, to the revolution, our people are the turning point of her history, the architects of her liberation"). I reflect on Martin Luther King saying, "I've been to the mountain top; I've seen the Promised Land..." The Nicaraguans are living their dream daily, right in the midst of Contra fire, and no horror diminishes their victory. They fight to defend their dream— that the poor live in dignity and security—even knowing that the rich will never leave them in peace.

I am left with the question, "What dream am I willing to defend with my life?" I feel so blessed, enriched, and challenged to live justice as they do, not reacting to how others are treating them, but ever focused on what they intend to create. I flash on the lessons from the wind that came to me at a young age, but seem so present here, where the stakes are so much higher than a gust of wind. Yes, I do know—as they so clearly do—how to aim for a far-off goal, yet respond to what arises in the present moment with courage, focus and intention. I have been embraced, encouraged, taught, and welcomed—not as an oppressor, but as an *internacionalista*—in their humble, pain-filled, yet wonderfully loving human community. I will carry their stories home to my people, and hold them in my heart forever.

III
Savoring Life's Journey
Into Wonder

CRONE

Alive to life
Aware of presence
On the move
Praying for acceptance
Saying "Yes" more than "No"
Gratitude, gratitude, gratitude…
Following my bliss, my purpose, my guidance
Journeying inward to soul, outward to grace,
Singing my soul song
Sharing power, vision, inspiration
Watching for the dawn
Marching for justice
Seeking peace within, peace without
Shouting hallelujah to the spring
Meeting my fear and befriending it
Welcoming love, radiating love
Cherishing solitude, stillness
Swinging in the hammock
Passing the torch, beginning again
Watching grandchildren grow, tending the garden
Living freedom
Traveling to foreign lands
Listening to the muse, awakening the writer
Celebrating beauty
Allowing time its due
Searching the heavens for home
Being home
Breathing in, breathing out
Now
Sandra

Journey to the Great Mother: Nepal
1989

I am standing in the Annapurna Sanctuary of Nepal before the sacred mountain called Machapuchare—The Great Mother. As our mighty but bedraggled band of nine commune before this altar of snow, ice, rock and sky. We are in the center of a ring of seven peaks over 23,000 feet (we are at 14,000 feet), and the light is changing from afternoon to evening. Just as the sun is turning the snow-covered landscape from white to gold against the still-blue sky, the full moon makes its appearance. The more it rises, the deeper the golden glow of the setting sun penetrates every crevice until the vast array of peaks pointing heavenward are singing to the sun and the moon, and our hearts join the

chorus. Deeper, deeper the glow fades as the sky goes from blue to cobalt to black. We stare in silence. The moon, catching the parting rays as the sun slips below the horizon, shines ever more mystically and mightily as it rises to adorn the prayerful peaks with its light.

This peak, higher than those on either side, somewhat resembles the tip of a whale's tail, culminating in a pin-point apex. The whole mountain is off limits to climbers by national decree. For the Nepalese, it is their cathedral in the sky. I ponder what it would be like to have a sacred mountain, held in respect by all of my countrymen. That would mean we held Nature as sacred and mountains as alive. I long for that kind of national identity. "Now I know where I will leave from when I leave this planet," my trekking partner Libby declares, "from the tip of Machapuchare." It does seem to beckon one to a home in the sky.

How does this one Sandra Waymer Boston de Sylvia celebrate her fiftieth birthday? I go to the highest mountains in the world to match my energy to the challenge of what is here—to meet my maker. This night, I have reached my destination. I have journeyed here with "Full Moon Rising," a group named after a song by that title that we have sung together in ritual gatherings for four years. We planned the timing of our trek to arrive in this sanctuary precisely on this Full Moon, November 9, 1989. We have been trekking for four and a half weeks around this ring of peaks called the Annapurna Circuit. The previous day we climbed from the main trail through a bamboo forest and up into the center of this ring, where we were greeted by a fire burning in the hearth of a welcoming lodge. This night is the culmination of a dream. We go back into the lodge to eat and warm up, but then we go back out into the magic of night and stars and moon in this top-of-the-world wonderland to stand and stare some more.

The grueling ordeal of the last four weeks hovers like a mirage beyond this shimmering moment. We have flown from

New York City, a mighty band of brave women determined to do a hard thing for a noble reason. Me, I wanted to test myself against a challenge unlike anything I had ever done before. I trained for twelve weeks before the trip. I found the steepest terrain in Deerfield, Massachusetts, where the departing glaciers 12,000 years ago had left a ridge of rock face towering above a river valley. I would park at the bottom, climb the steep road winding up the side of the ridge, mount the lookout tower on top, then run down to the bottom and do it all again.

How do you get ready for an untried challenge? I flash on my Lamaze training for natural childbirth. It was the same kind of challenge. I couldn't know when I was ready. I could only invest all I had in the training and then be drawn into the challenge of labor, knowing I had done all I could to prepare, but with no idea if it would be sufficient to the challenge. Trekking in Nepal, like childbirth, would be something to get through anyway I could, with the same relentless humility—the only possible way of proceeding. There would be no conquering the mountain; there would be only crawling, clawing, limping and aching into it.

I remember vividly reaching the opening of the trail. We have ridden a bus from Katmandu seven hours along a twisting, narrow road with rock face on one side towering out of sight, and a perilous ravine on the other side with no bottom in sight. When a bus would come from the other direction, both would slow down to about five miles per hour and pass with a finger's width of space between us. We all hold our breath, hoping one of us would not topple into the ravine gaping below (it is a rare, but predictable occurrence). No guard rail stands between us and eternity, only the experience (and sobriety, I find out later) of the driver. This is the first of many ordeals coming our way, all part of the challenge we have undertaken with such boldness, only to find our hearts thumping in our throats as we sit, powerless, in the hands of the Gods.

The bus stops in what seems like wilderness. No building, no people—there is simply an opening in a stand of trees by the road. Here is the trailhead where 20,000 trekkers in Nepal are dropped off each year. As we watch the bus depart, we begin five weeks of no bathrooms. We had been told to wear skirts for this reason—not my first choice for trekking comfort. After finding our first bush, we head out on this innocent enough, easy, mostly flat, open-vista dirt trail, surrounded by unfamiliar leafy tall trees, and a glimpse of the great mountains far in the distance. I feel like a freshman heading off to college, eager for the challenge awaiting us, while utterly naive about what really lay ahead.

We reach the foothills that evening. From then on, it will seem like we are dancing with a dragon, and the dragon will do all the leading. We are at the mercy of the mountain. There is no turning back—no bus would be there to meet us. The four Sherpas assigned to our group have our gear and they will always be miles ahead of us, hell bent on reaching the destination of the day so they can unburden themselves of 120 pounds of gear (two women per Sherpa) that they would carry over the daunting terrain. They are short and slight of build, maybe weighing ninety pounds, and they trek in flip flops! They are very friendly, but speak no English. In this country, children go to school in hopes of not having to spend their life carrying others' burdens for a living, but not all children are fortunate enough to go to school. We have one Nepalese guide who will go the whole trek with us, and one American guide from our group, Penelope, who has made this trek before, and a second American, Kathy, who is our first responder.

Luckily, one cannot get lost. The trail we will follow is the only road around the circuit. Sometimes it will be as wide as a one-lane road, other times it will dwindle to a footpath. It will rarely be flat for more than ten minutes. As we come into the full mountain terrain, we will be traversing all the rivers that come crashing down from the ring of peaks we are circling. Most of the rivers cut a chasm 1200 feet or so in depth. In the morning as we begin our trek, we might be looking down at a river way below us. Then we can trace the trail up the other side with our eyes to where we will be later that afternoon, back to the same elevation as we are at presently. Climbing up won't get us anywhere but nearer to the next down. Our accomplishment will not be in elevation reached. It will be in persistence. Each twist in the trail brings a new mountainscape into view. When the turn is abrupt, and you can't see where you are going next—it can seem like the path just trails off into space. You don't know if you will be going up or down, but you know it will be steep in any case. The biggest challenge is continuing to put one foot in front of the other and to keep on going. There will be no apex to achieve. We are not going to a top, we are going around.

Every few hours along the trail there is a lovely, one-story lodge constructed of logs and hand-hewn stones fitting perfectly so that no mortar is needed. These are the actual residences of our host families, who serve tea and British tea biscuits, and offer a one-room dorm space outfitted with twenty wooden beds that have straw mattresses. We have brought our own sleeping bags and use our sweat shirts for pillows. The hostess prepares a meal of rice (huge piles), dhal, a few greens (only locally grown), and occasionally a stringy, tough piece of a chicken wing (mostly for flavor). We stop several times a day at these lodges to rest and drink tea, but one lodge in particular is our destination. *Ah—* arrival means reprieve from our ordeal. As our altitude rises to 10,000 feet and October morphs into November, the nights get cold. A particularly charming and comforting feature of some lodges is the surprising warmth beneath the long, wooden table we all gather around for dinner. The table is set slightly above floor level. We bend down to sit on a bench, and when we swing our feet under the table there is a radiant warmth rising from glowing coals in the center of a space dug into the ground.

This is the only time in my life I remember sleeping twelve hours a night. I arrive at our destination about 6 p.m., exhausted. I wash and eat by 7 p.m., then drop into bed. Up at 7 a.m., with a breakfast of porridge, fruit and tea (five weeks of no coffee has to be good for me), I'm off with my trekking buddy, Libby, by 7:30 a.m. We have the name of our next destination in hand as we are sure to get separated from each other during the day because of our differing habits of hiking. Speaking of what is good for me, I have never had this amount of daily exercise—eight hours of relentlessly climbing and descending. I vow that whatever weight my body ends up being after these five weeks will be my ideal weight, regardless of what any charts might say.

There are stone walls, flat and wide—like shelves—along the trail, built at waist height and meant for trekkers to rest their packs on. I occasionally not only rest my pack (which only carries snacks, water, camera, TP and layers of clothing), but stretch out my weary body and take a fine nap for thirty minutes. Nepal is the only country in the world where I feel safe falling asleep in a public place with valuable possessions beside me. Is this because it is a Buddhist country where people would be concerned about their karma? Is it the happy "Namaste" greeting they extend to all they pass on the trail, meaning "I greet the God in you?" Is it their humble, open energy born of a simple life with little wealth of physical possessions, but mighty wealth in communal and family life? No one ever bothers me. The only time I have a moment of fear is when I am trekking alone through a field sloping sharply downhill, and I see an uncharacteristically large man carrying a machete the length of his arm coming toward me. I hesitate. He must have read my uncertainty, because he calls out "Namaste, mabutu!" from a distance of about thirty feet. "Mabutu" is their word for "Grandmother." It is a name of respect. I immediately relax—my trust in these people confirmed—even though no one has ever called me a grandmother before. Do I look that old?

About a week into our peregrination, a very strange and dramatic event gives us one of our most profound lessons. We arrive at our evening destination to discover that one of the Sherpas has disappeared with all the possessions of two women in our group. There is no explanation of what has happened. Everything draws to a halt. Did he fall off a cliff? Abscond with the goods to sell them? Drop dead of a disease? Was he attacked by a thief? A mountain lion? We are adrift like a boat that's lost its mooring as we huddle helplessly in the designated lodge, pondering what to do. It is decided that our Nepalese guide and the head Sherpa will head back to our previous destination in the morning and inquire along the way. That means they will have to do three days of trek for our one to catch up with us. We have to keep going in order to meet our rendezvous with the bus in the wilderness four weeks hence that will pick us up and get us to our return flight in Katmandu on schedule. There is no phone service in these mountains.

The Sherpa and gear are never found. That means our group has to share sleeping bags, clothes and toothbrushes with the two unlucky women. Here are the lessons we receive. First, there are no police in the mountains. There is no place to go and report such a loss. This is a Buddhist country. Whatever happens to you is just your karma. It isn't right or wrong, it just is, and nothing needs to be done about it. Now watch nine Americans wrap their minds around that one! There will be no search, no insurance, not even a report. We sit in the emptiness. Gradually the group remobilizes, figures out what we can muster together to share, and we prepare to continue on, now feeling more vulnerable, yet more bonded by meeting the challenge together.

The second lesson comes with the reaction of the two women to their misfortune. One is furious, bent on justice, protesting the lack of support from officials. She is going to report the loss to the American embassy and sue the Nepalese government to recover her losses. Besides that, none of our donated clothes fit her. She never overcomes her misery at her bad luck and she leaves the trek at the one place on the trail where an airplane can fly her out. The other woman surrenders to her fate. She is graceful and appreciative of all that is being done for her. Her good humor heals us all of whatever residual fears might be lurking beneath the surface of restored normalcy. In her borrowed socks and underwear, she continues to recite roles from Shakespeare (she knows them all by heart) every evening after dinner in the short interval before we sleep. The contrast of one woman aborting and the other bonding through the crisis is profound. No one is unchanged by this lesson that maybe only Nepal could have brought us—a kind of harvest of the soul.

Have you ever been unexpectedly confronted with a physical challenge you are going to have to accomplish, but your first impression is "I can't possibly do this?" Crossing the many rivers descending from the peaks we are circumventing is like a scene out of Indiana Jones. Picture a turbulent, crashing, icy cold river full of boulders. Sometimes it is a few feet below the bridge you are on, water splashing all around. Sometimes it is twenty to thirty feet below. Sometimes it is just twenty feet across; sometimes it is fifty. The bridges are mostly all hung on cables, so they swing with the rhythm of your step (we usually crossed one at a time). The freakiest part is what is available to place your footing on—narrow wooden planks, sometimes length-wise ahead of you, sometimes width-wise across the cables running below your feet. In any case, there are usually some planks missing, and often many—too many for comfort. With just cables to hold on to, leaping over gaps with either raging water or gaping space beneath you is a heart-thumping endeavor. Some of the crossings are among the most daring feats of my life. Being this close to the force of Nature, with so little distance between me and certain death (the water is icy in addition to being like a flash flood in speed), my survival depends on how firmly I hold onto the cable, and how deliberately I hop over the holes. To prove my triumph over fear to those back home, I begin a photo journal of the bridges, each daunting in its obstacles to be met and matched.

The other thing we have to watch out for are approaching mule trains. They are the only means of supply for all the lodges on the circuit since wheels don't work on bumpy, crevice-ridden rock face. They are a true hazard to the newbie trekker like me, who does not know the rules of the road. The animals rule. They don't move over for anyone. One side of the trail can be a drop-off of 100 feet. If you don't get safely out of the way, you can be pushed off the trail by a donkey who is simply doing what donkeys do—walk in the center of the trail with their big hips and wide loads. Luckily, you can hear them coming because they wear bells and there are usually at least twenty of them at once. It's an awesome sight from afar, a harrowing experience up close.

One day mid-way through the trek we arrive at a village late in the day ready to collapse, eat and sleep as usual, but there is a kind of wildness in the streets unlike any village before. Children are running and shouting to one another. The usual aquifer that runs through the main street at knee level for all to draw water from is red in color. It must be blood! As we walk farther into the town, I see a man squatting above the gushing stream washing whitish grey entrails (intestines), with a huge pile of more resting on the cobble stone street beside him. I stop to photograph this bizarre scene, and he explains that today the villagers killed fifty yak. Yak are large, long-haired beasts, a cross between a bull and a buffalo. The man looks up from his work with a knowing smile and in perfect English explains that this slaughter provides enough meat to feed the whole village for a year. How can this be? They don't have freezers. No, he explains, they smoke the meat to preserve it, and then stuff it like sausage into the intestines. Welcome to the non-western world! I breathe deep to calm my automatic reaction to the presence of blood and guts, and gradually take in that I am in the presence of—people who know perfectly well how to sustain life without electricity and gadgets in every room.

I wander slowly with my group through the narrow, cobblestone streets lined with two-story homes made of perfectly fitted stone with no mortar—only gravity and precision holding them together. I am amazed by the craftsmanship of these resourceful people, living in a world without cement. I see fires burning in every back yard. I am trying to wrap my mind around the enormity of fifty huge beasts being slaughtered in one place. Outside one front door, sitting on the cobblestones, I come upon a yak head. It comes up to my naval. Its black eyes—the size of plums—are still open, its black leathery snout still warm, its red blood pooled where it rests against the stone building. Soon I see a man carrying another head strapped onto his back, a trophy that will grace his homestead, I presume. What does one do with a yak head besides gape in awe? I have stumbled into another reality—of totems, rituals, and a people living in the raw nature of survival with animals. My initial repulsion is transforming into respect as I begin to understand the sacred dimension of this tribal communion with the body and blood that sustains these mountain people. Seeing blood running in drinking water appalls me as an American. For the Nepalese, it is a celebration of the Life Force. I feel my foreignness, but I also feel my kinship in the cycle of life in a new way. Just by being present I have unexpectedly received a profound gift.

I am also taking in the communal dimension of what has happened here today. These animals belong to the whole village and everyone will be fed as one family from their bounty. I have never witnessed this profound expression of being my brother's keeper before. I've been to Fourth of July picnics where everyone brings their own picnic, or one-time barbeques that someone has put on. But those events are nothing like this. I am in the midst of an ancient tribe, and the yak sacrifice is their ritual of belonging. I wish I could sit around their open fire and eat with them, but I'm not invited. Meat is scarce here, and not extended to foreigners—there wouldn't be enough to last the year for the village if they did. I watch the backyard feasts with envy, and give thanks for seeing such solidarity, care, and equality in action.

Another experience of raw Nature and my foreignness is living with no bathrooms. The Nepalese people are living on solid rock. One can't dig a hole with a shovel, and the donkeys don't bring jackhammers up the trail because there is no electricity (except for a few tiny solar panels). They can't even have an outhouse close to their dwelling. So each village has designated areas for elimination on the outskirts of town. After a few days of trekking, we realize we can tell when we are approaching a village because we can smell it. We carry our own toilet paper

and bag it for burning later. Unfortunately, many of the 20,000 other trekkers do not follow suit, so their trail of discarded multi-colored paper dots the entire area. TP is another luxury the locals don't have. By now I am convinced that my skirt is definitely the right attire for this trek.

At the beginning of the fourth week, we begin the ascent that will bring all of us to our knees—the Thorong La pass. At 17,900+ feet elevation, it is just shy of when mountain climbers put on oxygen masks. We trek to 14,000 feet and rest for two days to let our bodies acclimatize. Altitude sickness can be lethal. The dragon is now beginning to breathe fire. Our feet, hands and faces swell. We feel light-headed. One early morning during our time of waiting, I venture out alone near our lodge and come upon a trickle of water arising out of the rock. It forms a small pool and then spills out into a small stream that tumbles down into the valley far, far below. I imagine it joining the mighty Mariasanga River that propels through all of southern Nepal and joins the Ganges River far, faraway. I am standing at one of the headwaters of the Ganges, another Great Mother for the people of India. I am on holy ground. I take a photo of my 7 a.m. shadow, cast across this sacred pool as I reach for the sky in joy, and it becomes a life-long treasure.

On the third morning, we snap on our packs and ready our minds for what will likely be one of the greatest challenges of our lives. It's 4:30 a.m. and stars still shine above as we gather at the trailhead to begin our ascent of the pass. We have to make it over the pass by noon because the winds there pick up to gale force in the afternoon. Nervousness is mixed with good humor as we sing out "Here we go, into the wild blue yonder.." and step onto the uneven rock face path leading from the porch of the lodge straight into the mountain. We walk single-file. Talking ceases as the steep incline begins to take its toll on our stamina in this thin air. Climbing in the dusk to early light is like being in a mirage. Mist punctuates the landscape, disappearing some of our group, then suddenly clearing so they reappear like spooks. It is mystical. Each peak we see up ahead seems like it will be the top, but it never is. Another replaces it, drawing us farther into the mountain. A man passes us heading up the trail on a donkey. You can do it that way? We are incredulous! Only the locals knew (and, no doubt, our Sherpas). No one told us riding a donkey was an option, but that donkey would soon play a major role in getting our troupe over this pass.

One by one, women start reaching the limit of their stamina. I wonder what would have become of us if that donkey didn't appear again. The donkey only carries people to the top, never down the other side because of the stress that would cause to its knees. So as the donkey makes its way back down our side of the pass, our women begin to hire the donkey to carry them, one at a time, to the top (so many unexpected fees must have made the owner's day.) Me? No donkey for me. No, I am determined to meet this challenge. It is what I came to the highest mountains in the world to meet. No, I talk myself over that pass by taking ten steps, then stopping. Ten more. Stop. Then ten more. The counting is like a meditation. The air is so thin my heart is pumping twice its normal rate to get enough oxygen to my muscles. The count of ten equals the time it takes for my heart to pump and my muscles to work. Every ounce of me is fully engaged with the dragon and I can't tell who is winning. But I never give up.

Another lesson arises here: just put one foot in front of the other. Don't look up. Don't focus on the goal—only the moment. The goal seems unattainable, the moment a matter of persistence. I flash on the teaching of my tai chi instructor back in Greenfield, "The only skill of this dojo is persistence." I don't even notice the sun rising, or the vegetation changing around me from lush bush, to scruffy stubbles, to lichens, to barren gravel. I am fifty years old and I am still climbing.

Not having a clue as to where the top of this pass will be, suddenly I am there. This is as close to the top of the world as I will ever be. The sun is high. I look up for the first time in hours. The sky is clear and I can see for miles. We are surrounded by majestic peaks, but from here they aren't that much higher than we are. Under my feet is a moonscape of gravel on a gently sloping rounded crest. Far ahead I see a valley between two peaks that looks for the life of me like a perfect vulva. Am I hallucinating? Probably, but it is pleasingly familiar and anchors me to earth. No lodge welcomes us. I don't even remember a sign or any trace of the millions who have passed this way before. Up here, time stands still. Very still, except for the wind, and there are no trees to mark its presence.

Soon my elation at achieving the goal of my journey turns to an urgent need to get down from here. It's very hard to breathe. Quick, take a picture—another treasure of a lifetime—and let's get out of here! The dragon has now gone to sleep, and we are beating it down a steep trail of loose gravel that loops back on itself every thirty feet and feels harrowing in its own right. Above me I see two men who are skreeing down the slope between the loops of the trail. With just their boots for balance, they are skiing on the bare gravel, careening straight down this mighty mountain. Heaven help them if they stumble or lose their balance. Boys will be boys, and that's sure not for me.

We descend so fast that within an hour we are resting on a grassy knoll beside the trail, basking in a mid-afternoon perfect day and looking up at where we have been. Only then do I realize that what I did that morning was—next to childbirth—the hardest physical challenge I have ever faced. I am proud. I feel my strength, well really the strength of my mind more than my body. This is the challenge that drew me here, to fully feel my vitality and strength. I am satisfied. I am happy. I am complete with my assignment, but not yet with my destination. It is hard to believe that we have another whole week to complete the circuit and be released from the mountain. Still, it all seems downhill from here.

In the week after our trek off the main trail into the Sanctuary, as we are making our way gradually down from the mountains into the valleys of the foothills, we trek through the harvests of November. We see piles of grain as high as a house, some bright orange, others deep blood red or creamy white, all spread on the ground. The women are winnowing with large wooden rakes, casting the seed pods high over their heads to let the breeze carry the shell of the seed away. The beauty of the colors casts a spell of satisfaction and completion, knowing the harvest will secure them against the cold winter to come. Apples, apricots, and peaches are also abundant. Marigolds grow everywhere as we reach the lower elevation, and are now used as garlands to decorate the entrances to the many bridges we still have to cross. We dub one lodge the "Marigold Hilton" because it is nestled like a sleeping cat in a gigantic bed of marigolds. Everywhere we look is the color of harvest.

One day, just like a due date that finally arrives in its own time, there is a small town visible far below. What appears to be near is still hours more of climbing down around bends and in and out of ravines. Our knees complain, demand rest. Gradually, the descent mellows into foothills, then valleys with flat plains. A few easy-going streams meander and burble quietly across the land, no longer crashing and screaming, furiously tumbling. We are down. Trucks, cars and buses appear, making us aware that we haven't seen a wheel for five weeks. Flat looks good. Buildings, colors, women in saris, stacks of food on grocery shelves, music blaring over the sound of engines all spell comfort, familiarity, and return to civilization. The mountains are a quiet magnificent presence in the background, like a silent, smiling Buddha who knows equanimity. As I lay that night in a bed with a real mattress, clean sheets, and a pillow (not my folded sweatshirt), my body is half in the town, and half still geared up for travail. I notice I can't let it go—the thrill of challenge, the opening to the unknown each hour, the exhilaration of standing on the edge of the mountain in the non-human world of silence, wonder and majesty.

I will still wander the streets of Katmandu for another two days, where beast and human merge with a mind-boggling ability to go in opposite directions in close quarters with no line down the middle and not bump into each other. I will shop for lapis jewels, a drum, a carpet, a singing bowl, turquoise and coral. I will marvel at monkeys leaping from every wall and statue in the temple that rises above 100 steps overlooking the whole city. I will see the monks in their saffron robes with shaven heads moving deliberately through the streets as if they have an important date with destiny. I will stop to watch a woman weaving a twenty-foot long sash in the street, one end anchored by a stone the other wrapped around her waist. I will ride a rickshaw to the ancient palace square where 100 merchants spread their wares on the cobblestones and wend my way through the maze of Nepalese art– carvings, statues, bowls, baskets, jewels, tapestries, and masks. One hangs on a stairway outside my garage today—twenty-two years later—a daily reminder of this awesome journey. I will see the wild-looking holy man in the market, with his two-foot long white beard and long hair, beads around his neck, his orange robe declaring his identity, his sturdy wooden staff in hand. He stands astride temple steps pontificating to all who will pause in their busy bustling to listen. I take another precious picture to remember the gift of his ancient presence.

I will mount the silver bird, fly high above that merciless dragon in the mountains, and see all the Himalayan peaks at once shimmering like gold in the 7 a.m. sunrise. As I watch them reaching through the clouds toward endless blue sky, I carry the feeling of the top of the world in my body and in my bones— and I will carry it with me forever. I know the dragon's fire, its lush secrets, its pulsing aliveness, its ancient story of travelers, traders, beasts, rock, and beauty. I bid farewell to the sacred mountain. Machapuchare now sings to me from a picture on the wall above my bed, but when I close my eyes, I can smell her, the Great Mother. She is in the smile of the inn keeper, the harrowing bridge across the raging river, the rock under our feet, all around and above us. She is in the strong backs of the Sherpas, and the donkeys with their burdens of sustenance for remote villagers. She is in the marigolds adorning village entrances, in the mighty yak that gives its life for its people, in the hands of the Tibetan refugees peddling their wares along the roadside in this foreign land. She is in the ascent; she is in the descent; she is the trail itself. She now lives in me.

This Pilgrim Meets Her Good Samaritan
1993

Have you ever hit the road to truly wander, to leave the beaten path and go out of bounds? In September of 1993, I have just completed another Pilgrim Warrior Training. After eight years of weaving my work between this program, psychotherapy with clients, and teaching my communication skills course several times a year, I am looking for a change. I want to let go of the familiar, head out of town, and see what might arise in the empty space. This journey would not be about purpose; it would be about savoring being alive, free, and open. I don't have a destination other than the Southwest when I drive out of town. Now, just five days later, here I stand with the number 893 on a mail box that marks my destination in a suburban neighborhood of one-story adobe homes in Albuquerque, NM. I couldn't have known when I headed out from Greenfield that this address would be my home away from home for my sabbatical.

I knock on the door at 8:30 p.m. after a twelve hour drive from Oklahoma City. The woman who opens it bursts out laughing. "I wasn't go-en-ta leet you een if you are unda a hundred 'n feef-ty paounds!" Thus do I meet Esther Gammil with her heavy Texan accent. She will be my hostess for the next twelve weeks. I have met her daughter, Kate, in Kansas City, MO just two days before through a mutual friend as I was traveling the 2,000 miles across the country hopping from friend to friend every 600 miles or so. "Where are you headed?" Kate inquired, as we met over lunch.

"Albuquerque," I replied, "I'm planning to live in my car and visit friends studying at the Ayurveda Institute there."

"My mother lives there," Kate surprised me. "She's newly divorced and living alone in a three bedroom house. She might like company. I'll call her and ask."

I was astonished by this synchronicity. Later that night, as I was visiting our mutual friend in Oklahoma City, Kate called to tell me her mother lived in the southeastern section of Albuquerque and would be expecting me. "What did you say to her?" I wondered, in disbelief at my good fortune. "She just asked me if I would let you stay in my house," she reported with obvious glee. As I thanked her and said goodbye, I was amazed by this blessing and also by that mother-daughter connection that must be so unlike my own. My mother would never be amenable to taking in my friends, especially one I just met the day before. I was starting to feel the hand of fate working behind the scenes. I was eager to discover what this new opening would reveal.

I am about 165 pounds, so Esther lets me in. I am also a wild kind of woman, preferring to sleep on the ground under the stars and take women through ropes courses, vision quests and psychodramas. I have entered into a womb-like, cozy home with all the curtains drawn. Esther is a roly-poly secretary at a local elementary school. She finishes work every day at 3 p.m., goes straight to Kentucky Fried Chicken where she buys dinner, comes home, climbs into her recliner with her remote, and proceeds to spend the evening with her feet never touching the floor.

Esther has said "Yes" to adventure just as much as I have.

Our saving grace (or maybe the magnetism that draws us into a friendship) is our senses of humor. The first few days I am there I would say something like "Esther, do you have a grater?" and she would start to get up. I would stop her: "Oh, no, don't get up, just tell me where to look." But by the third day, the teasing starts. "Esther, you're going to have to get up. I can't find the—whatever." It feels good to tease her about her sedentary lifestyle, and she seems to enjoy it—or is it the company she likes? She is quick on the come-back. "I *can* get up if I *have* to."

I go off on jaunts to Indian reservations and national parks, and come home having slept in my car as I had planned. A few minutes after one such return, I hear the vacuum cleaner running. I must have tracked in some dirt. The next time I return from a journey, I come in and call out, "Esther, get out the vacuum cleaner, I'm home!" We are like the Odd Couple. I ask her if I can use the treadmill in the garage, and soon she is reporting that she, too, has used it. One day she even reports, "I was out of my chair more than I was in it today!"

Esther collects nativity scenes. There are at least ten of them located tastefully around the house. She talks a lot about her ex-husband leaving her one day—with no explanation—and how all three of her children are divorced. Being a mother of three sons myself, my heart aches for her, for them, and for wondering if I, too, will ever have to live through that. As I attempt to study Ayurveda with my friends, I begin eating tofu and tempeh, Esther occasionally passes by in the kitchen and peaks at my pot on the stove. "Whazzz thee-aat?" she inquires suspiciously, but she never takes a taste. Our worlds just barely touch, but never blend.

One day in my roaming I see a flyer on a bulletin board in Santa Fe and decide to take a leap of faith and attend a six-day workshop called "Multi-Incarnational Karmic Clearings" at The Light Institute, founded by Chris Griscom. In addition to being the most expensive workshop I have ever chosen to attend

($2300), this topic gives new meaning to my penchant for going out of bounds. The workshop takes place at an alternative high school in the little town of Galisteo in the middle of the New Mexican desert far from any other town. The first day, I enter a small room with a massage table and a practitioner sitting at its head. I lie down on my back. She puts soft synthesizer music on, and instructs me, "Go to a lifetime you want to heal." I am dumbfounded. I have never been asked such a question before, with the clear assumption that I have had many lifetimes I am unaware of in the present. I choose my mother. Then the practitioner asks, "What color is needed to heal that relationship?" My left brain is very busy by now with thoughts like, "How should I know?" and, "I've wasted all this money because I don't know how to do this." Then the practitioner touches two acupressure points on my temple, and suddenly there is an answer, "Magenta-orange."

Who said that? I don't know; it just popped out, and it is an answer to the question. It's not even a real color I've ever heard of, but it surely matches the astounding New Mexico sunsets I have been experiencing. The practitioner keeps asking me what color is needed as we move through a pantheon of relationships. I come to understand that recalling painful scenarios has a vibration, usually a low one. Primary colors have a high vibration. When I introduce the experience of a color into the memory, a physics of color is predictable—the high vibration works on the low vibration to break it up and bring it to a higher vibration in resonance with the color. The work is all about physics. I don't understand it, yet it changes me. I get used to being asked those questions and expecting an answer to emerge from a source beyond my knowing.

Later that week, the practitioner asks me again to go to a lifetime I want to heal. While my left brain is busy being befuddled again, suddenly a scene, like a vivid memory, comes to my awareness. My brother is sitting on a horse beneath a tree, with a noose around his neck. My mother is standing under the tree right in front of me, glaring at me. I am also on a horse. Suddenly I realize that I am wearing a badge. I am the Sheriff, and clearly what is happening is an execution that I am responsible to carry out. In that moment, I understand the dynamic between the three of us in this lifetime, and why they have bonded so tightly, and why they both seem to have disliked me from my birth.

Somehow the practitioner leads me from that scene to an awareness of how my brother's spirituality as a teenager was expressed in his love of flying, which my father had thwarted saying it was too expensive and too dangerous. I have a fantasy of finding a silver airplane model and sending it to my brother as a sign that I know that part of him and want to celebrate it. I would follow through with that compelling inspiration when I returned home. I found a friend who builds model airplanes, told him my story, and he gave me one that I sent to Sam through the mail in a shoe box. My brother never understood why I did that, nor did he ask, so I had to let the gift have my own meaning and what I wanted to express, and not be about inviting him into a different relationship with me.

Through the ensuing days of this mind-boggling experience, this jump from what I assume is left brain to right brain happens countless times, until I come to trust that it will happen, and I relax into meeting the healer within me. I have never met this healer before because I have never asked her a question. When she is asked, she answers! I also leave with a deeper compassion for my mother and my brother that would prove transformative in our relationships in the years ahead. In hindsight, the workshop did indeed guide me to break the karmic bonds I was in with these two family members even without their awareness or participation, which made the experience invaluable to me. I feel set free to fully love them in spite of a painful history, while needing nothing from them in return.

The week-long experience ends with a fire walk, my first and only crossing on hot coals. We have a three-hour preparation to ready our minds to go beyond our own powers of perception (i.e., hot coals burn bare feet). After rehearsing with a fifteen-foot long red carpet indoors, learning to say—and believe—"I can walk on these coals and my feet will be fine," we finally stand before the real thing. What had been a pyre of logs about eight feet high has now crashed and burned down to coals. We watch in anticipation while the fire tenders take rakes and smooth the coals out into, yes! a fifteen-foot long path. Then, one by one, members of the group step up to the edge, center themselves, and step forth onto the coals, walking briskly but confidently the whole way to the end. At some point it is my turn. I can feel the edge of doubt begging for a voice, but I hold to my focus. I take a deep breath, knowing the longer I hesitate the more likely I will fall back into fear. I affirm my altered state—the closest to a hypnotic trance I will ever be—suspend reality, and step forth. I keep my eyes riveted on the end point and just keep going, not thinking about anything but the mantra, "My feet will be fine." Toward the end, I feel the edge of fear, and I scamper the last five feet.

My feet are not burned, but they are not normal, either. Clearly the energy in my feet is strange, indescribable, like the molecules are racing on a bike with the chain popped off. Because I had scampered, I am disappointed in my experience. I need to know I can do it without fear taking over. I choose to go again. I want to be sure. I resolve to hold my intention, "I can walk on these coals and my feet will be fine." All that exists in that moment is my focus. I step out again. I do it without scampering. I am ecstatic! This time I go out of the bounds in my own mind, and what has always been the limits of possibility will never be the same again. I see what a receptor for fear my mind is, and now I know that I can choose whether or not to act on that fear. The amygdala part of my brain that masterminds fight or flight has been deposed as the expert on flight. Something more elegant has taken its place—perhaps that realm of limitless possibilities?

Is this the same source of "knowing" that had answered those first questions from the practitioner, and introduced me to a dimension of myself I may never have known without those questions? Getting beyond what has to make sense is truly liberating—if you don't die in the process. I have learned to trust a wisdom and a physics I may never have encountered anywhere but at this out of bounds Light Institute in the middle of the New Mexico desert.

Just before I head back to Albuquerque, I stumble across one more amazing gift. I am browsing in a mall in the art district of Santa Fe and I come across a hay wagon full of semi-precious stones milled into round "donuts" for making necklaces. I spend an hour perusing the wagon load of hundreds of stones, large and small—black onyx, lapis, amethyst, moss agate, aventurine, jade, Indian agate, desert jasper and so many more—each one unique and demanding to be picked up and chosen. I put together a necklace of desert jasper and Indian agate.

When I am at the cash register ready to pay for my precious new possession, I see a sign that says, "Business opportunity, inquire within." Out of curiosity, I follow the direction and inquire. The artisan says for $3000 she will give me an inventory of stones and beads, and teach me how to assemble the necklaces. I feel the rush of fun, of possibility, of anticipation. I have deeply enjoyed the last hour of creating and making something so beautiful, Once again, as with the workshop, I am willing to let money be a conduit to an experience every cell in my body is aligned with. Those who know me well will know how extraordinarily uncharacteristic of me this letting go of money is. Being a Taurus, "stubborn" and "practical" are my calling cards. But I do it again. I pay the money—using my last two nearly maxed out credit cards—and drive back to Albuquerque with my new-found treasure. This purchase will become another entrepreneurial adventure that will last for twenty years. Is the southwest casting a spell on me? Is this what wandering will get you?

When I return one last time to my dear home away from home, Esther is my first customer. She pours through the stones, finds one she likes, and together  we make her a necklace. I am leaving the next day. We are both sad that our time together is ending. I give her another nativity scene as a thank-you present. As I drive away, Esther has tears in her eyes and the beautiful stone around her neck. I know I have been very blessed by this woman's big heart, and that this Pilgrim had found her Good Samaritan. Because it is now just a week before Christmas, as I retrace my steps across the county, I would succeed in selling $750 worth of necklaces to my hosts. I was right, these necklaces are precious indeed, enhanced for each recipient by the act of creativity in putting them together. Within the year, I would be grossing $12,000, carrying the stones and beads everywhere I would go. That $3,000 was indeed a good investment. But did I learn the deeper lesson about the gifts that come in letting go, especially of money? I am a beginner, but I am learning.

As I travel back across the country toward home, I ponder what has come of my wandering out of bounds? I surely feel taken care of by Spirit. Crossing paths with someone like Esther might never have happened in my normal course of events, and I suspect she was as blessed by this unexpected liaison as I was. I communed with the beauty and stillness of the desert and swooned over the majestic sunsets. I watched three different lightning storms on the horizon booming their show simultaneously. I watched Native Americans with their indigenous cloth-ing and drums performing side by side with cowboys in their boots and tall hats with guitars—a picture of healing, mutual respect, and celebration of ancient enemies having fun together that made my heart happy.

I climbed the steep walls of Canyon de Chelly with my Ayurveda friends, following a Hopi Indian guide upward on a harrowing path far above the canyon floor. We scrambled up hand-lashed ladders perched on two-foot square surfaces that led to rounded cliff surfaces with no ropes or railings. Toe holds chipped into the surface held us precariously, with the canyon floor 800 feet below. "Don't bump me" the guide said to me as I navigated to the base of the ladder. Why were we doing this very dangerous climbing with no precautions in a State Park? What was she trying to get us to understand by putting us in such danger? Was she trying to show us how brave Indians are—this is a traditional path up the canyon wall—and how weak-kneed we newbies are by comparison? I flash on how the Native Americans are known for their fearlessness around heights while building skyscrapers. But why us, why here, why now? This was one of the strangest—and most dangerous—encounters of all my adventures ever. When we completed the ordeal, she invited us to sleep in her round house that night, an unexpected hospitality indeed after our experience in her hands.

I delighted in seeing a Virgin Mary statue in Taos where the locals change her clothing with the seasons, using the Native American traditional colors of the four directions. It was a lovely integration of two spiritual traditions. I wandered out into the white sands desert, marveling that such a place exists in my country. Signs warned me not to go out of sight of my car because there were no landmarks to find my way back. I stood in the cockpit of the Rover spaceship replicating the moon landing in the Science Museum at Alamogordo. I heard the actual dialogue and saw the video as if I were there. I gazed up at a replica of the international space station suspended from the ceiling, being built cooperatively by thirteen countries—who knew? Seeing it took the sting of competition out of what had been a "space race" my whole adult life. This endeavor seemed like a harbinger of possibility for humankind to find another way of co-existing on our one planet. I saw petroglyphs on the rocks left by the Anasazi 900 years ago, and photographed one of a woman's face staring back at me from antiquity. She was wearing earrings. I am filled with awe, intrigue, and gratitude for this time I have had to wander and wonder.

I return to my work in Massachusetts refreshed, content, and expanded in mind, body and spirit. Nothing about my work would change, which surprises me. I am what changed. There are deeper currents of knowing in me, more dimensions of curiosity, wider reservoirs of gratitude, and stronger trust in the guidance of Spirit. My soul is magenta-orange.

Women of the World Unite!
U.N. Conference on Women: Beijing, China
1974

Some unexpected events grab us like the cyclone grabbed Dorothy and carry us away from Kansas to the Land of Oz. One such event would lift me up over the North Pole and drop me down into the biggest gathering of women in the history of our planet: the U.N. Conference on Women. I am going to Beijing, China! There have been three such conferences before this one. I had heard about them, but I didn't imagine myself being a participant. This time I'm not going to miss it. It is September, 1995. I am fifty-five. I belong there. My decade of work with women stepping into their truth and their power has prepared me to walk among these leaders as a peer. My sisters from every nation are gathering. I find myself humming "I want to be in that number, when the saints come marching in "I long to be in their presence, hear their stories, cheer them on, and share my stories, too. I am thrilled with the prospect of being part of making history.

I write another fundraising letter to my web of sisters, inviting them to support my participation, and they respond in a matter of weeks. I am able to raise $6000, which will cover travel and the conference. Packing for this trip, I feel like I am readying to make another Pilgrimage, this time not to a place, but to the mythic Holy City of women in their power. I hook up with a Vermont women's theater troupe of nine and together we plan to fly halfway around the world through Anchorage, Alaska and over the top of the world to Beijing. I don't know these women, but that doesn't matter; we are sisters in spirit, and this is a journey made of dreams and passion.

We arrive in the middle of the night, bleary-eyed from the twenty-four-hour flight through twelve time zones. Through a blur of uniforms, customs lines, a maze of luggage, and forty-five minutes of congested traffic on a cramped bus, we reach a college campus dorm outside the city. We retrieve our luggage from the heap, find our assigned rooms and crash. I wake the next day in a tiny dorm room with bunk beds, a table and a single overhead light. The bathroom is down the hall. As I enter it and look into the faces of the dozen or so women standing at sinks brushing their teeth and grooming, I realize for the first time what I have joined. Unfamiliar languages are being spoken. Wardrobes range from simple sarongs to fancy satin garb. I notice for the first time—as I stare in delight—how common black hair is for most people on our planet. Here are old and young, large-boned and petite, with every skin tone of the human rainbow. A party-like atmosphere fills this otherwise ordinary place as women gather at the expected site: the source of water. Their footwear is mostly flip-flops—an unremarkably common denominator in this sea of diversity. I emerge from that bathroom into the company of somewhere between 35,000 to 50,000 women. No final count is ever taken. We hail from 196 countries.

I head out from the dorm still reeling from jet lag, but eager to meet whatever will cross my path. At breakfast in a college cafeteria with the usual buffet venue, everyone is buzzing about tickets to the opening ceremony. You need one, but no one knows how to get them. I locate my dorm parent, a young Chinese woman dressed in western clothes and wearing her long hair tied back in a ponytail. I ask her how I can get a ticket. "I have one for you, but I only have a few so don't tell anyone where you got it" she says in a hushed tone. What? Don't tell anyone?

I am incredulous and confused. I take the ticket and get on the appointed bus to the stadium, feeling a mixture of guilt for having something others do not have, anger at being put in such a position, and relief that after traveling halfway around the world to be here, by a seeming stroke of luck I will be able to attend the opening ceremony.

This is my first experience of being in a communist country with a population of over one billion. It is probably common place that there isn't enough to go around, and I imagine secrecy and connection are the common ways people get what they need. As I get off the bus outside a stadium on the outskirts of Beijing, my ticket says Gate 16, so I make my way to the appropriate long line—an inevitable part of this gigantic undertaking. As I get nearer to the gate up ahead, I can see a mountain twelve feet high of plastic water bottles. As women surrender their ticket, they are being made to relinquish their water bottles. I am stymied. It's 4 p.m. It's ninety degrees, and the sun is beating down on the stadium. I am particularly concerned because I am using iodine tablets to purify my water so I won't have to buy bottled water. I need my one-quart size bottle for this purpose. I drink all the water in it and beg the guards to let me keep my empty bottle for "medical reasons." I show them the iodine pills but do not explain what they are for. I succeed in persuading the guards to let me keep my bottle. Clearly, my stubborn Taurus personality is able to persist in this situation, but I am left wondering how those born under my sign in this land fare with having to accept this kind of authoritarian control on a daily basis. Later, when I ask my dorm "mother" why they did that, she just shrugs and smiles. No answer. Did they really think someone would throw a bomb? Were they just trying to show us who is in control?" We will never know. This is China.

The better side of China is their ability to perform ceremony. The opening this afternoon features about 1000 Chinese women dressed in sparkling white with flags and veils flying, performing

Tai Chi-like movement in unison on the field while an orchestra of hundreds—also dressed in pure white—plays Beethoven's Ode to Joy. It is an Eastern phantasmagoria performed to classical Western music, a fitting tribute to what we are all about. The heat is bearing down on us as young Chinese women move up the steep isles with trays of water in tiny paper cups, and women pass each cup down the rows of thirsty delegates. After many speeches, most of which remain a blur of words and formalities, the whole stadium (holding 12,000) sings "We're Gonna Keep on Moving Forward…never turning back…" as the words flash across the digital scoreboard at the end of the field. That song was written by Pat Humphries, who is from Massachusetts, and she isn't told until after the conference that her song was used in the opening ceremony. It is a glorious and poignant experience to sing it together in this place. It's too bad Pat couldn't be there to experience such a tribute.

The next six days are a feast of color, performance, speeches, workshops, and ceremony. Hillary Clinton, Sally Fields, Gloria Steinem—and many I don't know—bring perspective, depth, determination, outrage, silence, and connection to this global sisterhood in action. I never tire of staring at the outfits and the decorated faces with tattoos, scarring, eye makeup and baubles of every imaginable sort. I learn about the global movement to stop sex trafficking of women, something I previously knew nothing about. It is horrifying to hear stories of poor families across Southeast Asia selling their daughters into the trade for enough money to live on for another six months. I have never before encountered the stark devaluing of the life of a girl, which seems to be so prevalent in that part of the world. I sense the bravery of these women of Asia taking on the challenge of turning this trade around. They have documented how many women are being transported beyond their own country in this trade, that Filipino women are most at risk, and that Japanese men are the most frequent users of brothels worldwide. In contrast to this horror, I attend an international song swap and a fellow Pilgrim Warrior from Massachusetts (Robin Weingarten) joins me in sharing "Mother I feel you under my feet," "Earth My Body, Water My Blood," and "We are All One" (the Pilgrim Warrior prayer). Women from every continent join us, and we receive the only applause of the event.

I attend a symposium with a woman from each of the seven continents telling of their journeys into spirituality. Each one had begun her path as part of an institutional religion, and each has moved out beyond the scope of her tradition into a spirituality without form or following—spiritual independence. I resonate with their experience. I am so grateful to know I am not only not alone in my own quest, but clearly my intuition matches that of my global sisters who are living into their own authentic experience of Spirit without the trappings of power and dogma. We are all wanderers.

One rainy evening as I am making my way back to the dorm, I hear singing in the night. I follow the sound to a circle of about twenty African women in a parking lot. I stop to listen, unaware that my life is about to take a radical turn—the kind I have come here to find. "Where are you from?" I ask one of the women when they finish singing and the circle is disbanding. "Uganda. Would you like to join us for supper?" I am hungry, but this is a strange setting for such an invitation. The rain has miraculously stopped. Then another woman opens up the back door of a parked truck and there is a stack of dinners in Styrofoam containers.

I accept one and we sit down at a hastily set up card table. My hostess, a mature woman wearing her traditional dress and headdress, asks me where I am from and what I do—the most frequently asked questions at this jamboree. When I tell her I am a trainer in women's empowerment and conflict resolution her next words are, "Can you come to Uganda?" I say "Yes" without hesitation, and she takes me a few tables away to introduce me to the President of their organization, The National Association of Women of Uganda (N.A.W.O.U.) When the President, also gracious and open, hears that I have said yes, her next words are, "When can you come? How long can you stay?" My whole being is leaping with excitement. (I suspect my acorn is already packing.) No questions are asked about references, resumes, or fees, just an open-hearted invitation to share in the dance of life. I would follow up on this invitation a year later and spend a month visiting twenty-one of their 1000 member groups in thirty days, again being financially supported by my web of sister allies.

I return to my dorm that night feeling elated with the prospect of another Spirit-led adventure. Once again I find myself just saying "Yes" to what crosses my path. This would be my third venture in Africa, but my first with the focus of my new calling. I am excited about assisting women to burst forth from their self-protecting habits of silence, shyness, and acceptance of abuse, into the beauty and strength of their truth, their courage, and their vision for this world.

Imagine the assignment of choosing from 130 workshops and ceremony offerings each day. Now imagine six days of those choices, and you begin to feel into the dimension of women on the move—smart women with plans, teams, resources, and allies. In between workshops, I wander into such experiences as Chinese women teaching traditional Tibetan dances, but with no recognition of their conquest of the Tibetan people. I come upon an hour long silent vigil of a 1000 Women in Black who have come from South America. They are joined by others at the conference and their witness shows me the profound spiritual power of silence and presence. They are protesting governmental silence around the disappearance of their loved ones.

The artist in me revels in the craft village, the largest collection of women's' creativity I have ever witnessed. It is in a giant tent teaming with paintings, sculptures, musical instruments, hats, footwear, jewelry, the ever-present tee shirts and ethnic clothing—a visual feast of color, texture, and talent. I participate in Playback Theater with leaders from Australia, and worship at the twenty foot high altar to the Sacred Feminine constructed in the Peace tent. I meet a young American woman who is doing micro-loan work in Thailand. I meet a street artist from Poland.

I am wandering through a festival, choosing between workshops for skill-building and gatherings for cultural sharing and entertainment. I meet a woman professor from Uganda who had convinced her colleagues to join her in offering a free university to all the graduates of secondary schools in Kampala who could not afford university fees. (I would teach there on one of my future trips.) I meet a headmistress of a secondary school in Kenya who keeps her fourteen-year old girl students in her own home over holidays to prevent them from being married off for dowry when they go home. I meet the woman Chief of Police of Madagascar, and wonder if I would ever meet a woman chief of police in my country. Weave and spin, weave and spin, the web grows strong and wide as we meet and exchange our visions and commitments. We are mighty. I see it, I feel it, and I dance it at frequent spontaneous drumming circles. I tape record interviews with twenty-six women about how they got to Beijing and what they are doing for women in their home countries. The entrepreneur in me sees a great opportunity here, and upon return from the conference I would reproduce the tapes and sell them as "The Voices of Beijing." The tapes are also a wonderful way to bring the experience home to all those who have so willingly supported me to make this journey.

Amidst mud puddles everywhere and piles of plastic bottles spewing out of every trash container (no recycling is happening), I one day arrive for a workshop, so carefully chosen from the 130 offered that day, only to find that the designated room on the third floor does not exist; that building only has two floors. It does make me wonder who is in charge, and whether this is just the way things unfold in China, or whether the mix-up is because of the gigantic scope of what is being attempted on this ordinary college campus. None of the frustrations matter compared to the adventure of looking into the faces and seeing the array of foot-high headdresses and hand-woven foot ware. I am envious. Why don't we Americans have such celebration of the feminine in our wardrobe? It seems every woman is carrying a briefcase full of brochures. They are all community organizers. I sit in one gathering next to an old woman from Nepal. She has lady bugs tattooed on the palms of her hands. I take a photo. I long to have such a mark of the sacred on my body. When I ask the women of Somalia how they were able to get to Beijing their answer is that European women's groups have sponsored them. Now they who once were colonizer and colonized are moving together in solidarity for all womankind. It is good to know that the women are connecting and healing, making deserved reparations for all that was taken.

The women of Somalia also tell me about their having no government for seven years—only the rule of warlords. Their lives have no safety and no secure future for their children; all resources are in the hands of male power and all challenges are being decided by violence. They have no education, no property, and no social freedom, but they have an interior knowing that they have something important to offer and they follow it. They tell me their story of crossing tribal boundaries to meet and talk with the women of rival tribes, attempting to create the possibility of peace by simply knowing each other. I have never taken a risk like that in my life. I have never heard stories of such bravery before. I bow to their vision of what is possible in a world where it seems women have little power or influence—and their courage to act on it.

The six days of adventure that has been the UN Conference on Women comes to its inevitable conclusion, but my time in China is not over. I transition now from participant to tourist, and open to the vastness of China and its history. I visit Confucius' tomb and the terracotta warriors of Xian (a whole army, complete with horses and chariots, all life-size and made out of terracotta clay, buried with an emperor to protect him in the next life). I promenade on The Great Wall as it wends its way out of sight in both directions, and take in the storied pomp of the Forbidden City with its imperial throne room and silk-clad bedrooms. I take in the majesty of one of the most innovative, dynamic cultures ever to evolve. I see commuters on bicycles—six abreast—riding in heavy traffic like a school of fish, each one perfectly synchronized so as not to cause a pile up. No one is trying to go faster or pass another. It is like a dance performance. I eat fried grasshoppers and locust (well, I try...) as well as the most delicious food I have ever tasted, always served on a huge lazy-susan four feet in diameter in the middle of every restaurant table so you can taste from sixteen different dishes at one meal. I buy jade donut-shaped stones for my jewelry-making, and hand-painted silk for presents. I am immersed in the bigness of the geography, the depth of the ancient ways, the uniqueness of the architecture and prevalence of dragons guarding doorways. I also breathe the pollution that is China. I ponder how it is that the U.N. would hold its conference for the women of the world in a country with so little personal freedom, especially for women. I now have a deeper appreciation for the freedom I have had the privilege to enjoy, and a greater understanding of the painful struggles to rest that freedom from entrenched autocratic regimes such as the Communist Party in China.

I can't leave my story of China without including my encounter with an eighty year old Chinese man named Cicero. I'm in Shanghai, its 5:30 a.m., and I—like many early-bird tourists—

am out on the sidewalk in front of our hotel. The sidewalk is at least twenty feet wide, and as far as I can see in every direction the Chinese are out with their

neighbors clustered in small groups of ten to thirty people doing different forms of Tai Chi. One group is wielding swords, another doing very slow-moving gestures, and another making very athletic moves. I stop to watch in front of one group and a woman beckons me to join in. I had taken a class in Tai Chi in Greenfield in preparation for just such a moment, but I am not prepared for what happens next.

As I begin to move, a middle-aged woman wearing a street-length skirt, plain white blouse and a scarf covering her hair and tied behind her ears comes up behind me, reaches around and grabs both of my wrists. She begins to move my whole body the way I imagine they teach a child. She does the form through me. I just relax, surrender, and am amazed at her boldness to touch a stranger and give her gift so strongly. She scoops me down into a deep knee bend until I seriously doubt I will have the strength to stand back up, in front of a crowd of Chinese now watching in delight. Somehow—miraculously—we stand back up together— is it synergy—and the onlookers all smile with satisfaction and applaud us when we finish. Greatly humbled by this experience, I am grateful for such generosity of spirit and welcome into their circle, into their form, and into their ancient roots of tradition. I suspect nothing as intimate as this invitation I received would ever happen to a visitor in my country.

As I move on down the block there is a group doing ball-room dancing. A young man with a bullhorn is calling out "1-2-3, 1-2-3" to waltz music blaring from a boom box on the side-walk. About twenty couples are moving in a large circle. Cicero approaches me and asks me to dance. He is about my height, slight of build, and makes very tender and kind eye contact. He is wearing a cotton long sleeved shirt and black cotton pants. My only hesitation is that I haven't ballroom danced in twenty years. I am grateful for the remnant of sixth grade dancing les-sons that still lingers somewhere in my being. We move together

 carefully and in silence. Then we con-tinue with the next dance. This elderly gentleman is offering me the gift of his friendship. Moving slowly together, we communicate without talking. I have never danced with a stranger on a side-walk next to busy city traffic at six in the morning. After a while he speaks to me in English, which is not only a relief, but a haven. We can relax in each other's company. I am meeting another Good Sa-maritan who is about to shepherd me through a wonder-filled experience of the lifestyle of China's older people.

At 7:30 a.m. on the dot, the Tai Chi groups melt into com-muter traffic. Dancers collapse their swords, strap them to their bicycle racks, and take off for work. But not those fifty-five years old and above who have a mandatory retirement with a very small stipend from the state. They must make room for the young workers. So Cicero invites me to come with him—and mind you, it's still early morning—to a nearby hotel ballroom where we can continue dancing. Sensing an adventure off the beaten track, I accept.

After a brief walk through a neighborhood of high rise apartments (apparently the only housing in the city), we enter a ballroom off the lobby of a European-looking, multi-story hotel. The lights are dim. A strobe light is turning in the center of the ceiling, casting star-like patterns on the floor and on the faces of people sitting at little round tables lining the dance floor. I wonder if they got strobe lights from us, or we got them from the Chinese? The tables are filled with elders drinking tea between dances. Cicero goes off to get us tea and a Chinese woman (who does not speak English) asks me to dance. I politely accept, while harboring amazement at this cultural assumption that women who are strangers are open to dancing together in public. Following her strong and capable lead, I again relax into the old familiar waltz pattern as we move around the expansive dance floor, surrounded by couples enjoying retirement together. The degree of close physical contact with strangers is again a jolt of culture shock, but I am thoroughly enjoying myself. As the music ends, she bows to thank me and departs as quickly as she came. Her quick departure makes me wonder if she did that dance with me on a dare.

In the ensuing hours, between waltzes and refills of tea, Cicero tells me of his early life as a POW during WWII in Burma, where he was pulled from the ranks of slave laborers building the bridge over the River Kwai because he spoke English and his captors needed a translator. He had attended a missionary school, which he said was the smartest thing his parents ever did for him. It saved his life to know English. After the war he was a college professor for many years. Now he asks me to bring him the free western newspaper available only to guests in the hotel lobby because he has no access to the news. He is too poor to buy a paper.

I cherish my time with this dignified old man, who lived through the greatest cultural and political revolution of the twentieth century and is now an ambassador to foreigners who cross his path early in the morning. It occurs to me later that day as I am telling my companions about my encounter, that this is probably a daily practice for Cicero to pick up an American tourist, have a few dances, practice his English, tell his story, and get a free newspaper. What better way to spend a day in retirement in Shanghai?

I bow to the beauty, grace and generosity I have found in the people of China despite their lack of freedom. I have been very blessed by the people I met, the dimensions of history I saw, and the opportunity to be part of the women of the world coming together. That kind of gathering was never repeated. There would have been too many participants for any country to host.

Global Sisterhood:
The Essence of Grassroots in Uganda
1997

Dorothy's cyclone has struck again, and this time it has me flying directly south from London and over the Sahara desert. The late afternoon shadows fall on high sand castle-like mounds that seem barren and isolated, poking up and surrounded by deep, swirling craters. The shadows cast an eerie moonscape-like effect that makes it seem like I am journeying to another planet. In the idle hours of flight as I peer down on this vast emptiness, I find myself imagining ancient caravans travelling far below, matching wits with the forces of the desert to connect across perilous distances to hear each other's stories, trade goods, and learn new ways of wisdom, art, and relation to the mysteries of life.

From the comfort of my soft chair in the air-conditioned airplane, I contemplate how I, too, am making just such a journey—and for similar reasons. I have said a simple "Yes" to the women from Uganda that I met that night in Beijing, and here I am flying across oceans and continents to meet them. I have exchanged a few very formal but brief letters with the President of N.A.W.O.U. and we chose a date for my arrival. I packed my good intentions, my life experience, my willingness, and a portfolio of my most useful flipcharts as a trainer in communication skills and conflict resolution for twenty years. I got the shots, the visa, the $1300 ticket (with the help of my circle of sisters again), and headed out to answer the call of my sisters in Uganda. What will my month of volunteering involve? What lies ahead? Who will I meet? What stories will I hear around the ancient campfire of culture? What treasures will I gather to bring home for my kin to savor? I don't know.

What I do know is that I am joining a modern caravan of globe-trotting women reaching out to share tools, resources, and connections that will make our world bigger and more filled with possibilities. Three hundred Ugandans attended the Beijing conference, and—having been a British colony for 150 years—they are not strangers to women from afar. I am hungry for new perspectives on women's lives and our common struggle to move beyond cultural barriers to participation and influence in our own societies. I'm anticipating the adventure of unfamiliar food, music, modes of travel, lifestyle, art, and spirituality. I want to give and receive the precious gift of friendship. I know the culture of Uganda includes polygamy and arranged marriages where women are considered property and dowry is compensation for the bad luck of having a girl. With such a wide divergence of customs in our two cultures, what wisdom would I find? What wisdom would I offer that would be of value? Such thoughts fill the empty 13 hours as my plane crosses the continent heading for Central Africa. I would be landing just one border away from Malawi, where I lived and worked thirty-two years ago.

Andrew MacAdams, a middle-aged, balding Brit, meets my plane, and efficiently ushers me through customs and into his Jeep Rover. We pull out of the airport parking lot onto the modern forty-mile highway toward Kampala. Andrew is married to Irene, who is on the staff of NAWOU. We chat about my trip as I take in the land of palm trees and women carrying large baskets full of produce on their heads, their backs straight and strong as they walk along the road on a foot path. Some travelers are riding bikes alongside us, more ride scooters as they weave in and out of bustling taxis and cars. It is evening, and it is 90 degrees in January. I will live in the home of Irene and Andrew, a multiracial couple, for the duration of my visit. Their family includes their daughter Grace, who is six, their adopted orphan from the civil war, Linda, who is eleven (and who functions as a servant for the family), and Sarah, thirteen, who is a hired housekeeper. Andrew is a professor of economics at Makerere University in Kampala. Irene meets me at the door and ushers me directly to my room with little conversation as it is now way past everyone's bedtime.

I am given a room of my own (displacing Grace) and I fall into bed without even unpacking my toothbrush. The next morning I take in this simple yet elegant home a-top a hill in a suburb of Kampala that will be my home base for the next month. It is a one-story, five-room house constructed of lime-stone. Their large living room with multiple couches arranged along three walls can probably seat fifteen. The dining table, which seats six easily, is to one side of this room. Two bedrooms and a tiny bathroom are down a wide hallway. Their "water closet" is a tiny, narrow room barely big enough to stand up in, with a pull chain attached to a tank mounted on the wall above my head. This toilet tells me I am in a colonial-era house, unlike those the near-by Africans have, with tin roofs and outhouses. The kitchen here includes a small refrigerator, a sink with running cold water, a two-burner electric hotplate, and a three foot long counter for preparing food. One small metal cabinet above the counter holds all the dishes. Linda buys fresh produce and bread daily in a neighborhood market and Sarah boils grains on the hotplate. That is the majority of their diet, except for tea, fruit, and occasional small pieces of one chicken shared by all. Sarah and Linda—so young in my eyes—do all the cooking and cleaning for the whole family. They never eat at the table with us. Since the civil war in 1985 that ousted Idi Amin and cost 500,000 lives, every family in Uganda had to adopt orphans. These abandoned children, like Linda, are destined to be life-long servants, with no opportunity for education.

Breakfast, which consists of tea and bread with butter and

jam, is at 7 a.m. Dinner is at 10 p.m.—way past my usual bed-time—because Adam and Irene own a small convenience store that they go to after their nine-to-five jobs. Such is the work ethic in a developing country. To get to the N.A.W.O.U. office every day, I walk ten minutes through our neighborhood of mostly mud houses with tin roofs, to the bottom of the hill. On my way I pass a twelve-foot high termites' nest, a constant reminder of how far away from home I am. At the main road, I wait for a kat-utu, a VW van that packs in fourteen passengers at a time and charges ten cents per person. I squeeze into the next one that stops (they don't stop if they are full), and hand my money to a boy who is probably twelve years old and the son of the driver. We speed between stops into the traffic-bulging commotion that is Kampala. All katutus arrive in the same place in the very center of the city of 20,000. Just imagine 100 VW vans. Now have each one pointed in a different direction with no seeming order to how they are arranged, and that is what this bus station looks like. It seems the drivers just pull into this city block-square de-pot and come to a stop wherever they find room. Squeezing into the van earlier with a physical proximity that felt strange and uncomfortable was a mini-culture shock to me, but seeing this bus station is a doozy of a shock. When I inquire about how to find my way to the right bus to get back home, I am told, "Just ask someone." Simple solution. People don't need signs and pre-dictable systems here. They just ask. How unlike America.

From the bus depot, I walk three blocks along a busy urban street to the office, a two-story house in a tree-lined neighbor-hood. Even though laid out as a home, it is indeed an office, with desks filling every room, charts and posters of women leaders on the walls, telephones on every desk, and even a receptionist. There I meet the staff of about ten women, all with different job descriptions, who work on the various projects of N.A.W.O.U. which I gradually learn about as I travel through my assign-ments for the next thirty days. Every Thursday when I arrive I find the yard full of women with stacks of hand-woven baskets sitting on the ground. N.A.W.O.U. buys their baskets, and has a storage room on the second floor of the office from which they ship the merchandise to stores worldwide. Such cottage industry is the norm for women earning a livelihood here.

The Director, Patricia, is about forty years old and wears a black business suit, big loop earrings, lots of make-up, and low-heeled pumps. The rest of the women are all dressed in Western style as well. This seems to be a status symbol that indicates you are educated and you have "made it," as in having a paying job. Patricia sits behind a very big desk and calls me Mrs. Boston, a formality which feels awkward. It seems as if they are treating me the way they would a distinguished guest, which, in hindsight, I guess I was to them. When I discover that this formal way of relating is the norm everywhere I go, I gradually get used to it. After all, we really don't know each other, and they are as unsure about what is going to happen next as I am. I can't help but wonder if this degree of formality is an internalization of the British way which they perhaps interpret as more professional than their friendlier and more open-hearted style that I had encountered in Beijing.

One of my fears in coming to Uganda with so little introduction or preparation had been that there would be nothing planned when I arrive and my hosts wouldn't know how to make use of my skills as a trainer. Nothing could have been farther from reality. They throw me into a whirlwind routine the second day, and it doesn't stop until I have trained over 430 people in twenty-one different groups in the thirty days of my stay. N.A.W.O.U.'s focus is on women's economic empowerment, specifically creating village banks that make micro-loans typically for $100 per loan. The groups vary in size from seventeen to fifty-four. The members have development projects together and/ or as individuals. Everyone I meet seems very eager, motivated, and determined to succeed in their enterprise. Much later they would admit that they had no real sense of what I was going to do, but they just trusted that what I would do would be helpful.

To this day, I have very little feedback about whether or not this was the case, as it is not in Ugandan custom to be direct with anyone, or give critical feedback, or even make suggestions. The norm is "Everything is just fine." The Taoists would be happy here, but it is quite disconcerting to this American who likes feedback and is accustomed to using evaluation to improve my training. I fly by my instincts, use all of my flipcharts that focus on managing differences and negotiating solutions to needs, and hope for the best. Embarrassed laughter is the best signal I receive that I am touching on something important. I always receive a very formal "Vote of thanks for a most interesting workshop" at the close of each event. Politeness definitely rules the day in Uganda.

My third day on the job, I find myself standing in an elementary school classroom with mud walls, dirt floor, and black paint on the wall for a blackboard in a village thirty miles north of Kampala. I look into the eager faces of thirty women. They don't seem to mind sitting at the small desks on chairs built for children. These women are in traditional dress. I surmise the western attire goes with the urban life. Sarah, the facilitator of the session, introduces me in perfect British English. Everyone is smiling. Then she coaches them to one by one stand up, announce their name, and then PROUDLY tell what they have done in the last week to improve their business endeavor.

"I am Teddy Natukunda. I want to sell cakes and sodas in wholesale and one on one. I am from Bukuya Kasanda. I am forty years old and I have eight children. All of them are still alive. Eight years ago, my husband died and I don't get assistance from anywhere. I have big problems to look after these children because only one child got a chance to go to school. This week I got training in bookkeeping, and bought a goat. I will use the milk from the goat for my cakes and to feed my children."

"I am called Regina Namusisi. I am going to use the knowledge I have got from here to sell fish and bake cakes for sell. I am born in Kyunga Busana. I have a five year old daughter and I want to send her to school. This week I found another shop keeper who will buy my fish."

The energy in the room is electric as one by one they report their efforts and successes. They have each brought the equivalent of ten dollars towards the repayment of their $100 loan, plus ten percent interest and ten percent toward savings. These are the requirements to participate in the international micro-loan bank they are part of. When they have repaid their initial loan they can receive another. Some of the women are on their fifth loan, using the first to buy chicks, the second to build a coop, the third to raise chicken feed, and onwards. Some are growing mushrooms to sell to hotels. Others are baking cakes, catering, tailoring, or drying fish. One group had been so  successful with their mutual project they were able to start their own revolving loan fund, where the interest doesn't go to an outside agency, but to the lending members. Here is grassroots empowerment in action. The young entrepreneur in me recognizes their courage and determination to go out of bounds in a society that does not recognize a woman's right to own property. In this case, it is not one woman, but a group owning an asset together, something the men in their lives have not had to contend with before.

Sarah tells me that these village banks are built on social networks; women have to be invited to join. Then if a woman misses her weekly payment because she or someone in her family is sick, everyone knows the circumstances and her friends will pay her loan for her on time until she can get back to her work. I flash on a memory of sitting in a huge auditorium at the Beijing Conference on Women two years before. I was listening to the man who heads up the U.N. Development Program. He was reporting that the micro loan programs for women are the greatest force for change on the planet. It was not only bringing families out of poverty, but greatly increasing the number of children able to afford to go to school. He said women invest in the whole family, and have a repayment rate of 98%. He reported that his program was now focusing entirely on women, no longer lending to men who tend to use the money for personal gain (like buying another wife), and have only a 48% repayment rate.

One group of fifty-two women I work with during my sojourn has pooled all their loan money in a group endeavor. They had rented farm land and raised a crop of corn. They then used the sale of the corn harvest to buy the land. With their second harvest, they have a profit in a bank account which their husbands cannot access because it isn't in any one person's name. The challenge these women face the day I visit is new to everyone involved—what to do with that money. Will they divide it up? Use it for school fees? Hire a trainer to teach them a new skill to expand their business?

These women are not only learning business skills but also problem-solving and facilitation skills. It is a joy to lend my expertise in negotiation to their success as they debate the advantages and disadvantages of going into poultry or piggery. I think to myself, "Oh if my friends at home could see me now..." Knowing nothing about the content, I am able to show them a skill for exploring decision-making by staying open to all the ideas being offered without letting judgments stop the creative process. These women are building an economic base that is equipping them to participate in a bigger arena outside the home. Their business model is radical in a culture where women are still considered property and own nothing themselves. Typically the husbands here take control of any money their wives earn. The children even belong to the man's tribe and the women have no rights if they decide to leave an abusive marriage. I can feel the seeds of revolution—of autonomy—taking root in these circles of determined women. Now they have access to financial resources that they control collectively, and they will be the deciders about how it will be used. I quietly imagine that in the next twenty years this country will be led by these women.

With some groups I have the opportunity to move beyond the realm of business and go beneath the social fabric to the deeper issues of women's lives, where they are held back from their full power by norms that allow men to control how their lives are conducted. What I find is all too familiar. The number one issue groups want to discuss is "rumor-mongering" among women. This issue is a great segway into empowerment strategies, looking at why this phenomenon of women not supporting other women as leaders seems to be present in every culture. The second most prevalent topic is what to do when your husband brings home a new wife (50% of marriages are polygamous.) I will give up on this topic after trying about four times to use it to demonstrate problem-solving (brainstorming all possibilities without judgment) and getting nowhere. I realize they are not even interested in solving this dilemma. They are mad and they want someone to validate their feelings. So I do a lot of mirroring their pain and decide this is not a topic that we can use for training purposes. While I have some ideas about the importance of making and keeping agreements, this is one of the places where our cultures are too different for me to be helpful, and I might even do more harm by pursuing it.

Other subjects we touch on in exploring the negotiation skills are: how the profits from a successful project should be allocated; what to do if a husband is refusing to let a woman attend N.A.W.O.U. meetings and training seminars, or have an income-producing project of her own; what to do when men talk too much at meetings (facilitation skills); how to bridge the gap of power between elderly and younger women (so elders are not excluded); how to keep women from dropping out when they become a wife or mother; how to address gossiping without causing a split; what a couple should do who want to get married and their clan refuses to accept the partner.

All of these topics help illustrate the skills needed to avoid arguing and instead really explore the differences, seeking to create understanding as a basis for finding a solution that would work for all parties. I soon learn not to refer to my work as "conflict resolution" because, to Ugandans, that implies armed conflict with soldiers, armies, chaos and tragedy that took thousands of lives just twenty years ago under Idi Amin's rule. So I call my training "How to Solve Problems without Fighting" as well as "Group Management" and "Problems of Women Working Together".

I face some very typical dilemmas that show me what living in a "developing country" means. One day a driver does not arrive to take me to a training in a rural area (he had no phone to let me know he had fallen ill), and I have to hire a taxi and go hunting for the location on my own. Another dilemma is having to change the date of a training for a town about three hours

away. The telephones were not working for days, so a N.A.W.O.U. representative and I decide to go a day early and trust our luck. Well, I think we are trusting luck because I do not understand that these kinds of troubles are normal. When we arrive in the town, it takes an hour and a half to find the organizer who is very surprised to see us a day early, but without more than a blink of her eye, she says, "Well, just give me an hour." She hires a taxi and drives to everyone's house and tells them of the change. An hour later, we start a four hour training with twenty women. Welcome to the fluidity and spontaneity so necessary in this place where there is enough technology to raise expectations—like we will be there on Wednesday—but not enough to meet those expectations.

I lead a two day training with another activity of N.A.W.O.U., the Single Mother's Project. These mostly young women are in a very precarious social situation. They have proved they can "produce," which is highly valued, but their marriageability is jeopardized because no man is going to want to be responsible for another's children. Children are the property of the man; they are his responsibility, but often now in urban settings men will abandon a woman they have not married, and she is left with the responsibility. These women have varying degrees of education, but are considered prostitutes unless they are celibate. They are also blamed for the street children syndrome. I invite them to raise issues they are dealing with, and some of the topics we explore are: communicating respectfully with children, good parenting, goal-setting and self-esteem building, how to look for a job, how to relate to men, mothers, and bosses, stress-reduction techniques, and building support networks.

In this context, I become a jack of all trades. I am simply responding to the women's questions with whatever life experience I have to offer. I am crossing all kinds of cultural divides in the process. The familiarity of their questions (second wives aside) assure me that we have more in common as women yearning to be free of all that holds us back than we have differences. It appears to me that their greatest need is to find connection with each other in this urban setting—something that would have been a given in their rural communities. Without the support of community, they are adrift in an extremely vulnerable situation both economically and sexually. They have not inherited any role models of women taking care of themselves economically, and their families are often far away. The spirit of Beijing is alive in our interactions. The true meaning of that U.N. conference—the richness of women connecting around our common struggles and sharing our gathered wisdom—is the essence of why I have traveled almost half way around the world to be here.

You may be wondering "What about cultural differences?" as you read this list. I wonder that all the time. It seems to me that my very being here is giving the women a chance to broach these personal subjects publicly, maybe for the first time. So my clear intention is to facilitate them listening to each other as we American women often did in our early consciousness raising groups. There is always wisdom in a group that is being vulnerable and transparent. I am not an expert with answers; I am a witness sharing compassion for their struggle while also being willing to tell them stories of women in my country and how we address some of these same challenges in moving beyond accepted social norms in order to meet our need for greater autonomy and possibility. Story-telling is always a potent way to stimulate new thinking. Their vision for their lives would look just like those of young women anywhere—good jobs, a home, education for their children (and sometimes themselves), taking care of parents, being married, or being single (about half now choose being single, showing the changing possibilities for women as they become economically empowered.) At one point, they asked me what my vision for my life was. I answered, "To raise all women up." They cheered.

The director of this program, Joyce, is herself a single parent of six-year-old twin girls. She makes a meager living selling used clothes shipped in from charities abroad. She has to come up with $50 for one term (of three) for her two girls to start school. She asks me if I know anyone who would sponsor them. Here is the bridge I came to help facilitate. I tell her I will reach out in my network and invite that support. When I ask her how she manages to keep going, determined as she is to remain single, her comment is, "I have hope that things will improve at any moment." This is the voice from the edge of survival, a level of insecurity I have never known. For these women, there seems no other option than being in the present moment. Anything else is terrifying. One young woman looks me right in the eye and says, "What can I do when I have nothing?" We ponder together what it means to believe in God when you have nothing. What can she trust in when her social norms are changing around her and her society has no place for her to stand that is secure? Here before me is the real teaching about the cost of social change. It may bring greater opportunities in the future, but the present is fraught with danger. Suddenly my suggestions seem shallow and I am the one receiving the teachings about endurance and faith. All I have to give is to walk beside them, hear their fear, and open together to Spirit that holds us all.

In between these scheduled trainings, events flow in a graceful way quite outside my American experience of tightly over-scheduled colleagues. I go to a demonstration against domestic violence on the town square. About 100 people are gathered in the rain. One of the speakers is the director of Isis—W.I.C.C.E. (Women's International Cross-Cultural Exchange)—a great acronym since W.I.C.C.A. refers to the European pre-Christian culture of the witches who were healers. Isis was the Egyptian Moon Goddess who promised gender equality. They were on my list of contacts I wanted to make through the Global Fund for Women, so I find that woman after the event and make a date with her for later that day. Her vehicle picks me up as they are located outside the center of Kampala. I arrive at her office about 3 p.m. We talk about her program and the history of her agency for a few hours (begun in Europe in the '70s, hence the way-cool name, and moved to Uganda in 1994 because the government was so supportive of women's empowerment).

Then she takes me downstairs to their resource center. It has been a global think tank on women's issues for the last twenty-two years. It is full of publications organized on racks, filled library shelves, and tables for researchers to use. They are now the biggest women's resource center in Africa. It is awesome! They place people in cultural exchange programs related to particular issues and then the participants write about their experience in a journal the agency publishes world-wide. They network among 2600 women's groups in 152 countries. (Address: W.I.C.C.E. Box 4934, Kampala, Uganda.) Their next project is to take the information in their journals and repackage it for rural, semi-literate women, using music, drama, and art instead of written words. She, the center librarian, and I are caught up in an amazing exploration of what global sisterhood involves, showing me all the hands-on tools and statistics of women grappling with the ways their lives are changing socially, economically, and spiritually the world around. We go on until 8 p.m. I love the sense of availability these women show. They have time for something new, intriguing, and deeply satisfying to happen. Here, in the grassroots of one of the most under-developed countries, is a powerhouse of global sisterhood in action.

Another surprise comes one morning when I think I am free of any commitments and walk a leisurely route to the N.A.W.O.U. office only to unexpectedly find a journalist named Alice, who writes a women's supplement weekly, waiting to interview me. We spend over an hour exploring my impressions of Uganda and what I think about a controversial cover of a women's magazine featuring an African woman in short shorts, legs crossed, with the lens aimed at her crotch. Many letters to the editor are aghast at the arrival of pornography in Uganda that this photo represents. We talk about freedom of speech and the press, the movement against pornography in the U.S., the conflict between freedom and values, and the difference between influence and control in the marketplace. Alice tells me how gender balance is emphasized in the Ugandan Constitution with 50% of their Parliament mandated to be women. This is something they are very proud of but they have many problems implementing (just like we do.) She wants to know how we are working on this in the U.S. I tell her the embarrassing story of the E.R.A. failure and then the new law in California that kids above the third grade can be suspended from school for sexual harassment. She wants to know what I think would end domestic violence. Her eyes open very wide in disbelief when I tell her about the men's movement here, raising consciousness and providing services to help men change their abusive patterns. Her reaction gives me pause to consider how recently this change has come to our culture and how susceptible all women still are to the physical abuse of men who perceive themselves as superior.

Alice surprises me with her final question, "Do you think the women's movement in Uganda would drop if the present government drops?" I don't think so, I venture, because as so many women are in these village banks learning economic skills and they are also learning political skills–how to make decisions with long-range goals, deal with issues of justice, share power, and practice leadership. Also, with their international connections after sending 300 delegates to the Beijing Conference, they have a lot of external support. Visiting with Alice, I feel the kinship of a sister seeking to move women ahead by giving them strong images of themselves and important questions to think about and speak out about in public. Alice will help women provide leadership in setting the discourse for their society.

As my adventures continue, I go one morning at 8 a.m. to visit the Women's Lawyers Guild, located on two floors of an office building in a suburb of Kampala. The staff is a mix of Ugandans and Europeans, all dressed in the usual western garb. No dazzling head-dresses here like I saw in Beijing. The air of officiousness permeates the space. I am amazed again to find this

British-funded N.G.O. has one of the most comprehensive programs I've seen. There is a walk-in clinic with on-going daily
education on women's legal rights for women waiting to see a
legal officer. There is also rural education offered off site on children's rights, inheritance and property rights, and divorce rights.
Many archaic customs were changed in Uganda's new Constitution in 1986, which is a showcase of women's equality. But the
oppressive traditional practices—forbidding women the rights
to claim children, property, or a divorce—are still in full sway
in rural areas, in defiance of the law.. The work of this N.G.O. is
another outstanding example of giving women information and
support to stand in their power in the face of discrimination. I
am reminded again of the adage, "Together, we are strong." No
woman can make these changes alone. Perhaps my presence,
witness, and caring lends strength to their daily push for their
social customs to catch up with the increasing consciousness everywhere that women's rights are human rights. Right here—in
this agency—is where the U.N. Conference, with its vision and
passion, is grounded in change for women's lives.

I talk to the Program Officer for an hour. She decides to call
in the General Secretary and Management Officer (a Dutch volunteer), and the four of us talk for another hour about the fea-
sibility of a battered women's shelter in Kampala (seems impos-
sible because if they advertised free shelter and food, half the
women in the city would show up.) At some point the program
officer says, "You must do a training with our legal officers. They
deal daily with very angry people who are sometimes shouting
and fighting when they come into the clinic. Please help us with
this." I point out that I am booked that afternoon and the next
day, and am leaving the following day. They persist. I am baffled
that they will not accept my "No." I look at my watch, and say,
"Well, I am free for the next two hours." "Fine!" they respond,
"We'll call the legal officers together in the conference room in
five minutes" (they were all meeting with clients). So off we go

into an unplanned training. I have my flipcharts with me because I am on my way to a second group at 12:30, and a university class at 5 p.m.

At noon we stop and they drive me to my 12:30 group, a village bank I had already worked with before, where I am supposed to be until two. I stay there fielding more problems until 4 p.m. because it is my last time with them and they want to work out what to do with participants who do not attend every week as required. I have just enough time to catch a "special hire" taxi to the university, where I start all over again with a class of forty men and women. I wish I could remember all the examples of problems they came up with but my mind is a blur except for the one about their clan rejecting their sweetheart. They come up with seven possible solutions for that situation and see how the skill of negotiation opens up a problem and helps them explore conflict over time instead of jumping to win/lose solutions.

Although the class ends at seven, I don't get away until about eight as so many students want to ask about how they can keep learning these skills and get my address. Then I go to the home of one of my favorite human beings—sixty-year-old Byaruhanga—whom I first met in Beijing. As a professor in Forestry at Makerere University, she is a botanist who wrote the first text book in Uganda on plants. She also started a free university at night for young people who can't afford the university, using the proceeds from her book to finance the undertaking. This program now has an enrollment of 600 students and over 1000 graduates. We had arranged for me to lecture there earlier this last week. She has a pronounced limp from polio in childhood and a radiant personality. She says things like, "God gave me the mind of a lorry and put it in a Volkswagen," or "It's a good thing I limp or I would go too fast and push other people down."

As she tells me about convincing her professor colleagues to donate their time to the evening free university she adds, "I don't like little problems, I like big ones, the kind that take ten years to solve..." She just seems to glow with the satisfaction of what she has been able to create with her passion for education and her enormous determination to lead. I am not surprised by her simple humility when she adds, "God has given me everything I have; whenever I need something, I just ask Him and He gives it to me." Here again I contact the simple wisdom of those who have little in the way of resources and make things happen out of their sheer intention and trust in the rightness of their cause. I ponder why it is that we Americans always think we have to seek funding before we can undertake a dream. I listen, absorbed in her cascading stories, as she describes her marriage to a South African man, a doctor. They live in their respective countries because, as she continues, "We each have our work to do." She tells me with a quiet smile how they have been deeply in love for forty years. They talk on the phone weekly and see each other two or three times a year. I hang on her every word, knowing I am in the presence of a rare human being who understands the autonomy of love.

This would be our last evening together. We hold hands and just let the love flow between us, a love encompassing respect, adventure, and shared responsibility for the fate of our people and our planet. I tell her I will always hold her in my heart and hope to have the pleasure of her inspiring, courageous company again. I have not seen her again, but her picture hangs above my desk in Greenfield, a constant inspiration and connection to the love which is the source of our being.

Thus ends about the busiest day I have ever had leading three trainings with about sixty-two people. I have an eight hour training scheduled for the next day. Reflecting on Marge Piercy's poem where she says, "I want to be of use..." I think, "Ah yes, but what about being all used up?" I have never experienced such a hunger for learning. I feel deep satisfaction, knowing that being right here, in the heat of our exchange, is why I have come to Uganda, and it is good. I am witness to hundreds of young people going out of bounds, stretching their traditional society into new possibilities, new standards, and new roles and expectations for women. I am exhausted, amazed, and grateful.

One of the highlights of my month comes on the last day when I am working with a group of thirty-five women who each represent a district of Uganda for N.A.W.O.U. They have come to the capital city for three days of empowerment and organizational training, and we are gathering in a large, sunny meeting room in a governmental building. Western garb is again the norm, even though most participants come from rural communities. I miss the color and flare of the traditional dress, while I also honor how this dress represents progress to these women. Meetings like this one help them spread their web of support farther, learn from each other's successes, and make the force of women's voices have a stronger impact on their wider community. I am thrilled to be here.

When I introduce myself to a new group, I always bring greetings from American sisters, play a tape of "Home on the Range "made by my Pilgrim Warrior sisters, and pass around photos of my family and my work in the U.S. One photo shows a woman in the Pilgrim Warrior Training embracing herself. I tell them that I include that picture because I believe empowerment begins with a commitment to love ourselves. After a day of the usual topics, it is 4 p.m. I can hardly stand up and I am losing my voice. If I weren't leaving the next day, I would have had to go into recuperation. I say to the women, "I have one more hour of training in Uganda before I go home. What would you like to talk about?" A hand in the back row goes up and a woman asks, "Please teach us how to love ourselves."

What follows is a delightful hour with more laughing and high energy than I have seen in the whole month of my visit. The shyness has dissolved. We are women having fun together, seriousness aside. We are talking about our lives instead of our businesses, groups, husbands and dilemmas. Suddenly we are talking about sexuality, orgasms, circles of support, and transitions. I show them flip charts I have not pulled out of my portfolio until now. One is a list of behaviors of "Women Who Love Too Much" (from the book by that title). Then I show them a list from the back of that book of behaviors of women who have healed themselves from that affliction. They loved the vision of the latter list. It is truly about loving ourselves. We end the day with me teaching them the song, "How Could Anyone Ever Tell You, You Are Anything Less than Beautiful." I keep glancing at my hostess to see if her face would give me any sense of whether this unplanned turn of events is totally inappropriate or not. Later in the car going home I ask her. She says, "No, we need more of this personal development training." I am relieved, and very grateful for that true connection that seems to drop below all the roles and customary politeness to the authentic womanhood we share, perhaps touching souls as well as minds.

As I pack my bags—now full of souvenirs—say my goodbyes, and head back across the world toward home, my heart is full. I have given my all. I have been embraced and enriched by new friends. I have deepened my understanding of how human beings can live on the edge of survival and ban together to make powerful things happen, like changing laws in favor of women's rights and sending more children to school. I have seen the stark difference that education makes in the trajectory of a life here and the passion for learning that propels people across that barrier. I have been moved and inspired by seeing how many European women are invested in the development of possibilities for women here, with N.A.W.O.U.'s 1000 member groups and village banks lifting women out of poverty and into greater strength and trust in themselves and what they can accomplish by working together. I have loved the Ugandan women's spontaneous singing and dancing that imbues every gathering with sparkle, rhythm, and communion of spirits. I have enjoyed getting off the clock, getting lost, and being found by those who did not expect to meet me, but embraced me with full enthusiasm when they did. I have been surprised daily by the leading of Spirit in all my endeavors and the grace of being able to laugh together in the midst of critical challenges.

My world has gotten bigger; I now know deeper compassion for the pain of a woman who looks at me and says, "What can I do when I have nothing?" I can be present to the reality of a single woman sitting on the city sidewalk calmly selling individual pencils as her sole income. I know what her hopes and dreams are. I know the painful reality of the woman who said, "Things can change for the better at any moment."

My acorn is happily exhausted, my wanderlust assuaged, my heart full, my body tired, and my soul grateful as I return home into the arms of eight Pilgrim Warrior sisters ready to hear stories, goggle at treasures, and give nurturing touch to this weary traveler. Their presence, their blatant enthusiasm, and the resonance between us feels like home. Their caring feeds my whole being as I rest, finally able to ponder what such a trip, with all the pouring out of words, images, experiences, traditions, and new challenges, can mean for our future.

I would return to Uganda a year later for another month, this time with a team of four, including my now twenty-year-old son, Nathan, who would do work with men. I would bring $250 donated to programs, $565 towards school fees for girls, and $500 for the Single Mothers revolving loan project. I am being a bridge between those of us with the privileges of access to public education and legal rights that are only dreams in Uganda. I feel the strength of so many allies meeting me and building the bridge together, allowing them in a small way to participate in creating this web of caring and support that will make all women stronger together. This bridge is, indeed, the spirit of the Beijing conference, where this adventure all began with a Pilgrim following the sound of a circle of women singing in the rain, and saying "Yes" to the simple question, "Can you come to Uganda?"

I made a second trip the following January and Nathan accompanied me and joined in the mission to share our experience with groups in the N.A.W.O.U.'s network of community empowerment groups.

Healing the Scars of War: Russia
2001

Larissa, at twenty-six, is tall and slender, with long, straight brown hair to the middle of her back, and eyes that hold a thousand secrets. She speaks English slowly and softly. She is from Moscow. We are roommates for a five-week training program in multi-cultural conflict resolution led by Armold Mindell in Portland, Oregon in 1999. "Why do you work just with women?" she asks as we are getting acquainted and I am telling her about the Pilgrim Warrior Training. I explain that because of sexism and female socialization, in mixed groups women often become listeners and men dominate the discourse. "Oh," she replies with surprise, "In Russia, the men are silent and the women do all the talking." Now it is my turn to be surprised. What grows into a friendship over the weeks of training turns into an invitation to bring my training to Russia. Having already done international training in Switzerland with women from seven

Larissa is on the left, Marina on the right

countries, I know language will be a challenge. The profound sexism of Uganda was a challenge, too. I wonder what the challenge will be in Russia.

Now I am being invited inside the country that my country has been in a "cold war" with for fifty years. Moving toward the unknown is always an intriguing endeavor. I am surprised to learn that well educated women in the other superpower of the world have no personal resources; there will be no compensation, so fundraising is once again in order. My network of women warriors has my back. Over 100 donors would participate, connecting with our spiritual and political sisters across the world, determined as we are to lift all women up and heal all cultures from the ravages of male domination. This time we would have the opportunity to heal the poisonous stereotypes that have created suspicion and mistrust between our two countries. It is a big assignment.

I need my co-trainer, ALisa[1] Starkweather, because there will be eighteen women for ten days in the training. ALisa is twenty years younger than me, and has been working with me for six years. She is a powerful energy work healer and ritual artist, as well as a leader in Shadow Work. She brings a fierce presence born of matching wits with life as a young single parent on her own. She knows the assignment of day to day existence and she brooks no excuses. I am in awe of her clarity and her courage. She keeps me aware of the reality of those who have less privilege than me in their lives. We pack and repack all our training materials, get our visas, book our flight though Amsterdam, and arrive in August, 2001.

That night we sleep on the floor of Larissa's two room apartment in a high-rise building in a suburb of Moscow. My first culture shock is opening her refrigerator when, due to the twelve hour time zone change, I am hungry in the middle of the night. All I find there are a few eggs, a quart of milk and half a stick of butter. I open the cabinets. There are a few dishes, no food. I would learn that Larissa, who is a Jungian therapist, and a single parent of a six-year-old boy, goes shopping every day for fresh food. Her pay check only allows for small purchases. There is no stocking up.

Experiencing this scarcity of provisions is just the beginning. As we pack her four-person car with all our baggage and head into traffic the next morning, the impact of communist utilitarian austerity is stark to my Western eyes. There are huge high rise apartments many blocks long and ten stories high lining six-lane highways on both sides as far as I can see. There is no landscaping around the buildings, no playgrounds, and no parking lots for cars (the average person doesn't own one.) The dull plainness of this urban environment is offset by the startling beauty of a forest of silver birch trees lining the highway as we speed out of the city.

We drive through enough small towns to know we are off the beaten track. Small wooden houses line the roads with beautifully carved and colorful shutters that remind me of the Hansel and Gretel story. The training center is at the end of a long dirt road into an old growth forest with no other buildings in sight. The two-story building is a camp that will house our sleeping, eating, and all our other activities for the week. Our vision quest will happen in the surrounding forest.

Meeting the eighteen women is like opening the pages of a fairy tale. Each woman appears extraordinarily beautiful to me and seems to radiate health. They range in age from eighteen to forty-two. They have made a very difficult financial choice to leave families and work for eight days. One woman named Marina is a physician in a government clinic. She tells me she earns the equivalent of $30 a week, and she needed her husband's approval to take the time away from earning that paycheck to do this training. I am stunned by the disparity between her plight and that of doctors in my country, who are among the top earners, and who, unlike Marina, have the privilege of freedom of choice about where to live and work.

All the talk is in Russian as they eat their breakfast of raw milk, farm-raised eggs and cheese, and home-made fresh bread. All ALisa and I can do is watch. They are bonding with each other, and we, as teachers, are set apart (another cultural difference we would need to work with.) As we enter into the work together, we soon learn that they love to sing, full-throated, with traditional pathos and gravity in their tones. We teach them our songs, and they gladly share theirs. Most of them do speak a little English, but are more comfortable with translation, which has a gentle way of slowing everything down so there is more time to take in all the nuances of what is happening in the room. They are eager, alert, and open as we move into our usual first day of exploring differences among the group members, bringing normal feelings of insecurity and resistance to joining a new group to the surface, to transform into trust with group support. We assume everyone has these reactions to joining a new group, and that if we try to hide them, we are left with coping behaviors such as being silent, or being critical of others, that blocks our sense of power, influence, and belonging.

What we aren't prepared for is that when we finish the program at 9 p.m., ready to drop into bed and be up at seven the next morning, they are ready to head to the sauna for another four hours. They stay up until 2 a.m. because it doesn't get dark here until midnight. They get up at 10 a.m., which would have been halfway through our plan for that morning. So we go with the flow, and spend precious midnight hours hanging out. I become acutely aware of how work-oriented I am, and how good they are at relaxing and playing. They are so comfortable in their collective nudity, and I notice that—unlike an American group of eighteen—only one is overweight. Their sense of sisterhood is palpable, with much more physical touching than we Americans are accustomed to.

Early in the training, we hold a circle where people call out an identity like "Have you gone to university, worked on a farm, or traveled?" Women who have experienced that would step into the center, then back out again. It is a way to get to know each other. Most of them have gone to university. None of them have travelled outside the country. Then ALisa asks "Was your family affected by World War II?" Every woman steps into the center. We are stunned. This is 2001. The war ended fifty-six years ago. Everyone here had not even been born yet. But everyone had lost a family member. We are touching the tip of what would become one of the most profound aspects of our work with these women.

As the story continues to unfold, we learn why it is that the women always speak and the men are silent as Larissa had reported. These women are the children whose parents are the offspring of the post-war Russia, when twenty million people were lost, including just about every able-bodied man. The men of their grandparents' generation were the ones left behind because of frailty of body or mind, or they came home war-torn. Unlike our story, where the men came home from the war as heroes and women went from factory work to raising children and being provided for, Russian women had to continue to be the providers. The men were weak, and the women were strong—too strong—it turns out, for a healthy gender balance.

When you stop to consider, do you know any culture that has a healthy gender balance? I don't, but doing international training shows me the different lenses through which to see this. Our work in America is to support women to come into their authentic selves, find and speak their truth, and break the glass ceiling of female socialization that holds them back from taking up space, influencing what happens, and leading the lives they want. For these Russian women, their power is a threat. It overwhelms the men who have been without empowered role models for two generations. I am seeing in their distraught faces the truth that armistice days are never the end of a war. One of

252 Out of Bounds

my stereotypes of Russia—that alcoholism is a big problem—is transformed as I understand what these people have suffered. I feel compassion for the powerlessness that the men who survived felt, and for what these women have had to struggle with in the wake of such immeasurable tragedy.

The women are showing us their struggle to reclaim a power they have had to put away in order to protect the men. They are sharing with us their fear of letting their power show, but for different reasons than American women have. They know they are more powerful than their men, and how threatening this power imbalance is to the fabric of their society. Only in this group of like-minded women, deep in the forest, is it safe for them to feel their mightiness, and therefore realize what they have forfeited and are living over and around instead of through. When we collectively give them permission to step into their power, they do it with a clarity and authentic truth that is beautiful to witness, and mutually empowering to all of us.

It seems that no matter what a woman's personal story is, the deeper truth we finally birth into is that no one has the power to hold us back unless we give it to them. Cries of "I want to be free!" turn into "I am free, and I'm never going back!" as we cheer, hold each other, and cry tears of joy together. This transformation in our own perception of ourselves requires women's community—away from the men—to feel into the depths of that feminine power, and find the courage to break the unwritten rules of society that tell us not to stand out. It seems to me—after fifteen years of doing this same work across many cultural differences—that what holds women back the most is their belief that to be true to themselves will hurt someone they care about or want approval and belonging from.

Mothers may be the biggest challengers to women's power. Mary Daly's writes in *Gynecology* that mothers are the perpetuators of the rules of Patriarch—the domination of the Father, and by extension the husband and the brother. They do their training in the rules out of a care that wants their daughter to be acceptable, to be marriageable, and therefore to survive. So the mothers teach their daughters not to make trouble, not to stand out, not to be angry, not to tell the truth, and not to compete with men. Until we can face these internalized scripts and dismantle them, they run our lives, limiting us to playing by other people's rules at our own expense.

The cry, "I don't want to be your servant" sharpens into "I am not your servant!" The speaker is casting off the mantle of womanhood handed to her at birth, and hearing the sound of her own authority on what is true for her and what she chooses for her life. Going beyond these internalized limits together, we find the strength to trust our truth and risk our authentic selves. We are no longer willing to forfeit that authentic self in order to belong. We draw on the strength of the group to sustain the costs that inevitably come as our significant relationships have to now learn to adjust to our bigger selves. Once this truth-telling self is reclaimed in voice, body, and spirit, she will not go willingly back into hiding. How to take that powerful self back out into the world is a challenge for any woman in any culture. ALisa and I can only share our stories, and stand with them in their solidarity with each other. They will find their way forward together.

I can't end this account of my trip to Russia without reporting two of the most astonishing stories I have ever encountered. When the training is over, two of the women who live in Moscow offer to show us around the city. They take us to Red Square, the seat of power for the Communist Party. Inside this walled city called the Kremlin, there are seven cathedrals. This is quite a surprise to us, as Communism to our knowledge is atheist. One cathedral is considered "Mother Russia." As Elana tells the story, when Napoleon marched across Russia to capture Moscow for his empire, the residents of the city knew they were outnumbered, so they packed up all their art and withdrew from the city. Napoleon marched into an empty city, and there was no triumph to be claimed. He decided to blow up this cathedral in order to leave his mark on the city. His troops laid a trail of dynamite powder, and just as they were about to light it, a thunderstorm arose and rained on the powder. Napoleon left, deprived again of his display of power. I stand in this magnificent building today, with ancient murals covering pillars, walls and dome, because of that storm (or the powers that be behind the storm—Mother Russia herself—as the story is told.)

The second story is also about a church, which begs the question of how and why the Communist Party ever imagined it could stamp out religion. Marina tells us about this church that stands on the bank of the river that passes through Moscow. Its graceful dome and pure white edifice fill the sky with a sense of peace. The communists of 1917, determined to obliterate the "opiate of the masses," destroyed this church. A huge pool of water formed in the former foundation that prevented construction of any other building on that site. For decades it was a public park. After Perestroika[2] in the 1990s, when leniency toward religion returned, the original architectural drawings were recovered, and the church was rebuilt on the same spot. But what about the pool of water, you ask? It receded when construction began.

These are stories of Russia's intimate connection to Nature and to the numinous. They are told with great reverence. It is healing for me to replace my stereotypes of the Russian people as enemy with a deep sense of camaraderie in our love of Nature. There is one more story that opens my eyes to the truth about governments. As the cold war between our two countries was building during the 1950s, I as a school child was being taught to crouch under my desk in the event of a nuclear attack because "the Russians are coming." When I share this account of my experience with our two friends, they tell us, "The people in Russia were never told that propaganda. We never feared an attack by the U.S." One of the gifts of travel, it seems, is a chance to re-write history with more information than you had before. I see now with this new perspective that the conjured-up fear in my childhood was meant to keep us cowering, so we would support the greatest arms race in the history of the world to protect us, a race that put us on top of the heap of nations and weapons, but kept us separated and blaming our "enemy" for all the trouble. Here we are now, embraced in the bosom of these beautiful Russian women, who were never our enemy. What a sad story, when loving each other is so easy. The bonds of sisterhood we have created together have succeeded in transforming the past.

I return home with a deep sense of healing. My childish images of Russia as dark and menacing are transformed into the beauty of white birch forests, sparkling eyes, deep-throated singing, broken hearts over the ravages of war, and the presence of mystery.

---

1. ALisa spells her name with capital A and L because she used to be Lisa

2. Perestroika: a political movement for reformation within the Communist Party of the Soviet Union during the 1980s (1986), widely associated with Soviet leader Mikhail Gorbachev and his glasnost (meaning "openness") policy reform. The literal meaning of perestroika is "restructuring", referring to the restructuring of the Soviet political and economic system.
Perestroika is often argued to be the cause of the dissolution of the Soviet Union, the revolutions of 1989 in Eastern Europe, and the end of the Cold War.[2] From Wikipedia.

Pilgrimage to Ground Zero:
New York City After 9/11
October 11, 2001

Today, September 11, 2001, I am travelling down Route 91 south at 8:00 a.m. with two colleagues to lead an organizational development training for a non-profit organization in Springfield, the largest city in Western Massachusetts. When we arrive at the office at 8:30 a.m., the staff of about fifteen are all clustered around a TV screen in the conference room. Two airplanes have flown into each of the Twin Towers just minutes apart in New York City's financial center. We join the anxious circle of on-lookers, and stare in astonishment at the smoking buildings. Another plane is reported to be flying toward the Pentagon, and a fourth, over Pennsylvania, might be heading toward the Capital as well. No one knows for sure. Those planes have been hijacked, and there is no communication with the crew.

Standing in our tight, silent circle, we edge toward the realization that—yes, indeed—our country is under attack. Who? What? Why? It's too soon for any answers. In the midst of the ensuing confusion, I remember just such a collective angst I felt once before in my lifetime—when President Kennedy had been shot, and no one knew if he was dead or alive. We don't know what has happened, but it seems like war has come to our land, bursting into our busy day like a carefully aimed arrow hitting its target—us.

It is clear in minutes that our training team's role for this morning will change. We are no longer outside consultants. We

are fellow Americans, needing group support ourselves to integrate what we are witnessing, and to figure out what action each
of us needs to take next. We shift from trainers to facilitators,
providing a safe space to hold all the reactions that are occur-
ring in the room. One person wants to leave work immediately
to call a friend who works in the World Trade Center. Another
wants to talk about the significance of the attacks being aimed at
the control centers of global capitalism. Another wants to ago-
nize with those caught on the 82nd floor with no escape. Another
wants to go and get her children out of school before they are
exposed to the news so she can tell them herself, gently. We listen and listen, sharing our own responses as well.

Now a stunned population is glued to the TV coast to coast,
watching in disbelief as unnamed assailants hold us all hostage
for hours. Most of the country had not witnessed the first two
crashes into the Twin Towers because we had been travelling
to work, in parking lots and on elevators, or in a different time
zone, but most everyone sees the next plane fly into the Pentagon an hour later, helpless to do anything to stop it. The plane
over Pennsylvania eventually crashes, due to a revolt by a few
heroic passengers who had heard by cell phone what had happened on the east coast as they were flying west, and assumed
they, too, would become a weapon of mass destruction if they
did not stop the flight. With the culmination of the disaster, all
flights across the country are grounded for the next three days,
while officials try to piece together the dimensions of the calamity that has befallen us.

Feelings of grief and horror are mixed with rage as more
than 3,000 perish in the rubble of the highest skyscrapers in the
biggest city of our land. An attack of this magnitude pulls our
politically deeply polarized country into a feeling of oneness. I
imagine that this hypnotic trance of national unity is like what
happened sixty years ago after the attack on our forces at Pearl
Harbor that propelled our nation into war. Will that happen

again? I have never felt under attack before, or the trance of my country as one. We are all left wondering—in anguish and anger—what will happen next.

The drumbeats of war start almost immediately, before we can begin to understand the why of what has happened. As quickly as President Bush demands retaliation against Afghanistan (where it is believed the perpetrators originated their plot), families of some of the victims in New York City form the "Families For a Peaceful Tomorrow" that stands for a peaceful resolution to the crisis, not more violence. The warmongers win the day, and less than two weeks later, our troops are attacking the militant, Islamic Taliban half-way around the world in Afghanistan. The transient feeling of national unity is shattered. Once again, Americans are polarized: war vs. peace; retaliation vs. trying to understand what caused this deep resentment of American power and provoked this attack on our soil. As I join the local protests against retaliation, I wonder: does this split of consciousness exist in every society? Are the two camps just two aspects of the human psyche, one side that fears war, and one side that is entranced by the thrill of imagined power to conquer an enemy? Is this ancient drama as simple as the difference between those who believe war is the answer and those who know that violence only begets more violence and never solves a problem? Such attacks bring these age-old questions to the fore, demanding answers.

War has come so close it is just 150 miles from my house. In the midst of this national nightmare of right/wrong thinking, my housemate Irene and I decide to journey—to make a pilgrimage—to New York City on the one month anniversary of the 9/11 attack. We drive right into lower Manhattan and park on a street just ten blocks from Ground Zero. We stand in stunned silence among the crowd that has gathered to stare at the torn buildings and the gigantic cranes lifting rubble that is three stories high. I find my attention wandering through minute detail—tire marks in the white dust that covers everything;

a pigeon perched on a sill below windows with no glass; traffic lights blinking routinely as if nothing unusual has occurred; and the man with his portable hotdog stand doing business with the onlookers ordering: "Mustard, please."

The highest towers in Manhattan are now reduced to a pile of mangled steel and cement, like a slain dragon downed in defeat. I ponder the victims of bombing attacks that we have perpetrated on foreign lands that wiped out precious human resources in a moment, and changed or ended lives and livelihoods forever just like here. I have watched those familiar scenes on television from the safety of my home with a kind of numbness. Here it is, the same familiar sight, right in front of me. Now it is mind-boggling. The stench of burned plastic still clings to the rubble four weeks after the fire. White dust that had once been people, buildings, desks, computers and files, now coats store fronts, still-parked cars, tree trunks, statues, and building ledges. I stare, wordless, at the remaining nearby sky scrapers shrouded head to toe in black plastic to keep the dust of the removal work out of their buildings. Many blown out windows have not yet been replaced. Hawkers on the street are selling American flags with replicas of the towers stenciled on them for a dollar, and more and more sweat shirts, caps, tee shirts, and flags, flags, flags. The biggest flag I see—it must be five stories high—is hanging over the entrance to the New York Stock Exchange a few blocks farther down Broadway. Do the financiers really believe patriotism can heal this wound to our national psyche?

As I walk down a side street, I read children's letters to the fire fighters: "Thanks for taking care of all the hurt people, " posted on store windows. I weep. I stare at photographs of the fallen and give money to their families. I write "May we bow our heads together in our shared grief for your loss, and in our fervent hope for healing and forgiveness for all of us," and leave my note among the hundreds on the make-shift bulletin board on Broadway, along with people from San Antonio, Texas who have sent a collage of notes to the people of New York. So, too, have the 1,000 who journeyed here on Oct. 5 from Oregon and left their prayers. Was their trip a pilgrimage, too, I wonder? I photograph a sketch of Jesus who is weeping while he holds the twin towers, one in each arm, in front of his chest. The initials "R.I.P." are written above his head. I accept a handout from the Billy Graham Crusade that says "Hate will not win" over a photo of New York City shrouded in smoke. A few steps farther on, we come to a bus stop where the back wall has become a neighborhood shrine. We worship in silence on this holy ground. We read countless "God Bless…" in several languages, with lots of English spelling errors, each message recording compassion, love, and prayers for peace for all to witness. I feel compelled to read every one. Irene adds a placard she has made that says: "Wage Peace" added ti a U.N. prayer for peace she had.

As we approach Broadway, we see a barricade that now holds us back from Ground Zero, still two blocks away. National Guard are stationed at every intersection. Across Broadway is an old stone church with a high steeple that seems like a beacon of light and hope in the midst of this chaos. The fence around it is covered with banners pleading for peace. I ask a young National Guardsman if we can cross Broadway and visit the church to pay our respects. "No," he replies, "It's only for the rescue workers now to go in and rest and pray." A sign near the door announces that chiropractic help is available inside. I think about their twelve hour shifts, as the first responders dig and lift rubble and bodies through stench, dust, and continual smoke. I give thanks for the body workers volunteering to touch those tired, strained, grieving bodies. Irene and I don't talk. Words cannot convey the depth of sorrow we are both experiencing. I take another photo to memorialize what is being seared into my being as I stand there—the paradox of horror and kindness, of cruelty and sacrifice.

We pass a small tee shirt shop with no door. It is open to

the street. The owner has left the shop just as it was on Sept. 11. Everything is covered in white ash, now the hallowed dust of buildings and bodies co-mingled in eternity here beneath our feet. Thoughts of Pompeii come to my mind. Dust has a way of getting into every crevice. New York will be sweeping forever. I take another photo.

Some New Yorkers on the street still wear face masks, remnants from a time just weeks ago when that sacred dust was finding its way into each survivor's lungs, touching their deepest core. Make-shift phone centers are still stationed on street corners—about sixteen pay phones mounted on a kind of trailer—with signs saying, "Calls limited to three minutes," a reminder of how many are still without land lines in lower Manhattan weeks after the tragedy.

What do I call it, this scene of destruction? "Tragedy" seems too simple. "Devastation?" "Armageddon?" The dimensions of the wreckage are unspeakable. Mangled, maimed, blackened, crunched, buckled, torn-asunder, pulverized...I'm hunting for any word that can contain this sight of ruin. I imagine this scene, so bizarre to my senses, would look all too familiar to anyone who lived through World War II in Europe, or Hanoi in Vietnam. My eyes are unaccustomed to such horror; I am new to the putrid smell, and the acrid taste in my mouth. I have come to intimately know this face of inhumanity, to know in my bones what war really is. It is this: vaporized lives, tortured families, vanished livelihoods for millions; it is disruption, disconnection, discontinuity with the past or the future. It is limbo. The past is erased; the future not imaginable. There is only the smell and the smoking rubble. In a way, it is a relief to have to grasp only glimpses of the wreckage down narrow streets with traffic lights blinking normally, and typical store signs above people going about their usual business. One store, called "Odd Job," is a surprising synchronicity facing my camera lens as I peer down the block at the stack of rubble.

I am standing—still silent as if in Church— peering down yet another street with another angle from which to glimpse the enormity of what has happened, when, unexpectedly, I come face to face with someone I know from home. She is from Sunderland, just ten miles away. She has participated in groups I have held in my loft, and I have done some consulting with her. We hug. We both feel surprised by the instant camaraderie that arises with someone who is familiar in a bizarre place. The sudden connection contradicts the isolation I didn't even know I was feeling until she appeared. We share our feelings of horror, incredulousness, and grief. We are quiet together. She mentions that the hotel where she is staying for a conference is back to 70% of business before 9/11, but the taxis are only back to 50%. We part, waving goodbye as other pilgrims pass between us searching the streets for answers.

We don't find the armory I had heard about on TV, where the families have gone to wait for news of their loved ones. I wanted to see all the pictures of the missing. I wanted to witness the depth of their loss. I wanted to grieve with the families. I see maybe a dozen such pictures along the streets and at the shrines, tied, nailed and propped together by those hungry to mark the place, the lost loved one, their grief, and the unspeakable emptiness the pictures make real. We are making our way back to the car when we round a corner, and there before us is a tiny fire station, whose door is just large enough for one fire engine to back into and park. We might have missed it entirely, except for the shrine out in front displaying photos of each of the twelve missing men from that company. It is Company 15, ladder 6 on South Street. Six young men in uniforms with Bermuda shorts on (it is still 70 degrees this October day) linger out front near the shrine, with its tribute to their fallen leaders. The chief is among the dead. I stand before his photo for a long time, looking into his middle-aged, clean shaven face with warm eyes. I remark to Irene that his seems to be one of the kindest faces I have ever seen.

Among the other pictures there are dads with very young children. We feel the heart break as we witness that loving connection that is now lost forever. The mothers are there too, who now have to carry on with the double grief—their own and their children's. Buckets of flowers have flags sticking out among the bouquets. Crucifixes on long chains hang above the photos. Someone has made a collage of the fire fighters at the scene that day, with the quote from the Bible: "Greater love hath no man than this that he lay down his life for his friends." I weep again, so grateful to let the tears finally flow and flow and flow. I take another photo.

When Irene and I round the next corner searching for a landmark to locate our car, we ask a maintenance man who is walking toward us for directions. He launches into his story of that morning a month ago, with all the children on the street of his neighborhood going to their first day of school. Over and over, he replicates with hand gestures and sound of the first plane approaching and impacting the tower. He tells us how he looked up in disbelief, and how, when he looks there now, there is nothing—only space. Emptiness. Huge emptiness in the midst of other mighty towers. He says he still expects to see the towers when he looks in that direction. I recognize this instant storytelling to strangers as a mark of the trauma still ravaging the occupants of lower Manhattan. I feel his angst, his powerlessness, his struggle to believe what has happened. I say a prayer for him, that he might know peace once again as we move on.

As we continue the last few blocks to where our car is parked, Irene and I remark that in all the years the towers were there—built in the 1970s—neither of us ever visited them nor desired to go to the top. I suddenly really get in my gut how tall they were—more than twice as high as anything near them on the skyline. How frightening it must have been to work that high up every day, let alone think of running down that many flights of stairs…or jumping out of the window…

I have found what I came to witness: the broken hearts, the smoke, the tears, the sense of terrible loss, and the people who lived it and continue to live it. I also found, among the people who survived, the resolve to rebuild, to pull together, and to remember. New York is a more human place to me now. I see the neighborhoods, the languages, and the faces of its people. Through all the diversity, there is the common humanness of shock, loss, and resolve to live so that those who are gone are not forgotten. Now I, too, feel a part of that resolve.

Did the victims of this travesty sacrifice? Are they innocent? Are the people who did this evil? Could they have been dissonants from two countries—Egypt and Saudi Arabia—whose corrupt governments are supported by enormous U.S. military aid that prohibits liberation movements from being able to bring change? Are these killers perhaps the true freedom fighters of their land, and we—the proponents of freedom—the guilty ones? What is their message to us when the two institutions they chose to attack (the World trade Center and the Pentagon) are repositories of the very power my country uses to control other countries and their economies? It is time to listen. To ponder. To learn.

When we reach our car, it seems so normal sitting there right where we left it six hours ago. It feels like we have been away much longer. As we head home through late afternoon traffic, we listen on the radio to a ceremony of commemoration being held in Washington, D.C. A flag is presented to a six year old girl who's Mom—her only kin—was killed in the Pentagon attack. She will be adopted. Then we learn that one in three children in Afghanistan are orphans from the terrible wars that we have supported and waged in that land. How do we make sense of such human pain, such injustice, such rage and frustration, such passion for peace, such longing for freedom? It is a tragic shame that our government sides with leaders in those lands who withhold freedom from their people, and then the hijackers kill us for revenge. We are all losers today. The empty space where the twin towers stood will be a constant reminder that we are in a global community and that community is in pain. Now we share that pain. Perhaps feeling that pain will bring a new identity of interconnectedness and accountability that will become a greater blessing for our national soul.

We pull into our driveway in Greenfield, Massachusetts, and drop wearily into our soft, safe, warm beds. I realize as I settle in that this pilgrimage cannot end. My home will never seem as surely safe as it did before I made this trip. I feel more vulnerable as I am pulled deeper into the pain of the global community. That pain reminds me daily to look deeper into the reasons for this tragedy. I am reminded of Arnold Mindell's teaching that all people who are denied freedom will likely become terrorists, and that is why he insists that all parties to a dispute must be present for his Worldwork to happen. I am reminded of the senseless creating of enemy that happened between Russia and the U.S. because we the people had no way to know each other and could be manipulated by our governments into fearing the other. I am reminded of Gandhi's teaching that everyone has a piece of the truth and no one has the whole truth. These lessons are being lost on my countrymen who are rushing to war to retaliate, to get out of their vulnerability, to be right about those terrorists who are all dead now, so they have no voice to tell us why they did what they did. We are left with our own hunger for understanding, and our hunger for peace and sanity. I hear the words of Rumi's poem arising in my tiredness: "There is a field out beyond right and wrong. I'll meet you there." I say one more prayer, this time for the families of the martyred terrorists, before I fall asleep.

Transformation in the Rubble:
New Orleans
2005

We like to remember New Orleans for its flair, color, and sound—for being a party town, and "let the good times roll." Few remember that it was the slave trade capital of the world, continuing that black market long after it was illegal. The Plantation mentality—that was always just below the surface of awareness—has been exposed now, as the city gasps and reels from the worst hurricane in one hundred years that put the city under water, destroyed levies and washed away mostly black neighborhoods. As we witness the federal government bungling rescue efforts, and leaving a stadium full of thousands of black refugees to swelter in the hot sun for seven days, with little water and meager bathrooms soon overflowing—we call it ugly, shocking. It is history, living history. Has the culture of the South ever taken care of its black people? Now the whole world is watching as the homeless are moved to far away cities, others into tiny trailers full of formaldehyde. Schools and churches that were once the center of a community are empty. A huge national movement has arisen to meet the need to clean up debris, and clean out black, dangerous mold from houses still intact that were under water for days. I join this army of volunteers, knowing "There but for fortune go you or I. . . ." (Phil Ochs song.)

It's January, six months after the devastation. I feel acutely out of place as a northern white woman stepping off the plane into a culture I have never known. I am met by one of our team of twenty-one from Amherst College who are there for a week to volunteer in the United Methodist Storm Relief Center. Louise drives me to this very large, elegantly white church with a majestic steeple which will be my home for the next eight days. My housemate, Irene, and I are immediately put to work clearing a storage area outside for a delivery of sheetrock and other construction materials. This church is the hub of a very comprehensive recovery program for all the devastated neighborhoods of the city. The minister, Jack O'Dell, tells us later, "I've always believed the church is only about mission."

In the office of the Recovery Center, Leslie has a white board on the wall where she keeps track of all the volunteer groups in the city today—twenty-one from Mass, twelve from Oregon, 120 from New Jersey, fifty from Chicago, and thirty Mennonites coming from many communities in shifts. One shift arrives as the other is leaving, always on their own bus, and making it known they are there only to work with families who have no insurance, since that is their choice as well—they are each other's insurance. Our group forms two teams, each with a rented van. Every morning at 8:30 a.m. we gather with all the other teams in the parking lot of the church. Leslie has prepared a clipboard for each team, which holds an application from a home owner, with a description of work, a map quest printout of the location, a liability form for the recipients to sign, and a report for what work was done and still needs doing. There is a tool room next to the office, where teams can borrow whatever tools they need for their job that day, to be returned at the end of the day. A whole room full of tools for the taking is a handywoman's dream!

Our team of ten (the number that would fit into a van) go to a new location almost every day. We dub ourselves the "Extreme Makeover Team." That's what we feel like when piling out of the van in front of a strange house, tools, masks and gloves ready to do whatever is needed. The work entails mostly removing moldy sheetrock, sometimes only two to four feet up from the floor, but sometimes whole walls and even ceilings. One house we work on had stood in four feet of water for sixteen days. The owner, who is there to greet us, tells us, "I can't even go in the house anymore, I'm so afraid of the smell." When I go in, I am puzzled. It doesn't smell that bad to me. Then I begin to realize that the smell is part of the trauma for this homeowner. The flood was three months ago but it is still happening for him. The second day we come, he calls his wife, Cindy, who is living 160 miles away, and says, "You have to come meet these people." She drives the 160 miles, gets out of her car next to a pile of rubble on the curb that we had made the day before that is as long as the house and shoulder high, and she says, "Who are you people?"

One hundred and sixty hours of free labor later, with their house a shell of studs, Cindy has bought us a traditional New Orleans "King Cake," called that because somewhere in the batter is a tiny replica of the baby Jesus. She writes down all our addresses. One of our group has planted yellow pansies by their back door step. Cindy cries, saying, "Those flowers give me so much hope."

Everywhere we go, we roll up our sleeves and get to work, happy as the seven dwarfs. Sometimes we even sing "Hi ho, hi ho, it's off to work we go!" There is a simplicity about what needs to be done. No one gives any orders. We all take up a job, drop it when our hands are needed elsewhere, share tools easily, and feel the oneness of mind and heart that guides our work. We cook simple meals back at the church with menus that have been planned and shopped for by a support team back in Amherst. We sleep on air mattresses provided by the church, occupying the unused Sunday school rooms and bathrooms. The church comes to feel like the old settlement houses of Jane Adams' day (1900s), with the space open to meet multiple needs of the local community.

One day we go to the home of Pat, a fourth grade school teacher, who has taken the day off from work to meet us and show us what to do. Her home is paneled, but all the paneling has to come down because there is sheetrock behind it. We can't even see the mold, but we have to assume it is there as we rip out seemingly OK paneling. She tells us about the influx of children into her school since the flood who are reading way below grade level, and what it is like for her to work with children who are just sitting with glazed-over eyes. She says there are now counselors in all the schools, but they are overwhelmed because every child is in need. The schools are dealing with the huge drop in their own numbers due to evacuation, as well as the newly displaced children whose schools have been destroyed. New Orleans, once a population of 480,000 is now 60,000. Pastor Jack has also lost half of his congregation with all the financial implications of that. As we rip out the destroyed insulation from her attic, Pat leaves to go and buy us all lunch—Louisiana Po-Boys (ground beef and spices, dripping in oil.)

As we sit in the front yard eating lunch, Pat tells us about her next door neighbor, Miss Rose, who is elderly and lives alone. Irene and I, being social workers, decide to go knock on her door and see if she would like to fill out an application for a volunteer team. About a minute after we start knocking, a voice from inside grunts, "What do you want? Who are you? I don't open my door." We talk for about five minutes through a closed door before Rose opens it a crack and peers out. About five feet tall, with long gray hair under a wool cap, her brown eyes look in amazement at the two of us—also elders. She finally relaxes and lets us in. She shows us through her house, furniture piled in the middle of every room and sheet rock removed up to waist level everywhere. At least the mold is out of the walls, but the smell is still very strong.

She shows us out into her backyard, which is full of debris from the flooding of Lake Ponchatrain. There are layers of mud, leaves, branches, and her own fallen trees. Irene and I decide to stay and work in her backyard. Rose sits and watches us in a chair by her back door. After an hour, she comes out with two glasses of iced tea. An hour later, she comes again with two cups of coffee, and in another hour with a batch of freshly baked warm cookies. Finally she brings out her boom box and a tape of Ella Fitzgerald, and Irene and I continue our schlepping with a skip to the beat. From a locked door and the isolation of an 80 year-old living alone in the midst of utter disruption, Rose is now throwing a party! Her final act is to bring out her Comet and scour her plastic porch chairs so we can sit down. The next day we go back with the pansy lady who has brought enough flowers for Pat's and Rose's yard too. She has also bought a bird feeder and seeds for Rose. Those pansies we planted in Rose's backyard are planted in my heart as well, and I can still hear her "God bless you, God bless you" as she waves goodbye to us with her restored spirit and tidy backyard.

In spite of the bright moments of satisfaction and connection, we can still feel the presence of utter hopelessness as we drive through the ninth ward where there is total destruction. There are no people here now, and no renovation happening. This ward is where the storm surge washed houses off their foundations and demolished them. I see a house that had crashed into a huge tree and just wrapped around it. All the houses still contain furniture, which lays strewn upside down in muddy piles with everything broken. Here is where we find Common Ground, another relief operation. They are a tent city with a big sign on the curb that reads, "Solidarity, not charity."

They are providing food, free legal assistance, clothing, tools, and all kinds of cleaning and toiletries for the taking. They have 250 volunteers, again mostly young people, staffing their operation. They are really on the front lines, and unlike us, they are here to stay.

The day before I complete my week, Irene and I walk two miles from the church to a soup kitchen to volunteer. We find our way to a school kitchen where Operation Blessing is feeding 2000 people three times a day in three different locations. We open cans for an hour and stir two waist-high vats of beef stew. A group of students from Iona College in New Jersey are doing twelve hour shifts here. The head staff are part of a group called "Bikers for Jesus." They are really big guys with black leather vests and bare arms full of tattoos, driving fork lifts between eighteen-wheeler trucks full of donated food. Kim, from Florida, who is heading up the cooking, is a nurse and full time volunteer with Habitat for Humanity. She has been in the kitchen since Oct. When I ask her how she got here, her one-word answer is, "God." She had come up to do sheet-rocking for pay, but ended up volunteering here. When we finish our jobs in the kitchen, we sit with folks from the neighborhood as they eat, and listen to their stories. We tell them about the relief center and later we go back to the church to get applications for them to fill out.

I have never done disaster relief work before. Every day brings a new awareness of our lives of privilege and relative safety back home, with access to anything we need to live life comfortably. Being in New Orleans is like being in a foreign land, yet it is my own country. It is a face of my country I am meeting for the first time. I am experiencing not just the poverty but the blatant disregard for human suffering that is an ordinary part of life for the black people of New Orleans. I am also meeting this incredible army of compassionate people from unlikely sources such as these Bikers for Jesus, and the white suburbanite Christians up to their elbows in beef stew. And I am meeting the other Northerners like myself who, maybe like those freedom riders of the 1950s, are coming to the South for the first time to help change the story of discrimination happening here. I am way out of my comfort zone—way out of bounds from anything I have ever done before—yet I am finding ways to fit in and ways to lean into the challenge, even if it is stirring a vat of beef stew or hauling toxic mold to the curb until the pile is so high we can't heave the next load without it tumbling back down at our feet. Every night after dinner the melodic voices of the Mennonite men singing in four part harmony fills the church basement where we all eat and sleep together.

The people here don't need my training skills or my wealth of experience. They need my willing hands, feet, and strong back. Being of use in this way is so very different from anything I have done before, and has perhaps brought me closer to feeling our common humanity than most of the other endeavors I have undertaken. With the homeowners, I have lived the transformation from rubble to possibility. With the Bikers, I have celebrated the transformation from stranger to friend. Going from home to home, I have embodied the transformation from observer of tragedy to an agent of hope, of renewal, and of solidarity with those who are suffering. I am humbled by the service of the Mennonites and the Bikers, who give their all to aid strangers. I am blessed by Rose who opened her door and then her heart to our presence and caring. The night before we leave, our team from Western Mass has our own walk down Bourbon Street, and finds a great restaurant with a rip-roaring jazz band and we have a fabulous farewell dinner together. I am the richer for having travelled out of my normal life into this chaos, where I have found great beauty of spirit. Is it "God" who led me here as well? Is this, after all, Buckie Fuller's God as verb?

In the Hands of the Gods: Bali
2006

"Blam, bam!" The sound of metal crashing on metal disturbs my peace before 6 a.m. in safe, sleepy Greenfield as a garbage truck finishes emptying the bin near my bedroom window. I'm irate! It's against the law to disturb the peace before 7 a.m. I'm tempted to pick up the phone and call the police, but I already know it is a law that is not enforced. Waking a whole neighborhood at 5:45 a.m. is just business as usual, just "getting the job done." Focusing on my breath, my flash of anger subsiding, I wonder if I will get back to sleep. Suddenly I am surprised by a thought: it isn't a bomb going off. Now in my half-sleep reverie, I am pondering how the Iraqi people dare to fall asleep at night, with bombs exploding around them as our country perpetuates war in their streets for the last three agonizing years. How do they find the inner strength to keep their sanity in the midst of constant obliteration of their peace? Surely there is no one for them to call, "Hey, someone just dropped a bomb in my neighborhood and woke me up. That's against the law! Make them stop!"

Now I am wide awake. I imagine their pleas and once again feel my powerlessness to help them. Barbara Kingsolver's words in *Small Wonder* are still with me from my bedtime reading last night, "My heart's edge feels as dull and pocked as an old shovel as it scooped low to take on this new weight, the rubble and grief of war." I am struggling with that dull edge inside myself, too,

274 Out of Bounds

as I bear the psychic burden of crimes against humanity done in my name with no end in sight. No amount of protest seems to matter to the powers that be. Weary, hopeless feelings swell and subside in me, gnawing at my conscience to find relief, to find transformation. I am craving respite from this madness my country is perpetrating on the Arab world.

I want to go to Shangri-La. I want to find a place I can go with my hunger for beauty, calm, and kindness. I am ready to let simple peacefulness be the reason for a long, long journey away from the utter unpeacefulness of my life. I had heard Jean Houston report once at a conference that Bali is a country of artists, a vocation so common that there is not even a word for being one in their language. The people there work their fields in the morning and make art for the temple in the afternoon. That scenario sounds like just what I am needing. It is the fall of 2006, and I want refuge from the storms of war. I am longing for time alone, for time out, and an artist's date with myself. I book passage and journey far, far across my own continent, and across the mighty Pacific Ocean, to see what would arise on this tiny island of artists in the land of Indonesia.

A very soft-spoken, Western-dressed, balding man with a friendly countenance, whom I had contacted online, picks me up at the airport. As we drive north in his shinny SUV through the congested tourist area of the southern edge of Bali, we are heading for the artistic capital city of Ubud. After two hours of smooth travelling through rolling green hills, quiet palm trees and simple rice paddies, I know we are close when, gradually, both sides of the two lane road begin to be lined with wood carving shops. Life-size statues of animals, people, and plants of all kinds carved in beautifully grained mahogany and teak are displayed by the road side. It is as if we are driving through a museum, or a gigantic outdoor gallery. Arriving in the town of about 20,000, we come to the main temple at the center, with its towering, thin, ornately carved spires gleaming with gold paint in the sunlight. The four main roads of the town radiate out from there, all lined with small, one-story shops that double as homes and studios. There are also tiny specialty restaurants, and lush, blooming trees. People ride on bicycles, scooters, donkeys, trucks and taxis. Dogs, cats and chickens mingle with human traffic.

I find a small, one-room cottage for rent for about eight dollars a night. It is one of seven cottages located behind a store front that is also my host's home. The one-room cottages ring a tropical haven of ferns six-feet tall, trees two stories high, and a variety of tropical flowers blooming along the path that circles the enclosure and connects the cottages. We are completely hidden from the street with its bustling traffic. I have found my little Shangri-La! Every morning when I awake about 6 a.m., I find a prayer offering of a spoonful of rice, a cookie, one flower and a stick of burning incense all cradled in a banana tree leaf on my doorstep, along with a gentle knock from my hostess, inquiring what I would like for breakfast. I always ask for fruit, because she gives me such a full bowl of it that I can eat half and carry the other half for my lunch. The pineapple is always sweet, never disappointing, as is so often the case back home when it has travelled a thousand miles.

Wandering the streets of Ubud, I see shingles hanging out on signposts beside doorways, with invitations to join the resident artist in whatever their craft is—batik, silver jewelry, mask-carving, cooking, dance, puppetry, drumming, Balinese orchestra music—all the crafts of this art-centered culture. I have never seen anything like this in all my travels. The Balinese artists want their guests to join them by touching, making, and participating in performance, color, textile, sound, smell and taste. Instead of just buying crafts, I am being invited to learn how to make them. The artist in me jumps for joy. In this swirl of color, cloth, wood, metal, and textures of all kinds, I can forget the world of bombs, protests, and collective madness. Here I am surrounded by gentleness, kindness, welcome and generosity. The open-heart-edness of these Balinese people begins to sooth my own heart. They are offering me just what I need—time with the artist in me, and time to be with beauty.

I follow my fancy into different studios, trying my hand at batik, mask-carving, and Balinese cooking, complete with a shopping trip to the market to learn about their spices. Every evening I attend a cultural event of puppetry, Balinese music, or dance. I absorb the strength of ancient tradition in their extraordinary hand, eye and foot movements accompanying their clanging music and classical stories.

In the batik studio, where I would spend three days, I pour through texts of ancient Balinese art and find a magical bird perched atop a stout, short tree. I take it back to my quarters, lay out a plain white sheet on my bed, and proceed to replicate the bird and tree with a pencil, designing what would eventually become a floor-length dress. What comes forth that night surprises me with a talent for drawing I have never recognized before. In the presence of these generous artisans of Bali, something deep inside me is being invited to bubble up. I am discovering aspects of who I am that my own culture has never called forth. This awakening feels similar to meeting my healer within through the portal of the karmic clearing work I did in Galisteo, New Mexico with Chris Griscom. I am expanding to hold more of what Life is about. This is one of the true gifts of travel.

The next day, when I return with my drawing, I am led by the apprentice to the master through the process of outlining each stroke of the pencil with hot wax. He is at my elbow constantly, sometimes literally guiding my hand, as I learn to use the stylus containing hot wax. I flash back to the same feeling of surprise by the physical contact and sense of receiving something indescribable that I had felt when the Chinese woman in Shanghai stood behind me and moved my whole body through the gestures of her Tai Chi tradition. I know I am in good hands. I feel uncertain, as one learning a skill for the first time does, but relaxed and happy, letting this Balinese artisan work through me as I learn to meet my own artist self. I am fulfilling my dream about coming to this Shangri-La.

Next comes the painting. The master in the studio comes over to me now that I am past the first step and ready for his expertise. He shows me how, just as with watercolor, I can blend one color into another over the wax lines. When the paint is dry, the garment is plunged into boiling water to melt the wax away. What remains are white lines wherever the wax has covered the original lines on the fabric. Now the entire design must be covered with wax, following the exterior border exactly. When

that dries, the entire garment is dipped in blue dye to give a background to all that is not the design, and finally, another dip in boiling water eliminates the last wax coating. *Voila!* I have an elegant dress of my own making, complete with a tropical flower design on the back, also copied from the ancient text. I also have a few white blotches where I accidentally dripped hot wax, a telltale sign that an amateur has been at work. I laugh whenever I notice them, remembering this bold experiment for a beginner, and how proud I am of the outcome. I find a seamstress who for pennies sews my creation together into a dress. I will now be able to show off my Bali artist's date experience whenever I have an occasion to dress up.

My memories of dance classes as a child are mostly of awkwardness and feeling like I was out of my element. I loved tap dancing, but ballet was too slow and deliberate. I don't remember being aware that important cultural traditions were being passed on through the dance. It was for fun, but it was no big deal. Nor do I remember teachers coming up behind me to guide my movements into some precise gesture as if my dance required that my gestures be exact. But this is what I witness when I go daily to watch the traditional dance classes for children of all ages in the yard of the main temple. There are so many children present I wonder if they are all the children in the town, and if this is a mandated cultural practice. Grouped by age, I see adults leaning over children as young as four and as old as fifteen, moving their hands, heads, torsos and feet in the intricate patterns unique to this place. I marvel yet again at the intimate physical contact, and the sacredness of the tradition the teachers convey with their focus and discipline. I imagine the children must feel inducted into a sense of belonging in a long lineage anchored to this place. I notice a pang of regret in the back of my throat as I wonder what, if anything, anchors me to such a lineage. I can't come up with anything beyond singing hymns written long ago, or maybe Christmas caroling. But no adult ever stood behind me to show me how. I am witnessing how an ancient culture is living today through their children. It feels new to me; it feels sacred.

Early in my sojourn here I see a procession of as many as twenty women walking slowly, single-file, with their silk billowy-sleeved blouses and flowing sarongs, making their way through the main street to a local temple to celebrate the birthday of that temple. They each balance three-foot high headdresses made entirely of fruit and flowers on their heads. The elegance of their posture, combined with their silence, their gracefulness, and the brilliant colors of bananas, oranges, pineapples, mangoes, apples, and flowers is a work of art in motion. I think, "This is what Jean Houston was talking about. These women are making art for the temple." I hadn't thought before now that their art is not of objects; they make their art with their bodies. I would learn that there are more than 365 temples in Bali, so there is a birthday celebration such as I am witnessing every day on the island. I follow the procession for about twenty minutes down narrow streets that twist and turn to the outskirts of the town, where the temple of the day—constructed entirely of stone—is sitting in quiet majesty in the forest, surrounded by a high stone fence. The balance of these gorgeous but heavy adornments on their heads is unflinching. I am spellbound, mesmerized, entranced by this spectacle of grace, skill and beauty.

Tourists are not allowed to enter the temples when a celebration is happening, but we are allowed to lean over the chest-high stone wall with our cameras in hand, and photograph the event from a respectable distance. We see the women, one by one, mount a stone staircase in the center of the temple courtyard to an altar about twenty-five feet from the dirt floor. They each carefully lift their headdress and place it on the altar, and return by another staircase going down the opposite side of the altar. The men in their sarongs, with matching cloth headbands and bare chests, gather at the base of the altar with drums, bells and horns in what appears to be a support role. This seems to be a female ritual.

I notice how the Balinese women of my compound are also the ones who perform daily rituals at a small temple in the yard of their home, where images of Shiva and Shakti are honored. Around town, I see women gathered in twos and threes during the afternoons, weaving banana leaves into receptacles for the offerings—little packets of rice, flowers, and burning incense—that will be placed on every doorstep at the dawn of each new day. As I walk the streets, I try to be careful not to step on the remnants of these offerings that seem to be all over the sidewalk. One day I notice that they let the dogs eat the offerings, so I ask my hostess why. She explains, "Once the offering is made, the object is no longer significant. It is the act of devotion that matters." I take in this seemingly strange custom, wondering if my people have any such practice of devotion. Maybe the Catholics do with their rosaries, genuflecting and crossing themselves when they enter a church or are about to shoot a basket, but I am a Protestant. Communion twice a year comes to mind, but daily? I don't think so.

As the daily processions to the temple follow one after another, I begin to realize that for the Balinese, their whole life is lived in a very present relationship with their gods. Returning late one afternoon to my cottage, I come across a group of three women making the banana leaf receptacles as they prepare for the next day. I stop to ask them more about the meaning of their daily offering. "Our daily devotion is aimed at keeping our community focused on maintaining balance between the realms of the Gods, the humans, and the underworld (which means forces of evil.) Our daily offerings are acts of awareness, reverence, and prayerful intention." I understand. I am touched by their simple habit with its vast implications. I have never heard the dynamic push-pull of good and evil described so simply.

My hostess goes on to explain to me that they know they are not in control of what happens. Their devotion is a prayer for protection and good luck. Any disease, Al Qaeda bomb, or pest infestation is potentially devastating. They pray hard. I sense the humility in their acceptance of their naked vulnerability to the vicissitudes of nature and politics. They live with daily reminders of the rumbling Gods of the underworld, brought into present awareness through ritual danced with elaborate costumes, and bigger-than-life masks that usually feature mocking tongues sticking out, and mirrors. Ah, I catch the jolt of cultural wisdom! These Gods must be laughing at the humans, with their illusions of being in control. And the mirrors, are they for us to see our own reflection in the rumblings of the underworld?

Yet another dramatization of living life in the hands of the gods are the statues in the rotaries at the entrance to every small town. Where we might have a garden, or a statue of a military hero, the Balinese have larger-than-life replicas of their gods and goddesses, all carved in concrete. Some are either astride horses fifteen-feet tall or driving chariots. One Goddess figure is surrounded by a ring of fire reaching thirty feet in the air. Every time I come upon such a statue unexpectedly I am taken aback by their size and majesty, and I imagine that is exactly the impression they are meant to have. They shout their message: presence! At one of the rotaries, I see a large tree trunk wrapped in black and white checkered cloth, the same as we would use for a table cloth. I later see men who are processing to the temple using the same cloth as a sarong.

When I ask my hostess about the symbolism of this cloth, she explains that the black and white squares represent good and evil, and in Hinduism, the most they hope for is a balance. Something deep inside me resonates with this message, this choice about how to relate to unknown forces that do seem to come when they will and wreak havoc in our lives. I ponder what could possibly create balance with such hidden, mysterious, and unexplainable but real forces. I have been taught that by doing good deeds, good can triumph over evil. I have never seriously thought about a balance being possible, or even the desired outcome, but I am taking lessons. Their way seems more grounded in reality than mine.

Now the master in the batik studio, who I have befriended over the three days of working in his studio, is teaching me about Balinese culture. "The Balinese hold harmony in their community as their highest value," he tells me. "It is a sign of being in right relationship with the gods. Because we are so vulnerable to forces beyond our control, we are very mindful of the rituals that sustain right relationship." I can feel how much he wants me to understand this, as if he knows this is one of the most important teachings his culture has to give to the world. I am all ears. I want to understand this. It feels new to me, yet I can sense a resonance with the lessons Alejandra in Nicaragua was wanting to give me, the courage and clarity of her culture withstanding constant war-making by the hands of the Contra, funded by my government. Surely the best she could hope for was a balance of mindfulness with the mindlessness of daily killing. There are so many important lessons I have to leave home to learn. My heart and my mind are open, receiving the grace, humility and wisdom being offered.

Near the end of my time in Bali, I do a little wandering from Ubud, and find myself at the seacoast waiting for a ferry to carry me to a near-by island. I realize I don't want to leave Bali. Being fluid and spontaneous in the moment, I hire a taxi and ask the driver what there is to visit in the vicinity. He drives me up a nearby mountain to a small village that has an old palace, now a hotel and restaurant. On the grounds of this palace, I happen unexpectedly onto one of my most treasured experiences. There is a very large pool, with a rectangular shape maybe fifty feet long and twenty feet wide, and a cement edge. Scattered throughout the pool are life-size statues of gods and goddesses on pedestals that are placed right at the water's surface. As I come to the edge of the pool, I discover that there are stepping stones wandering among the statues, meant for people to walk upon. As I step out onto the first one, I see green plants living below the surface of the water and fish swimming in and out among the ten foot long ferns. As I move out from the edge on the stepping stones, I have the sensation that I am walking on water! I spend an hour repeating this experience over and over, entranced by the magical feeling and the wonder of the world beneath my feet. My dream of Shangri-La comes to life again. I am here. Paradise is really happening.

As I am returning to the lodge where the taxi driver dropped me to inquire about a room, a young man on a motorcycle approaches me and offers for a few dollars to take me on a ride through the rice patties around the village. Being up for adventure, and feeling totally safe in this island paradise, I hop on the back of his cycle and off we go. This is just the kind of travel I love! After half an hour of bumping along the dykes of the patties, and seeing rice growing up closer than I ever have before, we end up at his mother's thatched roof hut in the midst of a forest. With chickens and pigs wandering around the fenced-in compound of her homestead, she welcomes me with an offer of tea. She doesn't speak English as her son does, but we make the best of two open hearts meeting around the ancient ritual of welcome: food. Here I am again, way out of bounds, on the back of a stranger's motorcycle, drinking tea in a Balinese forest. The welcome I feel is so archetypal, reminiscent of Esther in Albuquerque, the village women of Jordon, Ghana, Malawi and Uganda, and Alejandra in Nicaragua. I feel at home. I am grateful.

The date on the calendar gently but firmly nudges me to prepare to return to my home. I pack my bags with jewelry, carvings, twenty-five Balinese ponchos to sell to my friends (ah, that ancient Bontecou merchant blood flowing through my veins— I never pass up an opportunity!), a camera full of precious moments to share, wisdom to ponder, and of course, my very special batik dress. I bid farewell to my little bungalow, my quiet space in which to savor all that this tiny Shangri-La has gifted me with. I thank my hostess, who has made me a special offering for my journey home, and head for the airport. The long flight home gives me time to ponder much about what I have seen and learned while among these conscious, care-full, religious people. I have just spent two weeks among people who seem to understand how to create peace. They understand the assignment of walking between the worlds of right and wrong, seeking balance instead of control. They have no illusions about good conquering evil. They seem to understand how to see themselves in the mirrors of the underworld gods and respond with humility, prayer, and acceptance of what is. They are not espousing perfection, dominance, or righteousness, all so familiar in my cultural story. I wonder what my leaders, with their "Shock and Awe" claims to righteousness and power would see if they were confronted with mirrors from the gods of the underworld?

I marvel at how the Balinese embody art; they know how to make it an experience of walking on water, and how to put it in service to their relationship with their gods on a daily basis. It is not a commodity to possess; it is a means to an end: relationship. They know how to keep an ancient culture alive by passing it on to their children through dance, from very early ages through the teens who, when they finish their classes, whip off their sarongs and take off on modern bikes in flip flops and cut-off jeans. They know that making an offering is what matters, not what happens to the offering a minute later when the dogs come along and eat it all up, leaving the burning incense and empty banana leaf to blow away in the wind. They are not embarrassed to pray for good luck, just like the Arabs I knew in Beirut, who wore a replica of an open palm around their necks as a protection from bad luck. I guess we Americans have the four leaf clover and the horseshoe, but last time I checked those symbols calling for good luck don't have any relationship to the gods of the underworld.

The Balinese have shown me what it means to live your life in the hands of the gods. They are prepared, as we are not, for the inevitable struggle with the forces of the underworld. They meet trouble pre-emptively and collectively, whereas we are usually caught unsuspecting and alone in our individual crisis. Our cultural belief about good triumphing over evil leaves us all feeling like failures when trouble hits. I wonder if perhaps we come closest to understanding that balance in the Serenity Prayer of the Twelve Step Program, when we pray–that is, humbly ask to be given—the serenity to accept the things we cannot change, the courage to change the things we can, and the wisdom—there it is, the balance—to know the difference. I would like to believe that my people could come to understand that peace in our communities begins with peace in our relationship with our gods, but I am afraid we have too much diversity in our beliefs about gods for it ever to form the rock bed of our society. I treasure the wisdom I have learned from the Balinese about being peaceful, and how it comes through in the way they walk, the gentle tones in which they speak, and their easy smile for a stranger.

I cross the great Pacific Ocean and familiar continent, and I am finally home again. The treasures I found in Bali are now a living part of me. I find myself praying more. I dream of the Goddess surrounded by a ring of fire beaming protection with her mightiness. Every time I put on my gorgeous batik dress, I experience again the amazement of what I was able to create under the tender care of those artisans. I have exotic spices tucked away in my kitchen cabinet. I have a beautiful carving in my entry way and one on my bathroom counter greeting me every morning with her headdress of fruit, reminding me of the importance of devotion. A carved and painted mythical bird sits on my back porch greeting visitors. I am full. I am content. The artist in me has found her place in the scheme of my life. I bring home a sense of living peace that is sacred and transformative, even as I re-enter the daily drumbeats of war.

> *May I find the humility to walk between the worlds as the Balinese people do, mindful that my life, too, is lived in the hands of the gods.*

> *May I strive for the mindfulness to create balance that comes from respect, devotion and authentic, humble petition.*

> *May I remember daily that communal harmony is a mirror of right relationship with the gods, and make that a living truth in all my relationships, as the Balinese strive to do.*

> *May I cherish the many blessings I received from this Shangri-La that is Bali.*

Cry for Justice: Palestine 2012

"What is the purpose of your visit?"
"To visit the Holy Lands" *(it's a lie.)*
"Where are you staying?"
"The Jerusalem Hotel." *(Another lie.)*
"Are you going to the West Bank?"
"Are there any Holy Lands there?" *(I'm not answering the question.)*

W hy am I not telling the truth—that I am a peace activist coming to support the Palestinians, to help pick their olive harvest, and to meet other peace activists in Israel as well as the West Bank? I would be refused entry into Israel and be sent home on the next plane. Our group leader, Sherrill, has prompted us well. She is retained by the authorities for an hour of questioning before she is allowed to continue her journey because she has been here many times before.

I have never had to lie at the border of a country in all my fifty years of world travel. But I am entering an apartheid system (so named by President Jimmy Carter during his visit in 2006) that is tightly controlled by the Israeli government. This is a land of rules, check-points, uniforms, guns, gates, walls, permits required to pass, and permits denied. My first impression of Israel is that of a land steeped in militarism that derives from a long history of a people threatened with annihilation wherever they went, matched with Zionism's message of being a chosen people

who are entitled to return to their historic homeland. In May
of 1948, the contemporary land of Palestine—where Palestinians and Jews had co-existed for millennia through many foreign occupations—was transformed overnight into the Jewish
state of Israel, rendering eleven million Palestinians refugees in
what had been their own country. Those who stayed have been
languishing since then in U.N. refugee camps, their coming and
going controlled by the Israeli government. The land called "The
West Bank," designated by the U.N. to be the state of Palestine,
has been occupied by Israel, and Israeli "settlements" are being
built on that land to house the increasing Israeli population. No
amount of international support for a peace process to end the
turmoil of on-going retaliation has succeeded.

Ten minutes after leaving the airport in Tel Aviv, our band of
four (soon to join seven others) is heading toward Jerusalem on
a highway lined on both sides with twenty-foot high concrete
walls. Barbed wire lines the top of the wall should a Palestinian
dare to try and scale it. Walls are always about fear. I ponder
the plight of both of these two peoples—Palestinians and Israelis—living in such proximity, with so many issues unresolved
and the threat of retaliation a constant reminder of injustices
perpetrated so many decades ago. Or is the timeline of retaliation longer? Are the Arabs of Palestine paying the price today
for the centuries of pogroms, displacement and Holocaust done
to the Jews in many lands over centuries, that makes them feel
so unsafe and need such walled-in defense today? I am traveling
through a war zone of ancient origin.

We speed along the highway in a van driven by our guide,
Muhammad, a sixty-year-old Palestinian. He explains as we
drive that this highway effectively cuts the country in half east to
west. Only Israelis are allowed to travel on this road, unless a
Palestinian happens to have the coveted green license plate
which is given only to those Arabs who live in Israeli-controlled
Jerusalem. All others have a yellow plate and need permits to

even drive between cities in the West Bank—an echo of separate drinking fountains, bathrooms, and restaurants for Blacks in our country not so long ago. As Muhammad continues his orientation, I begin taking on the painful role of witness. To live for a time inside this system of Israeli control of a whole people, to feel into the history of these two groups of people living face to face amidst such animosity, mistrust, and brutal force, is why I have come to the West Bank in September, 2012. I had visited here in 1960 as I was returning from my year of study in Lebanon. That was just twelve years after the Israeli take-over of the land that was Palestine, a routing of the indigenous people that left 534 villages bulldozed to oblivion. The Palestinians fought then for their "right of return"—a United Nations' international law—and they are still fighting for that right today.

The land on either side of the walled highway is desolate desert, with little to see beyond gently sloping hills of brown dirt. In stark contrast, the Israeli "settlements" begin dotting the horizon. They are gleaming white, walled cities of 20-50,000 people. The buildings—almost all two to six-story apartments—are uniformly white, and nestled in lush green landscaping (in stark contrast to the dusty Palestinian villages which are deprived of their own water source and must buy water from their occupiers). These Israeli cities are always on the crest of a hill and surrounded by a high wall. They look militant and intimidating in their dominance of the landscape.

It is evening when we arrive at the Siraz Center (meaning "the light") in Beit Sahir, a few miles north of Jerusalem. It is a two-story limestone building surrounded by a high fence which also encloses a small olive orchard. This will be our home base. Siraz was a convent attached to a small, simple church, and now has been revamped to be a guest house. It includes a large kitchen and dining room, where we will take almost all of our breakfasts during our sojourn. We meet the rest of our group of eleven, all from the U.S. We will spend the next ten days climbing in and out of a van many times a day as we traverse the 150 miles north to south of the West Bank, home to four million Palestinian refugees struggling to keep their sanity and to survive under occupation (the other seven million have left the country.) Each day will take us to several organizations—including ones that are Israeli-led—working to make life tolerable under painful and precarious conditions.

The stories that pour forth from these resource people tell of war in the streets, demolition of Palestinian ancestral homes, smashing of "illegal" wells, and homes deprived of public water situated right next to Israeli homes that are connected to it. We stand beside towering concrete walls that separate neighborhoods from stores, homes from work, and children from schools. We learn how harassment of Palestinians by Israeli settlers goes uninvestigated and unpunished, and how permits that Palestinians need to travel to cities beyond their own are arbitrarily denied, always on the grounds of "security," even if the travel is for a medical emergency, a family wedding, or a funeral. Some days we feel as if we just can't hear any more painful stories. Then we remember why we have come. It is the assignment of the witness to hold it all, and to validate how painful and unjust the plight of the Palestinians is in what used to be their own country. Somehow we go on to the next place-people-story, and open again to what needs to be understood. Our listening is a vital part of their sanity. We also struggle to understand how it can be that, though not as extreme as a Holocaust, similar tactics of isolation, control of movement, and deprivation of basic needs that the Jews suffered throughout Europe in the 19th and 20th centuries are being turned on the Palestinians now by the Israeli government. Is this what fear for survival does—turn the victim into a perpetrator? I feel profound, deep sorrow for both groups of people.

Twice, while walking through Palestinian neighborhoods, we are swept off the street into a living room by mothers call-

ing from their doorstep, "Fudlah, Fudlah," meaning "Welcome, come in." We are served
sweetened tea or Arabic coffee
while they tell us stories of loss,
despair, and struggle. We are
the witness, as they provide the
ancient hospitality for the traveler from afar. In the time before books or newspapers, the
traveler crossing their path was
the news-bearer, as well as the
treasure-bearer, and the teacher
of new ways of thinking and being. I feel drawn into that archetypal custom as I sit around the

coffee pot with these open-hearted strangers. Yet now we are being asked to be the news-bearers. Our hosts want us to tell their
story so the world will listen.

A week into our journey, we arrive at the home of a widow
with two teenagers who owns a small olive orchard. She doesn't
have enough hands to harvest her crop, and there is just a week–
long window for the harvest. We are there to help. She opens her
home to us, introducing her two daughters and their aunt who
lives down the street. She shows us the portrait of her deceased
husband hanging above the couch in the living room next to a
portrait of Jesus. Yes, this is a Christian family, and Christians
make up about 20% of the Arab population here. Her sixteen-
year-old tells us about her recent trip to New Mexico with seven
Palestinian girls and seven Israeli girls to do a peace-building
program. She is radiant as she talks about her new Israeli friends.
Then she explains that they can visit each other only in Israel because the Israeli girls are too afraid to come into the West Bank.
She seems undismayed by this, as if it is normal. She hopes she

will be able to get the necessary pass to get through the Israeli checkpoint to visit her friends. She doesn't know what will happen, but she is still smiling from head to toe. I feel so grateful as I look into her young face and see the hope for the future I find there.

Our hostess's home is full of couches, chairs, and a big dining room table that seats all eleven of us. She has done all the cooking to feed our caravan with rice, delicious spicy lentils, lamb, pita bread and peaches. Olives and hummus are on the table as well, along with yogurt, olive oil for the bread, and fruit jam. We are filled to the gills by the time we bed down in our various nooks and crannies. Our hostess is beaming with pleasure at our presence in her home, which seems to me even more important to her than the twenty-two helping hands she will have for the next two days.

Some of the olive trees we climb into as we begin our service are over a thousand years old, putting me in intimate touch with ancient roots. Olives are to the Palestinians what corn is to the Latinos, or rice to the Chinese. They are the lifeblood of a people, a deep connection to place, to soil, to ancestors, and to culture. We spread huge black tarps under a tree and ten people pick all around that tree, some standing, some climbing into the branches. We pull the olives off with wooden hand rakes, and they tumble like rain to the ground, collecting in ankle-deep piles. Lively conversation accompanies pokes and scratches from the dense branches as hundreds of olives plop loudly onto the tarp. When the tree is stripped clean—meticulously clean, to prevent gleaners from entering the grove—the tarps are gathered up and the olives poured into large white bags.

It takes twelve of us eight hours to fill five bags. When our guide comes to pick us up at the end of an exhausting day, he comes with a story of Israeli settlers pulling up in a pickup truck, grabbing the bags harvested that day in a nearby orchard, and driving off. We can deeply appreciate what was stolen—not only a day of work, but a staple of the food supply for the coming year. No one has to tell us there will be no law enforcement to right this wrong.

Leaving this village, gifted by our hostess with a pound of Arabic coffee each to take home, we head to Hebron, perhaps the oldest continuously inhabited city in the world. At first it seems like any other Palestinian village we have visited, with narrow, winding streets lined with two-story contiguous homes. Only front doors indicate where one home stops and another starts. Balconies all have laundry drying on the railings and plants cascading down or climbing up the exterior wall. Our van pulls up right next to the most ancient mosque in the town—maybe even in the whole Middle East. It is located alongside the main road of Hebron. The Israelis have commandeered the main road for their use only, blocking all the ancient roads leading to it with concrete barriers. They built a sidewalk with a waist high wall to allow Palestinians to walk on a few blocks of this road to reach the main mosque from their sequestered neighborhood.

This mosque is also a Jewish Synagogue, as the site is sacred to both religious traditions. If the sidewalk isn't enough of a symbol of apartheid, entering this building with its dual constituencies is another stark symbol of separation. The two groups had previously shared the building, using separate entrances. But since an Israeli massacred twenty-six Muslims during prayers in 2009, a partition was erected cutting the sanctuary in half. Between the two areas is an enclosure where the tomb of Abraham, sacred to both traditions, is located behind barred windows. Each group can peer into this inner sanctum only through the bars. The beauty and majesty of the space—with sweeping arches holding up domed ceilings, intricate wood carving on altars, stairs and pulpits, mosaic mandalas on the pillars, and the brilliant red carpet covering the vast floor where worshippers bow to Mecca—is permeated with the energy of separation.

Hebron is considered by some to be the oldest inhabited city in the world, which explains why Jews as well as Palestinians claim it as their ancestral home. As we walk that main road (foreigners are, of course, treated differently from Palestinians), I ponder how my town would react if a segment of our population commandeered the main street for their exclusive use, blocked all access roads, closed the businesses on that street, evicted families living there, and gave the homes to their own group. What authority would we turn to if that same group usurped Washington and Congress? Most of the Palestinians—whose ancestors have lived here for 5,000 years—having lost their livelihoods, have left the city. One of the groups we have come to meet with in Hebron is trying to create conditions that will allow these Palestinian refugees to return to their ancestral home by offering free rent and electricity, funded by international organizations.

As we walk farther down the road, we unexpectedly come across international peace keepers from Denmark, Sweden, the U.S., and Australia. They are sitting outside a Palestinian elementary school to protect the children from harassment by Jewish settlers. The children have to traverse a small stretch of road that crosses "the line" between Israeli and Palestinian neighborhoods. These young activists sit at their station all day for eighteen month tours to prevent violence against Palestinian children. Their presence gives full meaning to the saying: "The whole world is watching." Placing their bodies in harm's way is an act of solidarity. I give thanks for their courage, their dedication of more than a year of their young lives, and the ripple effect their actions will have on the Palestinian children, the parents, their own families where they come from, on me—the witness—and perhaps on the Israeli settlers as well. I flash back to how the women of Seneca changed the way it felt to be at the armored military base, and I feel the same power here in their simple act of sitting like a beacon of light radiating from this place.

Journeying on to nearby Jerusalem, we meet Imbal, a twenty-three year old slender and soft-spoken Israeli woman wearing jeans, a flowered shirt, and carrying a backpack over one shoulder like any twenty-something from anywhere. She tells us of her refusing compulsory military service at eighteen, and choosing instead to work to prevent Israeli demolition of Palestinian homes in East Jerusalem. She leads our van to a hillside overlooking the whole city. We can see the gold-gilded Dome of the Rock—sacred to Muslims, Jews and Christians—which is now off limits to Muslims except on holy days and then open only to Muslims living in Jerusalem. We can see the Mount of Olives outside the ancient wall that still circles the city. We see a bustling metropolis, a mix of old and new buildings with modern highways leading in and out through ancient gates. Jerusalem was intended by the U.N. to be a shared city in a two-state solution to the partition of Palestine in 1948. Now it is surrounded on three sides by Israeli settlements, and controlled by occupying forces who are systematically demolishing Palestinian houses. In the foreground, outside the wall, we see a Palestinian neighborhood which has no services of trash disposal, road repair or water supply. Imbal tells us this is part of the Israeli strategy to push the ancient residents out—to simply make life too miserable for them to survive.

Why are their homes being demolished? As Palestinian families add generations, their traditional way is to add floors to their homes. When they apply for a permit to build an addition, the Israeli authorities deny them a permit to do so. They are then faced with the option of leaving or building illegally. They are then subject to demolition for illegally building. Imbal goes on to tell us how her organization helps families with legal representation when they receive the three- day advanced notice of the impending demolition (with two of those days predictably being the Jewish Sabbath when no court is open). The family usually loses their appeal, and they are charged by the Israeli government with the cost of clean up after the Israeli military destroys their home. The coalition helps the family with this cost, and the cost of rebuilding after the demolition is carried out. She tells us the Israeli government limits the demolitions to two or three a month so as not to attract international attention to this persistent act of ethnic cleansing of the capital city. Imbal's quiet clarity shows us the resolve of some Israelis to reach across the walls and barbed wire, to go out of bounds in her own society, in order to answer the cry for justice. I am reminded of a quote by Holocaust survivor Eli Wiesel that says: "There may be times when we are powerless to prevent injustice, but there must never be a time when we fail to protest." Imbal is living that truth. There are many organizations both within Israel and around the world working in solidarity with the Palestinians to bring pressure to bear on the Israeli government to work toward a two-state solution that would end this occupation of Palestinian territory.

Imbal's organization does international fundraising to draw attention to what the Israeli government is doing here, as well as building solidarity with the Palestinians who want to rebuild and stay where they have ancestral roots. We are told of one woman, an outspoken Palestinian activist, who has had her home in Jerusalem destroyed by Israeli tanks seven times. Each time, it was rebuilt by a team of international volunteers. We ask Imbal, "How is it with your peers in Tel Aviv where you live? What do they think about what you are doing here?" She replies: "It's OK, because we just don't talk about what I am doing." She tells us her family is also not supportive, so we can appreciate the price she is paying daily to follow her conscience.

I wonder what it takes to dance with such despair, and yet keep its clutches from swallowing your spirit whole. As we journey on day after day, one of Rumi's poems comes to mind:

Come, come, come, come,
Wanderer, worshiper, lover of leaving,
Ours is not a caravan of despair.
Come, though you have broken your vow a thousand times,
Come yet again, come, come.

Ours is a tired and stretched caravan; we certainly feel the presence of despair. Those we are meeting seem to have made their peace with the temptation to despair. They seem radiant, relaxed, and open to enjoying our presence. Their temperament is amazing to me as I struggle with feeling overwhelmed by their plight.

We meet another Israeli woman, Hagid, who is working to monitor and report settler violations of Palestinian persons and property in order that these violations not go uncounted and unacknowledged by the wider world. The eleven of us fill her tiny office, which holds nothing but a desk, the chair she is sitting on, and lots of posters and charts on the walls. I read stamina on her face, hear it in her voice, and see it radiating from her strong body. This woman tells us, "I am an Israeli. I love my country, and I want there to be a safe place for Jews to live in this world. But I hate what my country is doing to the Palestinians. You don't let a friend drive drunk. My country is driving drunk. My country is committing suicide by perpetuating violence against the Palestinians." She explains to us that the intention behind continuing to build settlements on land belonging to the Palestinians in the West Bank is to eventually equalize the number of Jews with Arabs (they are up to 600,000 Jews now). This will make claiming the land for a state of Palestine highly compromised because there will be too many Israelis claiming it as their home to get them to leave. With little hope of preventing the land grab, Hagid is determined to make it as difficult as possible for the Israelis to deceive the world about what they are doing.

While in Jerusalem we also meet Palestinian social workers running a day care center for disabled and emotionally challenged adults. The workers have not been paid for five months because the Israeli government cut off foreign funds meant for Palestine when the Palestinian leader, Mahmud Abbas, went to the U.N. seeking recognition as an independent state. We ask them how they can afford to work with no pay for that long. They reply: "We must. This is our work. We love these people. We cannot abandon them." This is life under occupation.

As we stand next to the twenty-foot high concrete wall surrounding East Jerusalem, learning about the systematic monthly destruction of Palestinian homes, I am looking at the writing on the wall. It has become a blank canvas for the soul of these people. What I see is, "This lie cannot live," "Love Wins," "HOPE," "Peace for Palestine." I notice the messages are mostly in English, which is their second or third language after Arabic. I surmise that these words are addressed to the European and American constituencies that support the policies of Israel. The Palestinians are using this instrument of domination as a message board to the world. There is no hatred here, no condemnation, only prayers, and pleas for freedom. I find myself wondering what my own people would write and draw on a wall such as this if we were captive in our own land, penned in by such a wall.

In another place I see a mural stretching the full height and fifty feet long, the Palestinian flag waving above faces depicting struggle and determination. I ask who painted these testimonies and hear of famous artists coming from afar to support the Palestinians by painting their story for the world to see. I sense the spiritual strength and the resilience behind their words. I see how they maintain their dignity through this art, even when caught in such terrible vulnerability. I am reminded of the Sandinistas in Nicaragua, who also carried on with dignity while under daily attack by the Contra within their own borders. They, too, had the same source of dignity—spiritual strength and clarity of purpose.

298 Out of Bounds

My awareness is expanding, deepening my understanding of the same struggle for Black liberation among those caught in an apartheid system within my own country. Martin Luther King's words, "I don't hate any man. I've been to the mountain top and I've seen the Promised Land" has new meaning now that I have seen the same injustices in action here. I can feel the spiritual strength of reaching beyond reaction, defense, or vilification of the oppressor to a place of not forfeiting one's own dignity by stooping to retaliation or victimhood. I understand more about the immediate urge of the young to throw stones at armed soldiers, and what a surrender of spiritual power that is.

How often do we get to experience that "Love wins," especially in circumstances of domination? One mural I see on the wall stands out more than any other. It is of a fifteen-foot high white dove of peace with the traditional olive branch in its mouth. But this dove is depicted wearing a flak jacket, and there is a bull's eye target superimposed on its heart, along with the cross hairs of a rifle barrel. The image is shocking; it conveys a story far beyond what words can tell. In an instant, I feel what Palestinians feel daily. They, like the dove, have a gun pointed at their human spirit, their love of life, of land, of home, of family, yet they choose to call for help and paint "Love Wins" on their oppressor's turned back. This gives new meaning to the Serenity Prayer for me—to accept the things we cannot change, and the courage to focus on what we can change. We can choose to love, even when we are being deprived of justice. This is a very brave choice. I am listening. I am learning. I feel very blessed by their witness to these challenging truths.

I know from the media that there are other factions of Palestinians such as Hamas in Gaza who have taken a more militant tactic to dealing with occupation than those in the West Bank. We are not being told their story on this trip. I don't presume to know the whole story of the Palestinian people and their struggle, or of the Jewish people and their millennia-long search for a safe homeland. I only know I am seeing my own country in a new light. I see with more clarity now that we did the same thing to Native Americans in the settling of our country that the Israeli government has done to the Palestinians. First, we took their land as if it didn't belong to anyone. Then we called them savages for fighting back. Then we destroyed their villages and put them out of sight on reservations in remote areas so we and future generations would not have to confront what we had done. We have broken every treaty we made to gain their compliance. They have shown some of the same reactions as these oppressed people—some seeking retaliation or sinking into despair, while others are making the spiritual choice to maintain their dignity and deep embodying of their own goodness and wisdom.

Seeing these similarities in our experiences of forming a nation where another people inhabited the land is making my own history come alive for me. What I knew intellectually before about our expansion into Indian Territory now has faces and feelings. The "Trail of Tears" that expelled thousands of Native Americans from their homes in our southeastern territory is happening before my eyes as I witness people driven from their land, their homes bulldozed, olive trees uprooted, and laborers forced to sleep on sidewalks overnight at check points in order to be able to get to work on time on the other side of the wall in the morning. Why is this occupation and oppression tolerable to the American politicians who support Israel and its policies so persistently? Where is our conscience as Americans when we give $6 billion in aid to Israel yearly to enable them to carry out these apartheid strategies and build more and more settlements on stolen land? Where are the reparations we owe to the Native Americans for the land we took from them? I sit with my own powerlessness to change the choices my country is making that seem so cruel and unjust. I notice the anger that arises so easily. I reach for the deeper truth—love wins—and know what hard work it is spiritually and psychologically to choose and main-

tain that conviction. These Palestinian people I am meeting—
and their Jewish allies like Imbal and Hagid—are warriors of the
heart.

On our last day we journey outside the city of Bethlehem to
a remote hilltop where the Tent of Nations, a Palestinian homestead and youth camp, is located. The hill is surrounded on three
sides by huge Israeli settlements, and the land owner has been
constantly harassed for over forty years by settlers trying to
drive him to abandon his land. We have to park a quarter of a
mile from the entrance, as Jewish settlers have rolled boulders
into the access road to block passage. We make our way past the
rubble of demolished buildings and rolls of barbed wire marking
the perimeter of the homestead. When we arrive at the gate, we
see carved on a knee-high, limestone boulder in English, Arabic
and German the words, "We refuse to be enemies." A deep smile
arises in me; I am entering sacred ground.

When the gate is opened by a volunteer from Denmark, we
enter a magical kingdom. The arid land is planted with grapes
and olives. We are met by Daoud, who, with his brother, is continuously occupying this hilltop purchased by his great-grandfather during the Ottoman Empire in 1916. If the land is not con-

tinuously occupied and worked agriculturally, it can be seized by the State (the occupiers) as "abandoned." Scattered around the camp on the ground we see four murals, each twelve feet square, painted on concrete by the young people who attend camps here. Each one depicts the motto of the camp, "With heart and hands we heal the land." Why would they paint murals on the ground? Daoud explains that when the water cisterns built by his great-grandfather were smashed by the Israeli government—which insisted that he buy water from them rather than "gather the gift from God"—those cisterns were secretly replaced by underground cisterns that are fed by the surface of the murals. Only then did we notice that the surface of these murals slopes gently (not visible to Israeli aerial inspectors) down to one corner that has a hole about three inches in diameter. As we pass by one of the murals, a head pops out of a trap door. It is a young man—an Austrian volunteer—who has been underground repairing that cistern.

We also see solar panels, compost toilets, and harvested honey products for sale. Daoud explains that he and his brother intend this camp to be self-sufficient energy-wise very soon. They don't want charity, he says, but they welcome donations that promote these energy-efficient improvements. We see a large tent where international volunteers are housed, and we see the cave where Daoud and his brother sleep—the same cave where his great grandfather slept. We meet as a group in a larger cave, about twenty feet by twenty feet. The walls are white-washed and covered with silhouettes of children leaping and playing.

Here Daoud tells us of the program he conducts with the help of volunteers. "What do we have to offer our young people?" he posits. "The Israelis have taken our land, our water, our freedom to move. They are expecting that over a generation, our young people will decide to just leave because there is nothing here for them." He goes on to explain how the young people are not experiencing the traditional connection to the land that

has been the bedrock of Palestinian identity, and that he, too, fears
they will leave. His mission is to
restore that connection. "This is
what we have to offer: We refuse
to be enemies." I feel as if I am in
the presence of a saint. This is the
most deeply moving moment of
my journey to Palestine. Gandhi
had taught that when you align
yourself with the Truthforce you
need no other defense. Surely that
Truthforce is what I am feeling so
strongly in this place.

So this motto is their response
to those who treat them like enemies. I am reminded of Vic-
tor Frankl's writing from a concentration camp in Germany
when he said the one thing the Nazis could not take away was
his freedom to choose his attitude toward what was happening to him. Frankl called this the "Will to Meaning." Daoud is
teaching this same wisdom to his Palestinian young people. My
heart breaks for these young people who have to learn such a
demanding lesson at such an early age. There is no surrender,
no power struggle, only the choice to retain one's own dignity
when another would want you to relinquish it. The courage to
make this choice, grounded in such suffering, is the heart of the
transformation I feel so strongly in this place. It is a profound
gift to witness this truth being lived, and perhaps to internalize
its meaning and its power for our own lives.

For me, this Tent of Nations camp embodies the Biblical beacon of light on the hill that no amount of oppression can put out.
As we prepare to walk back down the road to our cars, the sun
is setting over the distant Mediterranean Sea, muting the persistent whiteness of the surrounding Israeli settlements. The glory

of the sunset-red rays matches the radiance of this place. I am filled with gratitude for the ministry of these people. I will carry what I have seen and heard in my heart forever, and pray for the spiritual strength myself to live this truth when I am sorely pressed by climate deniers, Tea Party Republicans, inconsiderate neighbors, or a Congress hell-bent on world domination no matter the costs in lives and resources. Many times I, too, feel like picking up a stone and hurling it at a perceived enemy. Now I have learned (again) that there is no power in that act. It is a capitulation. "We refuse to be enemies" is full victory. When King says the long arc of history bends towards justice, this man Daoud's testimony and action is what that arc looks like.

I return home changed. I went to give support. I received so much more.

Epilogue

I have led an abundant life. As I opened the book of possibilities in my youth, a path kept opening before me. I could never have planned this most amazing life, but I guess my acorn could! I could not have known that the first journey to Grinnell, Iowa would open me to the Universal Church, and that opening would call me to work camps in Ghana, Jordan, and Zimbabwe. It would call me to Lebanon, Malawi and Switzerland under the wing of the Presbyterian programs that Margaret Flory created, each one defining anew what the mission of the church was. I, along with hundreds of American young people, followed her lead, with her vision of a church without walls that meets people in transition on the frontiers of change in God's beloved world. She made us ambassadors rather than preachers. She taught us what the Church truly is meant to be, a community of compassion, respect and service.

I could not have foreseen how the wave of women changing the norms of our cultural values and behaviors would challenge all my assumptions about Christianity and the Church, until gender equality became more important to me than devotion to "Sons of men and angels sing, glory to the new born king." I was in need of my own resurrection, and it came through joining Movement for a New Society when I was thirty-two, coincidentally the same age Jesus was when he started breaking the rules of religion.

In hindsight, this journey of consciousness and service simply opened before me as I responded to what crossed my path. The experience of the peace camp at Oak Ridge, with its radical Catholic warriors, showed me a faith at work that was fiercely political, yet nonviolent. I found myself drawn to yet another frontier—facing off with the social evils of war, inequality, and poverty in my own country through nonviolent direct action.

Moving into an urban commune in 1973 was probably my most profound experience of going out of bounds. The enormity of leaving a ten year marriage with three little boys was matched by the intensity of purpose and possibility I felt. I was joining what had—without the words—become Church for me. Here the Gospel was being lived in the midst of Quaker traditions, singing, potlucks, shared house chores and endless meetings leading to actions that we dreamed would usher in a new society. We called our mission "'decentralized, democratic socialism," a big mouthful and a big assignment. We would "live the revolution now." We would not try to change the present social/political system, but rather focus on building alternative institutions that people would simply choose to shift their allegiance to because they made more sense (as Bucky Fuller taught.). As with the Susan B. Anthonys and the Frederick Douglasses of history who did not live to see their causes triumph, we gave our all. We changed countless individual lives, yet our new society still alludes us. The personal transformation I experienced while living communally, joining in civil disobedience, and becoming a trainer in nonviolent social change tactics, gave me the inspiration and tools to become the Pilgrim Warrior that I would go on to call forth in hundreds of other women.

As I reflect on our M.N.S. dream today—forty years later—decentralization is happening by fiat because the federal government is so polarized it has become unable to govern. Cities are going bankrupt and states are taking single payer health care into their own hands. Climate change is pushing us into focus on the local economy for our sustainability. Polls tell us the word "socialism" is having a comeback among the twenty-somethings, who have the perspective of forty years of socialism in post-World War II Europe. It seems to make more sense for the common good to them than our rampant free market system that fosters the inequality we are experiencing today with the top one percent of our people owning forty percent of the wealth.

The next wave of radical change, climate disruption, is already working its way into our social fabric, threatening to upend our belief systems, our lifestyles, and our politics. I know the price such disruptions will exact, and I also know the rewards of facing into change with a positive vision and community at your side. The privilege of living a suburban lifestyle supported by a fossil fuel economy will probably end in the next fifty years (or less). How scarce resources like food, energy, and water are distributed will become the challenge of the second half of this century. What will the new frontiers be then? How will the Universal Church make sense of what has happened because of human greed and denial? What will going out of bounds look like under intensifying pressure to simply survive, let alone thrive? Will we have learned, like the Balinese, to live our lives in the hands of the gods?

I believe that those who survive these coming changes will be those who have learned how to live in harmony with the laws of Nature. I believe the sacredness of life will once again become the ground of our Being. The God of the Bible will become the God of the Soil, of all living things, and we will find our oneness again in the web of life. The vaults of silver will be useless. The sweat of our brow will once again be what connects us to meaning, to love, to each other, and to our God.

Those of us who see this new paradigm emerging are banding together. We call our local group of twenty-five "The Neighbors." We meet in our living rooms, with the now habitual monthly potluck, and talk of raising food and chickens, sharing tools and skills, tending the sick among us and each other's animals. We sing and pray together. We give leadership to what will build sustainability out of the looming environmental crisis. We call ourselves Green Heroes as we adopt new ways of living more lightly on the Earth. We are a voice for simplicity, for recycling and composting, for shutting down dangerous nuclear power plants, and for shifting to renewable energy. We are the five percent known by sociologists as the "trim tab," that little rudder mounted on the edge of the big rudder that turns a mighty ship to an altered course. We will turn the rudder that will eventually turn the ship of culture and lifestyle toward sustainability.

I once heard it said, "You can't break the laws of Nature; you can only break yourself against them." It seems apparent that, for now, that is exactly what the majority of humans, including most of our politicians who could be heroes of innovation, are hell-bent on doing. But from a distance, I see that time is on our side. We *will learn*, as the feedback loops of Nature's laws will inevitably teach us, to stop trying to outdo Nature's design of balance and sustainability. I believe we will be reborn in the experience of losing our 20th century privileges. Private property producing food for the few will simply not survive the demand to share resources as food becomes scarce. We will once again find ourselves, like kindergartners, having to learn to share.

The humanity that created vast disparities of wealth and poverty will be remade by the humility, compassion and simplicity that the 21st century will demand of us. The humility of the Balinese who understand how to live without certainties, always relating to the hidden forces they can only seek balance with, can show us the way. The ingenuity of the Ugandan village bank women can show us how to build on community for survival. The Russian women can model for us not being drawn in by propaganda that creates false enemies, drains resources, and reinforces unjust power structures. The Nicaraguans can show us the persistence to live a revolutionary spirit and commitment to equality for all even in the presence of internal enemies bent on their destruction. The women warriors of Seneca, the non-violent warriors of M.N.S., and the displaced people of Palestine bear witness to the power of a vision to generate the courage and inspiration to keep on believing in what is possible against great odds.

The morphogenic field generated by our struggles in the 1970s for shared leadership, consensus decision-making, nonviolent discipline in confrontation, and a culture of inclusively has shown up in Technicolor in the Occupy Movement of 2011-12. As I walk among the young people building this new movement, I am thrilled by their competence, their solidarity, their creativity, and their vision. My acorn is quiet now; theirs is pushing out. The torch has been passed. All the skills and consciousness we struggled so hard to learn seem so easily accessible to them. We gave them a pathway to this revolutionary consciousness. They will build on it. Another mighty march for justice is underway and it is in good hands. May their acorns push together, thrive, and bring this world closer to what we all cherish—a world at peace, with justice for all.

Acknowledgements

My thanks goes out to all my readers of this manuscript, especially Becca King, Cheryl Fox, Bruce Boston, Jannie Dziadzio, Robin Weingarten, and Gaella Elwell, and my writing partner Alison Taylor, as well as Marian Kelner and Gurunam Khalsa who readied it for publication. My thanks to Jim Sadler for a creative cover that so well expresses my journey, and to Maureen Moore for guiding me through all the gates of self-publishing with kindness and patience.

I thank my partner-in-blended-family-nurturing, Jean Boston, for her open heart in allowing me to continue to be a part of Bruce's life as family with our three sons and her two daughters. Without Jean's gracious welcome in their home, my journey would have been much harder. I honor my three sons—Aaron, Nathan, and Kyle— who had no small assignment, sticking out ten years of communal living which made them different from their peers, not to mention having a mother that kept choosing to get arrested, and who now have to tell their children it's OK that their grandmother lives with housemates, still likes to sleep in her car, and all she eats is vegetables. She's still weird, but very loved—thank goodness.

I am grateful to my dear friend, ally, and chosen-family, Dakota Butterfield, who—when she asked me to become Grandmother to her children—gave me the gift of belonging in a family that sees and welcomes who I am as normal, wonderful, and a role model to emulate in a way that is deeply healing for me.

I have deep gratitude for the wide sisterhood that has had my back every turn of the way—some ahead of me—Starhawk, Audre Lourde, Holly Near—showing the way; some beside me— my co-trainers, Julie Devon Dodd and ALisa Starkweather, as well as my Full Moon Rising sisters of twenty-five years—sharing the learning; and some following in my footsteps on this sacred journey.

And finally, to my enchanting acorn—an amazing mix of mystery and intention—that brought such adventure, meaning and purpose to my life—Gass Ho (I bow to you), and thank you.

Sandra Boston lives in Greenfield, Massachusetts where she has a psychotherapy practice (which includes phone counseling) and offers board and staff training in conscious communication skills. She is also available for motivational speaking engagements. She can be reached by email at bostons111@gmail.com or by phone at 413-774-5952.

For additional copies of this book go to www.createspace.com/5149857

Other books by Sandra Boston are

Aiming Your Mind: Strategies and Skills for Conscious Communication, 2005.

Aiming Your Mind: Strategies and Skills for Conscious Communication with practice exercises

For copies of these titles contact the author via e-mail or her website:

www.ccitraining.org

Made in the USA
Lexington, KY
30 November 2015